Competitive Dynamics in the Global Insurance Industry

Markus Schimmer

Competitive Dynamics in the Global Insurance Industry

Strategic Groups, Competitive Moves, and Firm Performance

Foreword by Prof. Ming-Jer Chen, Ph.D.

Springer Gabler

RESEARCH

Markus Schimmer
St. Gallen, Switzerland

Doctoral Thesis, University St. Gallen, Schweiz, 2012

ISBN 978-3-8349-3991-3 ISBN 978-3-8349-3992-0 (eBook)
DOI 10.1007/978-3-8349-3992-0

The Deutsche Nationalbibliothek lists this publication in the Deutsche Nationalbibliografie; detailed bibliographic data are available in the Internet at http://dnb.d-nb.de.

Springer Gabler

Cover design: KünkelLopka GmbH, Heidelberg

Printed on acid-free paper

Springer Gabler is a brand of Springer DE. Springer DE is part of Springer Science+Business Media.
www.springer-gabler.de

Foreword

The term "competitive dynamics" may be used to describe rivalrous behavior in any number of contexts. In business and economics, it stands for the ongoing struggle between firms for competitive advantage – a process central to the economic development not only of firms, but of entire economies.

For many years, however, scholarly research fell short of its potential to cater to managers' interest in means and patterns of competition, favoring more static industry-structure analyses. Aware of this shortcoming, several scholars set out about two decades ago to pursue the sort of competition research that would be more relevant to strategists. They forayed into the study of competitive actions as vehicles for rivalry, and thus into empirical data that directly relates to managers' competitive decision-making processes.

As one of these pioneers, I have worked to advance the field of competitive dynamics along four cohesive thematic lines: (1) the action/response dyad, (2) firm-(business-) level competition, (3) theoretical and methodological concerns, and (4) corporate-level competition. Across these themes, several findings stand out. In contrast to the structural school of thought, competition is not a symmetric market characteristic uniformly spread throughout the market, but a relational phenomenon that exists between rivals. Further, competitive behavior follows patterns that can be elicited from the stream of firms' competitive actions. Within these sequences, actions tend to be direct responses to prior rival actions and can, given knowledge of these rivalrous actions, often be anticipated by a firm.

The action-oriented approach to the study of competitive dynamics has mitigated the static legacy of structural industry-level research. Its micro-view turned interfirm rivalry dynamics on its head and reconciled it with the central propositions of Austrian and Schumpeterian economics. Despite these important contributions, however, competitive dynamics research remains underdeveloped in several important ways. It lacks an integrative framework that can organize the field's many facets; its potential to bridge the micro and macro perspectives has not been fully realized; it has yet to establish important links with other disciplines in the management field; and it suffers from lack of "contextualization".

Markus's dissertation takes several steps toward addressing some of these issues. In its first study, the dissertation shows how human agency links the direction of a firm's strategic change with the firm's broader industrial environment. The study provides not only an innovative and far more comprehensive perspective on strategic group dynamics, but also one that remains anchored in behavioral thinking.

The dissertation's second study contextualizes the competitive-behavioral patterns of firms by explicating the impact of environmental shocks on the firms' competitive choices. Its analyses initially discuss the impacts market shocks have on how managers determine competitive actions. The study also pioneers a very useful empirical approach by tapping the online press release archives of firms in a scalable and replicable manner.

The third study, focusing on interrelationships in action sequences, provides a more granular level of investigation, scrutinizing the performance implications of strategic interrelationships among individual competitive actions.

This body of work represents a comprehensive effort to close significant research gaps pertaining to competition and competitive dynamics. Not only does Markus's dissertation address a thematically wide range of research, it is highly entrepreneurial in its empirical approach, utilizes a varied set of methods, and is truly collaborative in character. I offer Markus my most sincere congratulations on his work, and send my best wishes for the future from the Darden School of Business.

Charlottesville, January 2012 Prof. Ming-Jer Chen

Fellow and President of the Academy of Management (2012-13)
Leslie E. Grayson Professor of Business Administration
The Darden School of Business, University of Virginia

Acknowledgements

Writing this thesis has been a very rewarding experience. It allowed me to meet exceptional people, explore different topics and distant places, and grow with the challenges the task implied. I feel very grateful to those who supported me during this experience and would like to take the opportunity to thank these people.

First and foremost, I am indebted to my doctoral advisor, Prof. Dr. Günter Müller-Stewens, who enabled this research. He further provided me with guidance through the inevitable ups and downs while leaving me the creative freedom to develop my own research agenda. Further, I owe to Prof. Dr. Hato Schmeiser, who kindly served as co-advisor and challenged my research from the industry perspective. My most sincere thanks go to Prof. Dr. Matthias Brauer, who helped me to narrow down my research scope, and ensured with his thorough feedback and continuous advice that my research stayed on course. I offer further gratitude to Prof. Ming-Jer Chen at the Darden School of Business, under whose guidance I completed my thesis at the University of Virginia in Charlottesville. My time at Darden truly completed my "dissertation journey". With respect to this stay, I gratefully acknowledge financial support from the Swiss National Science Foundation.

I also want to give thanks for the generous support I received from my former employer, Allianz SE. Prof. Dr. Volker Deville and his team not only willingly served as a sounding board in the early stages of my dissertation project, but also helped me to overcome some of its empirical challenges. In this regard, I also thank Mr. Bryan Martyn of A.M. Best Europe for his efforts to bring A.M. Best on board. One step further back in time, I owe to Mr. Martin Wricke and the CPO-team of the "Sustainability Program" of Allianz SE, who taught me the quantitative skills and practices that inspired the research strategy of this dissertation and allowed me to pursue my scholarly interest in a methodologically largely unconstrained manner.

Further, I want to thank those people who nudged me into the right direction at the right time during the last years. These people are (in chronological order) Ann Currlin, Prof. Dr. Jan-Marco Leimeister, Damir Cacic, Martin Reich, Roman Simschek, Andrea Olivieri, Jennifer Gunther and Alexander Gebauer. Without any of you, my life would have taken a different course and I would most likely not have written these lines. Thank you for your advice and invaluable friendship.

Working on my dissertation would have been much less fun without my colleagues, friends and fellow PhD students at the University of St. Gallen and the University of Virginia. I want to particularly thank Sven Kunisch, Christian Welling, Dr. Markus Menz, Dr. Lisa Hopfmüller, Petra Kipfelsberger, Dr. Christoph Tyssen, Johannes Luger, André Blondiau, Nicole Rosenkranz, and Dr. Florian Hotz for the joyful moments we shared. In Charlottesville and at the University of Virginia, I want to particularly thank Caroline, John and Damaris Jimenez, David Dobolyi, Vincent Kan, Xin Chen, Sebastián Alcain, Betsy Chunko, Dr. Eusebio Pires and Adrian Keevil for their great company, which had a fair share in turning my stay in the United States into an unforgettable experience.

My final acknowledgements belong to my parents Lydia and Heinz, and my sister Nicole, who trusted my decision to journey into uncharted waters despite the many twists and turns encountered. Thank you for your unwavering support and love during these exciting years.

Charlottesville, July 2011 Markus Schimmer

Table of Contents

List of Figures

List of Tables

List of Appendices

List of Abbreviations

ANOVA	Analysis of variance
BTOF	Behavioral theory of the firm
CAAR	Cumulative average abnormal return
CAR	Cumulative abnormal return
CATA	Computer aided text analysis
CD	Competitive dynamics
e.g.	exempli gratia (for example)
EBIT	Earnings before interest and tax
et al.	et alii (and others)
etc.	et cetera (and so on)
EUR	Euro
GWP	Gross written premiums
H	Hypothesis
HTML	Hypertext Markup Language
i.e.	id est (that is)
IO	Industrial organization
n/a	Not applicable
N.B.	nota bene (note well)
OECD	Organization for Economic Cooperation and Development
OLS	Ordinary least squares
PCA	Principal component analysis
P&L	Property and liability
PRA	Performance relative to aspirations
ROA	Return on assets
ROE	Return on equity
S-C-P	Structure-conduct-performance
s.d.	Standard deviation
SCD	Strategic convergence-divergence
SE	Standard error
S&P	Standard and Poor's
U.S.	United States
USD	U.S. Dollar
UK	United Kingdom
VBA	Visual Basic for Applications
VIF	Variance inflation factor

Abstract and Keywords

This dissertation develops and tests theories on temporal dynamics of interfirm rivalry. It comprises three empirical studies that contribute to different discussions within the competitive dynamics research strand of the strategic management discipline.

The first study contributes to research on strategic group dynamics by pioneering a behavioral theory on how managers reposition their firms vis-à-vis the strategic group their firm is part of. The study reveals how the managerial process of contemplating repositionings within strategic groups is connected to feedback from performance benchmarking, behavioral biases, stimuli from the external environment, and the individual position of the focal firm within its strategic group. Based on a unique longitudinal dataset covering the yearly repositioning moves of 1,191 firms over a 10 year period, this study provides the first large-scale empirical test of the behavioral mechanisms that underlie the evolution of strategic group structures.

The second study adds to the action-response stream of competitive dynamics research and complements recent efforts to develop an action-based theory of interfirm rivalry that goes beyond the firm-dyad and thus remains valid in markets that are characterized by a larger number of competitors. The study initially incorporates the external environmental context into the discussion and explicates the different effects market shocks have on interfirm rivalry. It finds that market shocks offer new competitive opportunities to firms and thus increase rivalry. Further, the study suggests that market shocks temporarily abandon the mechanisms that generally drive the competitive behavior of firms and thus punctuate the process of interfirm rivalry. Our results are based on an event history analysis of 2,467 competitive actions pursued by 37 firms.

The third study contributes to research investigating the performance implications of competitive actions by revealing how strategic interrelationships between individual actions, as well as experience transfer and timing effects, impact the stock market responses to these actions. We test our theory on a distinct action type (i.e., divestitures) using event study methodology on a sample of 160 divestiture announcements. Our research suggests that well-conceived and strategically linked competitive actions are better received by the stock markets than isolated actions.

Keywords: Competitive dynamics research, strategic group dynamics, action-response patterns, interfirm rivalry, market shocks, divestitures, insurance industry

1 Introduction

Ever since the early days of research into the functioning of economic markets (Smith, 1776), there has been a vibrant academic debate on the role of competition. While this debate has traditionally been led by economists and centered on the welfare effects of competition (Hayek, 1968; Schumpeter, 1934, 1943), strategic management scholars turned the focus of the debate toward individual firms, and their competitive strategies and advantages (Porter, 1980, 1985). Even though they initially adopted economic ideas, management scholars soon developed their own perspectives on interfirm rivalry that were better suited to explain performance differences between firms (Baum & Korn, 1999; Chen, 1996; Hunt, 1972). These theories and related work became known as "competitive dynamics research" within the strategic management discipline (Ketchen, Snow, & Hoover, 2004).

Competitive dynamics research comprises several sub-streams – such as competitive action-response, co-opetition, multipoint competition and strategic groups (Ketchen et al., 2004). These different areas of interest are united by their common empirical focus on the real competitive behavior of firms. Further, they consider the competitive action as the constituting element of competitive behavior and thus as the vehicle through which firms engage in rivalry, reposition themselves, and eventually create competitive advantages (Chen, 2009b; Chen, Smith, & Grimm, 1992; Ferrier, Smith, & Grimm, 1999).

With its distinct focus, competitive dynamics research produced various important insights on the causes and consequences of different patterns of competitive behavior. However, the research strand also faces some challenges that go beyond the research gaps within its sub-streams (Ketchen et al., 2004; Smith, Ferrier, & Ndofor, 2001b). In light of its past successes and an increasing degree of differentiation in the questions competitive dynamics research asks, the future progress of competitive dynamics research requires novel dynamic theories, innovative empirical strategies, and methods that are better suited to capture temporal dynamics (Baldwin, 1995; Chen, 2009b; Daems & Thomas, 1994). Furthermore, the progress within several sub-fields of competitive dynamics research is currently impeded by the dominance of certain theoretical paradigms or research practices – such as the focus on firm dyads within the action-response sub-stream. To overcome these challenges, scholars have suggested future research to challenge these dominant theoretical ideas with novel arguments from a wider range of theoretical perspectives (Smith et al., 2001b; Thomas & Carroll, 1994).

The main part of this dissertation consists of three individual studies, which mitigate the overarching issues of competitive dynamics research while addressing research gaps within the field's sub-streams. The dissertation's first study, for example, contrasts the dominant research practice to perceive strategic group dynamics as consequences of industry-level events and variations (Mascarenhas, 1989; Zuniga-Vicente, Fuente-Sabaté, & Suarez-Gonzalez, 2004b). The study instead suggests a behavioral theory of a firm's repositioning vis-à-vis its own strategic group that centers on the managerial decision-making process and behavioral biases. The second study contributes to an emergent body of work in the action-response sub-stream of competitive dynamics research (Hsieh & Chen, 2010; Zuchhini & Kretschmer, 2011) that challenges the validity of the dominant research paradigm (i.e., the focus on firm dyads in predicting competitive moves) for markets that are characterized by a large number of rivals. The third study reveals shortcomings in the extant practice of studying competitive actions and underlines that competitive actions should not be studied in isolation but in a manner that considers the interrelationships within action sequences.

This chapter serves as a broad introduction to the dissertation and proceeds as follows. After presenting our general research objectives and guiding questions (1.1), it provides an overview of our research strategy and method (1.2), and concludes with the outline of the dissertation (1.3).

1.1 Research Objectives and Guiding Questions

This dissertation addresses gaps within competitive dynamics research (Ketchen et al., 2004). Specifically, it focuses – as its title suggests – on strategic groups, competitive moves, and performance. The dissertation represents a cumulative work and contains three individual studies that contribute to different academic discussions. Since we present these discussions in great detail within the subsequent chapters, we do not elaborate on them at this point, but instead open up a broader frame that explains our general research objectives and guiding questions.

The most general objective of this dissertation is to improve our understanding of the nature and consequences of the competitive dynamics among firms. This objective inherently relates to the challenges that currently impede the further development of competitive dynamics research (i.e., the need for novel dynamic theories and more multilectic thinking) (Baldwin, 1995; Chen, 2009b; Daems & Thomas, 1994). To help overcome these issues, the dissertation pays particular attention to temporal aspects of rivalry and challenges or renews the theoretical perspectives that currently dominate the academic discussions it contributes to.

In order to derive a set of guiding questions that sets the bounds of our research scope, we first considered those fundamental questions prior research has related to the study of competition and rivalry within strategy and competitive dynamics research: "How is competition conducted? What are the performance consequences of particular types of behavior and strategies? What are the dynamics of competition among existing firms? How do new firms enter an industry and what impact does their entry strategy have on future dynamics? How do firms change?" (Pruett & Thomas, 1994: vii). Based on these broad questions and in light of current trends within major sub-fields of competitive dynamics research (see chapter "2.3 Toward a Research Agenda"), we further narrowed down the research scope of this dissertation to the following questions:

(1) Why do firms change their competitive positioning?
(2) How do firms compete? What external factors affect interfirm rivalry?
(3) What are the performance implications of different types of competitive behaviors?

Answering these questions guides us to research gaps within strategic group research (relating to question 1), the study of competitive actions and responses (relating to question 2), and the performance implications of competitive actions (relating to question 3). As a consequence, the dissertation spans different levels of abstraction and analysis – stretching from the ideas of positioning and strategic groups, which are industry-related, to the narrow and much more granular analysis of competitive actions. The order in which we present our subsequent studies reflects the order of our guiding questions and represents a progression toward higher levels of granularity.

1.2 Research Strategy and Method

We designed the research strategy of this dissertation in a way that would allow us to answer the dissertation's guiding questions and abide by the research practices of the discussions to which we contribute (see Ketchen et al., 2004 for an overview). These two goals mandated our studies to investigate the real competitive behavior of firms based on quantitative research designs. We further aimed at creating synergies between our individual studies and decided to focus on a single industry, the insurance industry.

Since this dissertation contributes to academic discussions that apply different operationalizations of competitive behavior, our research strategy needed to accommodate these variants. The study on strategic group dynamics refers to competitive behavior in terms of repositionings within an industry (Fiegenbaum & Thomas, 1990); whereas the other two studies refer to competitive behavior in terms of the competitive actions firms employ (Schumpeter, 1934; Smith, Grimm, & Gannon, 1992). These operationalizations appear disparate at first sight, but on deeper reflection, they are inherently linked by the idea that competitive actions eventually transform the (strategic) profiles of firms, which in turn alters the firms' positionings within the industry (Durand, 2006; Smith et al., 2001b). Figure 1-1 illustrates the central role a firm's competitive actions assume within competitive dynamics research and conceptually relates it to the firm's resource profile, the industry structure (e.g., the strategic group structure) and the competitive action(s) of its rival(s) (Smith et al., 2001b).

Figure 1-1: Important Elements Driving Competitive Behaviors

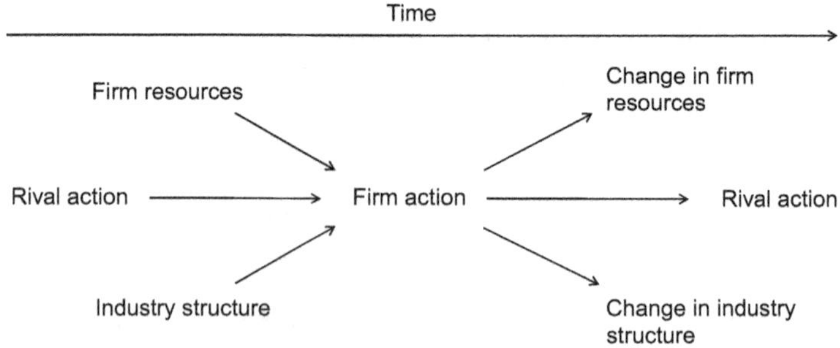

Figure adapted from Smith, Ferrier and Ndofor (2001b: 348)

By mapping these empirical elements and making their interrelationships explicit, the illustration conveys the empirical challenge our research strategy needed to solve – i.e., to collect the depicted types of information and relate them to each other. We accomplished this task by compiling a comprehensive longitudinal database on the global insurance industry (see Appendices 1 to 4 for details). The database combines three major categories of information: information on the competitive actions of firms; highly granular accounting data on all globally listed and most non-listed insurance firms active between 1999 and 2008; and information on contextual events, such as catastrophes and stock market developments. We obtained the data behind these categories of information from three different sources. To collect and identify the competitive actions of firms, we tapped the firms' online press release archives and processed their websites by a sequence of self-developed computer programs. With respect to the accounting data of firms and also some industry variables, we relied on the leading proprietary database on the insurance industry, A.M. Best's Global File Statement (A.M. Best, 2009) – which was provided by our research partners Allianz SE and A.M. Best. We further complemented our database with data on contextual events, which we retrieved from Swiss Re's formerly public research portal (Swiss Re, 2007). Figure 1-2 sketches the empirical foundation of this dissertation and presents the data sources and procedures we have deployed in its development.

Figure 1-2: The Dissertation's Empirical Foundation

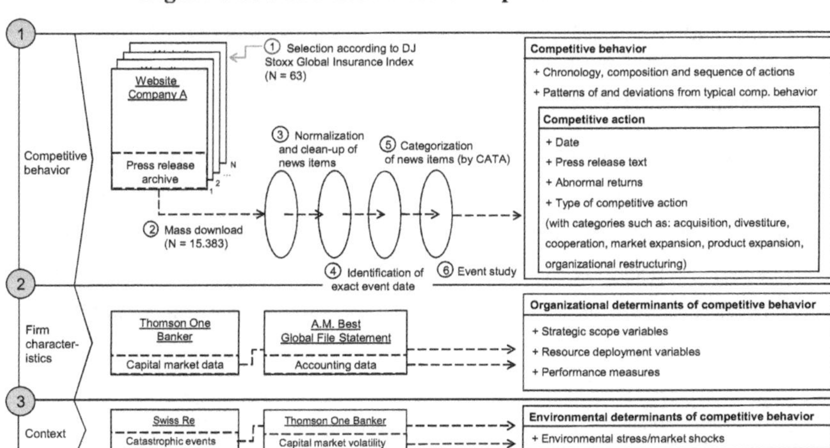

We applied two statistical methods during the development of this empirical foundation. First, we used computer-aided text analysis (CATA) (see Hilliard, Purpura, & Wilkerson, 2006 for an introduction to the method; consult the second study for a detailed description of our implementation) to transform the qualitative data collected from the firms' websites into a format that allowed for the statistical analysis of the firms' competitive behavior. Second, we applied an event study analysis to produce an objective performance measure for the competitive actions in our sample (see MacKinley, 1997 for an introduction to the method; consult the third study for a detailed description of our implementation).

The individual empirical studies of this dissertation draw on the dissertation's empirical foundation in different ways. While the first study on strategic group dynamics benefits from the large sample size and variety of data items available in the A.M. Best database (see line 2 in Figure 1-2), the latter two studies mainly take advantage of the extensive and detailed record of competitive actions that is available for a smaller sample of firms (see line 1 in Figure 1-2).

We test our theoretical propositions with those statistical methods most appropriate for addressing the questions we ask (Hair, Black, Babin, & Anderson, 2009; Tabachnick & Fidell, 2006). For studying the repositioning of firms vis-à-vis their own strategic groups, we use fixed effects panel regressions (Baltagi, 2005). For analyzing the antecedents of interfirm rivalry in competitive markets, we apply event history methodology (Box-Steffensmeier & Jones, 2004). For evaluating the sequences of and relationships between distinct moves, we run multiple regression analyses on the stock market responses that we have generated by the event study analysis mentioned above (Aiken & West, 1991).

In order to assure that our results can be reproduced, we programmed all transformational steps and analyses in self-contained sequences of Visual Basic for Application (VBA) macros and Stata Do-files. Whenever possible, we preferred the latter since Stata Do-files can automatize the full cycle of the analysis workflow, including the organization, analysis, and documentation of data (Long, 2009).[1]

[1] The VBA macros and Stata Do-files can be requested from the author. One module of an exemplary macro is provided in Appendix 4.

1.3 Dissertation Outline

This dissertation is structured in six chapters, with three chapters accommodating self-contained studies. These three studies represent the core of this dissertation and are framed by two introductory chapters and a concluding chapter.

The first chapter ("Introduction") holds a general introduction that provides easy access to the dissertation. It begins by positioning the dissertation within strategic management research and laying out its research objectives and guiding questions (1.1). It then describes the empirical research strategy of the dissertation and the methods applied (1.2) before giving way to this dissertation outline (1.3).

The second chapter ("Theoretical Background") provides a broad theoretical background to the overall theme of the dissertation – competition and interfirm rivalry. The chapter has two major goals. First, it intends to resolve the ambiguity that surrounds the notions of competition and rivalry (McNulty, 1968). Second, it relates the discussions to which we contribute to a wider set of perspectives and thus explicates their overall relevance for our understanding of competitive dynamics. The theoretical background is structured as follows: We briefly review the economic roots of competition research (2.1) before tracing the development of strategic management's competitive dynamics perspective (2.2). The chapter concludes with a short discussion of current trends and challenges in competitive dynamics research. This serves as the dissertation's research agenda (2.3).

Chapters three to five represent the body chapters of this dissertation. Each of these chapters contains an empirical study that addresses one of the research gaps identified in the research agenda (2.3). Chapter three ("Convergence-Divergence Within Strategic Groups") resolves gaps within strategic group dynamics research. Chapter four contributes to research into interfirm rivalry in competitive markets ("From Crisis to Opportunity: How Market Shocks Impact Interfirm Rivalry"), and chapter five ("Performance Effects of Corporate Divestiture Programs") contributes to prior work on the interrelationships between competitive actions. The studies in these chapters were designed in a manner that allows for their individual publication. Hence, they are self-contained and possess an internal structure that consists of an introduction, a theoretical background section, a section deriving the study's hypotheses, a method section, a section presenting the results from the statistical analyses, and a discussion.

The sixth chapter ("Discussion and Conclusion") synthesizes the preceding chapters' main results (6.1), theoretical (6.2) and practical contributions (6.3), and presents the dissertation's major limitations (6.4) and research implications (6.5). It ends with a final conclusion (6.6). Figure 1-3 provides a graphical illustration of the dissertation.

Figure 1-3: Dissertation Outline

1 Introduction

- Research Objectives and Guiding Questions
- Research Strategy and Method
- Dissertation Outline

2 Theoretical Background

- A Short History of Economic-Thought on Competition
- Competition Research Within Strategic Management
- Toward a Research Agenda

3-5 Self-Contained Studies

3 Convergence-Divergence Within Strategic Groups

4 From Crisis to Opportunity: How Market Shocks Impact Interfirm Rivalry

5 Performance Effects of Corporate Divestiture Programs

6 Discussion and Conclusion

- Synthesis of Results, Theoretical and Practical Contributions
- Presentation of Limitations and Implications for Future Research
- Conclusion

2 Theoretical Background

"There is probably no [other] concept [...] that is at once more fundamental and pervasive, yet less satisfactorily developed, than the concept of competition"(McNulty, 1968: 639).

Clearly, the term competition triggers different associations among theorists, policymakers and businessmen. While theorists and policymakers oftentimes relate competition to broad industry states and market structures, businessmen tend to conceive the concept as a rivalry between competing firms. Similar to these different stakeholder perceptions, there is also no unified notion of the concept within the social sciences. Instead, during the more than 200 years of academic discourse in economics and, more recently, in management research, various contrasting perspectives on competition have been promoted, leaving us with a somewhat ambiguous notion of the concept (McNulty, 1968).

There are three broad categories into which the extant body of research on competition can be divided (Blaug, 2001; Budzinski, 2008). First, philosophical research on the nature of competition (Hayek, 1968; Schumpeter, 1934; Smith, 1776). Second, structuralist analyses that investigate competition as abstract equilibrium-based states of rest in the rivalry between buyers and sellers (Bertrand, 1883; Cournot, 1938). Third, studies on the competitive process with its constituting actions and the actors involved (Schumpeter, 1934; Young, Smith, & Grimm, 1996). While economists have legitimized and advanced all of these categories of research, management scholars have mainly engaged in the last category with their distinct interest in interfirm performance differences (Chen, 2009b).

To position this dissertation and its three empirical studies, and to provide clarity on the notion of competition to which we refer, we briefly lay out the academic discourse on competition and rivalry. Since this discourse has traditionally been led by economists, and since economic theories underlie those of strategic management research, we first synthesize the evolution of economic-thought on competition before presenting how management and competitive dynamics research approach the topic. We conclude with a research agenda based on the current state of competitive dynamics research.

2.1 A Short History of Economic-Thought on Competition

Adam Smith's "The Wealth of Nations" (1776) not only marks the birth of modern economic analysis, but also of research into competition. Smith's *magnum opus* describes how competitive forces – metaphorically labeled as the "invisible hand" of the market – organize individual economic activities in free market economies and thereby reconcile the self-interest of market participants with the general public good. Adam Smith uses the term competition in a manner close to the term's semantic meaning, describing "an inherently lively process that, with its rivalry and the mutual incentive and stimulus to innovate and improve, is the driving force of [...] [positive] welfare effects" (Budzinski, 2008: 297).

Following this classic conceptualization, however, economists developed a contrasting perspective on competition. From the mid 19th century onwards, economists tried to turn economics into an exact science and, inspired by Newtonian mechanics, promoted the idea of markets in equilibrium (Blaug, 2001; Budzinski, 2008). Thus, scholars began using the term competition in a new way; namely, to describe equilibrium end-states of markets in which market participants finally resolve their contests by adjusting their quantities of production and consumption (Blaug, 2001). As a consequence, the concept of competition lost its behavioral character and became reduced to an endogenous force in empirically empty models (Bertrand, 1883; Cournot, 1938). While these models yielded some very important theoretical insights into broad mechanisms of competition, they, and the neoclassic paradigm they represented, failed with the arrival of the Great Depression in the early 20th century (Budzinski, 2008; Friedman, 1962).

Economists hesitantly began to accept that real-world competition may not live up to the faceless force they had conceived, but is inherently flawed with imperfections, such as geographical distortions or product heterogeneity (Budzinski, 2008). In recognizing these flaws, they replaced the ideal of perfect competition with the idea of workable competition and re-introduced firms into their theoretical equations (Clark, 1940). For the next three decades, however, industrial organization (IO) scholars managed to maintain the primacy of the market by claiming that structural market characteristics would mostly drive the conducts and performance levels of firms (Bain, 1956, 1959; Mason, 1949). Even though firms had thus re-entered the argument with this structure-conduct-performance (s-c-p) paradigm, they remained annexed to the industry level and deprived of their autonomy and diversity.

Proponents of Austrian and Schumpeterian economics criticized both the neoclassical and the s-c-p paradigm for being inherently static and missing central aspects of competition, such as innovation, change, endogenous growth and heterogeneous capital/firms (Jacobson, 1992; Nelson & Winter, 1982). To overcome these deficiencies, these scholars abandoned the end-state focus of extant research and revived the behavioral notion of competition by focusing on the very process of competition with its diverse actors and their competitive behaviors over time. Seminal conceptualizations described the competitive process as a discovery procedure (Hayek, 1968) or a process of creative destruction (Schumpeter, 1934), in which entrepreneurs and market incumbents grow markets by innovation and fight over market shares by means of competitive actions. Empirically, this process-focus suggested a less abstract and less analytic discourse than neoclassic theories – a factor which caused it to face criticism for not being rigorous enough (White, 2008) – and, instead, promoted a focus on the competitive actions of firms. Through this, it stimulated the development and evolution of competitive dynamics research with its distinct interest in the competitive behavior of firms (Young et al., 1996).

Most recently, the study of competition has been informed by game theory (von Neumann & Morgenstern, 1944). While game theory was originally merely a mathematical discipline concerned with deriving optimal strategies within simple strategic games, its obvious relevance for competition-related questions motivated scholars to advance the game-theoretic models and apply them to complex competitive issues such as tacit collusion or predatory pricing (Baumol, 1982; Kreps, Milgrom, Roberts, & Wilson, 1982; Kreps, 1990). Besides these specific contributions, game theory needs to be credited for providing an approach that is useful for describing competitive situations in which a strategy is sought that explicitly acknowledges that rivals will respond to one's actions in a manner optimal to them (Chatterjee & Samuelson, 2001). Since most competitive situations ask for such strategies, game theory has become a valuable lens for studying interfirm rivalry and rightfully informs competitive dynamics (McGrath, Chen, & MacMillan, 1998) and business literature (Brandenburger & Nalebuff, 1996).

2.2 Competition Research Within Strategic Management

Since its inception as an own academic field in the late 20th century (Schendel & Hofer, 1979), strategic management has developed a particular interest in how individual firms can achieve and sustain superior performance. To trace this question, management scholars also turned to economic theories on competition and found that the rivalry between firms needs to be a key element in their answer (Thomas & Pollock, 1999; Young et al., 1996). Based on the theoretical legacy from economics and the various perspectives common to the strategic management discipline (Hambrick, 2004), strategy scholars advanced our understanding of competition and its outcomes at the firm- and industry-level. Figure 2-1 organizes the major theoretical lenses through which management scholars have viewed competition along a scale that indicates the perspectives' levels of reasoning.

Figure 2-1: Theoretical Perspectives on Interfirm Rivalry

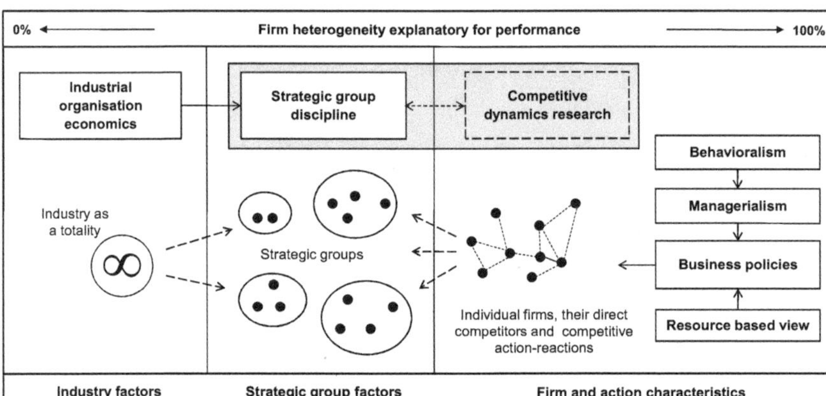

Figure adapted from Killström (2005: 7)

As the illustration shows, strategic management research has paralleled the conflict between equilibrium and process theories of economics and referred to competition both in terms of industry-level characteristics and dynamic firm-level processes. To reconcile the disparate notions, management scholars have conceived the strategic group discipline as a mediator between them and promoted the idea that both structural market and idiosyncratic firm characteristics drive interfirm rivalry and its outcomes (Hoskisson, Hitt, Wan, & Yiu, 1999; Hunt, 1972). As a theoretical and analytical link between the disparate firm- and industry-levels, the strategic group concept fastly assumed a pivotal role in the study of industry dynamics (Huff, Huff, & Thomas, 1994; Mascarenhas, 1989), and became, despite its origin from the "static" industrial organization perspective, part of process- and firm-focused considerations. It is thus nowadays also considered as a distinct strand of competitive dynamics research (Ketchen et al., 2004).[2]

Industrial Organization and Strategic Groups

The most traditional perspective in studying competition and its outcomes is the industrial organization perspective rooted in economics (Bain, 1959; Mason, 1949). The theory of competition it suggests proposes strong reciprocal causalities between the competitive conditions of the industry (structure), the business policies of firms (conduct) and the performance levels firms experience (performance). Within this set of interdependencies, the stimulus of change originates from variations at the industry-level, relegating the competitive behavior of firms to an annex of industry events. Combined with neoclassic assumptions on the rationality of managers, firms were presumed to show identical or at least highly similar conduct and performance levels (Bain, 1959; Mason, 1949; Porter, 1981).

Since these assertions could not be empirically confirmed, IO scholars stepped down to a lower level of analysis for defending their s-c-p paradigm. They conceived a within-industry structure to which the variations in firm performance and conduct could be attributed (Caves & Porter, 1977; Hunt, 1972). Strategic groups form the constituting element of this industry structure and represent clusters of firms that closely resemble each other in key strategic dimensions. It was reasoned, that such groupings exist due to structural barriers within the industry that hamper the repositioning of firms (Mascarenhas, 1989; Porter, 1980). These structural barriers, also termed mobility barriers, were portrayed as walls around strategic groups that would protect member firms from external competition, leading to homogenous conduct and performance levels within the groups.

[2] It is important to note that "competitive dynamics research" has initially only described studies on competitive actions and responses, but nowadays also refers to research about contextual aspects of rivalry that shares the interest in dynamic aspects of competitive behaviors – such as strategic groups, regional clusters, and multipoint competition.

However, also within strategic groups, performance differences prevailed (Cool & Schendel, 1988) and the strategic group concept became severely criticized (Barney & Hoskisson, 1990). In answering this criticism, scholars largely replaced the concept's IO-based theoretical fundament and gave up the idea of homogenous performance levels within groups. Strategic groups became reconceptualized as "cognitive communities" of firms that share a common recipe for competing and doing business in an industry (Porac & Thomas, 1990). By this, strategic groups also turned into cognitive reference points and landmarks that inform the temporal dynamics of competition within industries (Fiegenbaum & Thomas, 1995; Hodgkinson, 1997).

Competitive Dynamics and the Study of Competitive Actions

Contrasting IO's interest in structural industry characteristics, the competitive dynamics perspective focuses on the nature and consequences of competitive dynamics among firms (Ketchen et al., 2004). The perspective generally assumes a notion of competition matching the idea of Schumpeterian and Austrian economics (Kirzner, 1997; Mises, 1949) that "the fundamental impulse that sets and keeps the capitalist engine in motion comes from the new customers' goods, the new methods of production of transportation, the new markets, the new forms of industrial organization that capitalist enterprises create" (Schumpeter, 1943: 83-85). It thus opens up the black box of firm behavior and considers firm performance levels resulting from an ongoing struggle among firms (Kirzner, 1973).

To better express the action and turbulence inherent in the competitive interplay between firms and to set their interpretation of competition apart from the static notion present in economics, competitive dynamics scholars have revitalized the term "interfirm rivalry" (Bettis & Weeks, 1987; Porter, 1979) and created certain useful metaphors that illustrate the personal, goal-driven and dynamic notion of rivalry they maintain (Chen, 2009b). Scholars described rivalry as a boxing-fight (Ferrier & Lee, 2002), or, with a focus on a larger number of competitors, as a race where multiple rivals compete against each other, while accelerating from time to time to overtake a specific opponent (Zuchhini & Kretschmer, 2011).

The inception of the competitive dynamics perspective dates back to the mid 1980s, when scholars initially put the dynamic, process-oriented notion of interfirm rivalry to an empirical test (Bettis & Weeks, 1987; MacMillan, McCaffrey, & Van Wijk, 1985). They pioneered an empirical approach that studies the competitive actions and responses of firms as the central vehicles of rivalry. Fueled by the research program of Professor Chen (1988, 1996; Chen & Hambrick, 1995; Chen & MacMillan, 1992; Chen & Miller, 1994; Chen et al., 1992), this research strand soon gained momentum and became an established area of research named "competitive dynamics research".

Early competitive dynamics studies investigated the defining characteristics of competitive moves and how these relate to responses by competitors (Chen & MacMillan, 1992; Chen & Miller, 1994; Chen et al., 1992). Important findings suggest that a shared market interest and similar resource profiles raise competitive tension between firms and that action characteristics, such as irreversibility, visibility and competitor dependence on the challenged market, have predictive power for the competitor's response behavior (Chen, 1996; Chen & MacMillan, 1992; Chen & Miller, 1994). Scholars subsequently complemented the analysis of action-and-response combinations with the study of longer sequences of competitive moves (Chen & Hambrick, 1995; Ferrier, 2001; Gimeno & Woo, 1996; Hambrick, Cho, & Chen, 1996; Miller & Chen, 1994, 1996b, 1996a; Rindova, Ferrier, & Wiltbank, 2010). In comparison to the analysis of individual moves, which draws on the isolated characteristics of actions, the analysis of competitive action sequences sheds light on the effectiveness of competitive strategies as a whole. Ferrier, Smith and Grimm (1999; 2001a), for example, find that challengers have better chances to dethrone their market's leading firm with sequences of aggressive actions if the leading firm fails to keep up with the challenger, applies narrower action repertoires, or responds in a less aggressive way.

Most recently, competitive dynamics research has taken a novel direction. It set out to expand its reach to market situations where the dyadic relationship between a focal firm and its main rival is not sufficiently instrumental for explaining the firm's competitive behavior (Hsieh & Chen, 2010; Zuchhini & Kretschmer, 2011). In other words, the most recent research efforts aim at developing an action-based theory of rivalry valid in competitive markets, where interfirm-relationships are numerous, and individually less relevant for the choice and timing of competitive actions than presumed by prior research (Chen, 1996;

Chen & MacMillan, 1992). Hsieh & Chen (2010) have pioneered such an expansion of the field's theoretical fundament and identified the recent competitive activity of all rivals as the major antecedent of a firm's inclination to take competitive action.

2.3 Toward a Research Agenda

Directly connecting to the preceding discussion of competitive dynamics research, we now provide a summary of those issues within sub-streams of competitive dynamics research that give rise to our main research studies. Since we elaborate on these issues in great detail within the following chapters, we limit ourselves at this point to relating them to their wider context and explaining why they need to be addressed to progress the theoretical discussions they pertain to. Our assessment of the relevance of these issues grounds on a thorough literature review and on meta-reviews of the current state of competitive dynamics research (Ketchen et al., 2004; Smith et al., 2001b). Figure 2-2 summarizes the research agenda as it will be discussed hereafter. The pictograms the figure includes link to the theoretical perspectives of competition research which were presented in Figure 2-1.

Figure 2-2: Research Agenda

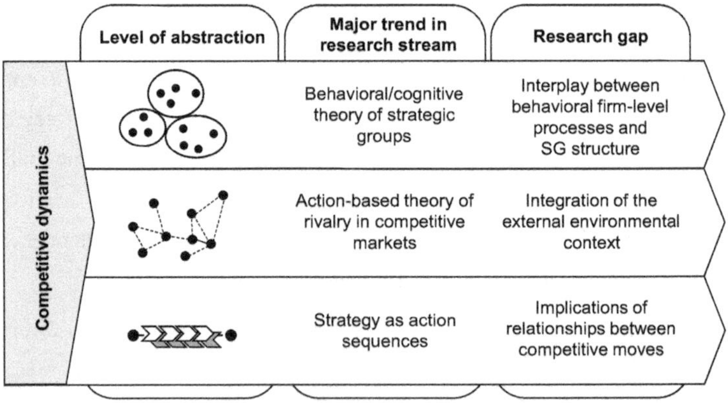

The future challenges of strategic group research originate from the recent evolution of the strategic group concept. The rise of the notion of cognitive groups that function as key reference points for managers when contemplating strategic change has fundamentally changed the questions we need to answer (Fiegenbaum, Hart, & Schendel, 1996; Fiegenbaum & Thomas, 1995; Reger & Huff, 1993).

Instead of further investigating performance implications that are presumed to result from mobility barriers, we should focus on the behavioral implications strategic groups have as reference points. Despite an evolving theory on these implications (Fiegenbaum & Thomas, 1995; Hodgkinson, 1997), there is a lack of large-scale empirical work that tests even the key substantive claims of the theory (Hodgkinson, 1997; McNamara, Deephouse, & Luce, 2003; Nair & Filer, 2003; Reger & Huff, 1993). To overcome this issue and to progress our understanding of the evolution of strategic group structures, we need to investigate their impact on the behavioral firm-level processes that underlie the repositioning moves of firms.

Similarly, the study of competitive moves and its research agenda have recently undergone an important change. In response to the criticism that dyad-based research designs fall short in competitive market settings, scholars suggested to go beyond the firm-dyad and to develop a new action-based theory of interfirm rivalry more valid for these settings (Hsieh & Chen, 2010; Zuchhini & Kretschmer, 2011). So far, however, this novel theory of interfirm rivalry is in a very early stage and neglects factors that are characteristic to the level of abstraction it argues on. This neglect especially applies to the environmental context, which hosts various factors that co-determine a firm's competitive choices (Chen, Lin, & Michel, 2009; Ghemawat & Cassiman, 2007). In contrast to dyadic research, research contributing to the novel theory on rivalry is not characterized by an empirical and theoretical scope that justifies an incomprehensive consideration of environmental factors.

With respect to research on competitive actions, further issues exist. Despite a few exceptions (Ferrier & Lee, 2002), scholars abstract from the relationships between the actions of an individual firm. Research on action-response dyads, for example, merely draws on the characteristics of an individual competitive action, the rival's response and the characteristics of the involved competitors, and thereby disconnects a distinct pair of actions from other actions throughout time (Chen et al., 1992; Smith, Grimm, Gannon, & Chen, 1991). Research that considers action repertoires over time, instead, may account for the heterogeneity of moves, but still abstracts from linkages between them (Chen & Hambrick, 1995; Ferrier et al., 1999; Gimeno & Woo, 1996). Competitive dynamics research thus misses out on an important dimension and may assume a micro-view on how relationships between competitive actions impact the actions' performance and other consequences.

3 Convergence-Divergence Within Strategic Groups

3.1 Introduction

Since Hunt (1972) initially grouped strategically similar firms within the appliance industry into sets of direct competitors and dubbed these clusters "strategic groups", numerous strategy scholars have adopted the strategic group concept. While early studies mostly applied strategic groups as a middle-ground between the industry and the firm for predicting profitability differences between firms, more recent studies turned toward investigating the internal structure of strategic groups (Cool & Schendel, 1987; McNamara et al., 2003), the groups' roles in guiding managerial decision making and the competitive behavior of firms (Baum & Lant, 1995; Bresser, Dunbar, & Jithendranathan, 1994; Fiegenbaum & Thomas, 1995; Porac & Thomas, 1994), as well as the temporal dynamics of strategic groups (DeSarbo, Grewal, & Wang, 2009; Fiegenbaum & Thomas, 1993; Lee, Lee, & Rho, 2002; Mascarenhas, 1989; Oster, 1982).

This paper contributes to the study of strategic group dynamics, a sub-field of strategic group research, which focuses on the evolution of strategic group structures and investigates the processes that either generate strategic groups, change the strategic positioning of such groups, affect the distribution of firms across different strategic groups, or alter the number of strategic groups an industry carries at a distinct point of time (Lee et al., 2002; Más Ruíz, 1999; Mascarenhas, 1989). While the initiation of strategic groups has been attributed to random differences in firm preferences (Caves & Porter, 1977), their ongoing evolution is considered as a function of various factors at the firm and industry level. Changes in the strategic positioning of groups, for example, were conjectured to take their origin both in environmental discontinuities and successful initiatives of firms, which are matched by imitation activities of competitors (Cool & Schendel, 1987). Movements between strategic groups, instead, were theorized to be largely driven by variations in firm performance and mobility barriers (Mascarenhas, 1989). The number of strategic groups an industry carries at a given point of time, in turn, has been controversially discussed with arguments either favoring structural environmental characteristics or strategic choices of firms as the main source of change (Fiegenbaum & Thomas, 1990; Más Ruíz, 1999; Mascarenhas, 1989; Oster, 1982).

Even when arguing from the firm perspective, most prior research subsumed the theorized firm-level antecedents of strategic group dynamics, such as variations in firm performance, under broad states or characteristics of the industry. In consequence, our empirical knowledge on respective phenomena, such as shifts of strategic group strategies or increases in the aggregated number of movements between strategic groups (i.e., mobility rates), has remained linked to periods of decline and growth (Mascarenhas, 1989), disruptive industry events such as market liberalization or crises (Más Ruíz, 1999), or gradual industry change accrued over time (Fiegenbaum & Thomas, 1990). The argumentation of many studies thereby still follows the structure-conduct-performance paradigm's notion that it is mostly environmental changes that mandate variations at the firm- and strategic-group level (Bain, 1959; Mason, 1949).

As a consequence, we know little about the strategic interaction mechanisms between firm-level processes and strategic group characteristics "that result in different strategic groups and competitive structures over time" (Fiegenbaum & Thomas, 1995: 462). Recent contributions in strategic group literature encourage us to explore these and test how strategic groups as cognitive references guide individual firms within the multidimensional competitive space of their industry (Hodgkinson, 1997; McNamara et al., 2003; Nair & Filer, 2003; Reger & Huff, 1993). Most notably, Fiegenbaum and Thomas (1995) provide valuable directions. With their finding that firms constantly track their own strategic group, they provide the first empirical evidence on the notion that strategic groups guide their members as direct references and benchmarks.

The purpose of this study is to advance prior theory on how firms move within their industry's strategic group structure (Fiegenbaum & Thomas, 1995). We center on the relationship between firms and their own strategic group and explicate how the interplay between strategic group and firm factors drives the managerial decision-making process preceding the repositioning of firms. We investigate strategic convergence-divergence as the extent to which firms draw closer to or further away from their strategic group over time. In this vein, our theory acknowledges that strategic group memberships are a matter of degree and subject to constant change (e.g., Más Ruíz, 1999; Wiggins & Ruefli, 1995).

Based on the behavioral theory of the firm (Cyert & March, 1963; March & Shapira, 1987, 1992), we propose that managers adjust their firms' positioning and turn toward promising business models available in adjacent strategic groups when their firms' financial performance levels decrease or are below the managers' aspiration levels. For high-performing firms, instead, we propose that managers are reluctant to change their firms' strategies. Also, we propose that high-performing firms will be imitated by other firms and thus be moved into the center of the strategic group (Lieberman & Asaba, 2006; Park, 2007). Furthermore, we argue that the relationship between a firm's level of performance relative to aspiration and its convergence-divergence toward its strategic group is moderated by the firm's environmental context and its within-group positioning. We test these relationships on a sample of 1,191 firms and their strategic groups within the U.S. insurance industry between 1999 and 2008.

The study advances our understanding of why and how firms converge or diverge vis-à-vis their own strategic groups (Fiegenbaum & Thomas, 1995; McNamara et al., 2003). It initially explicates and empirically tests the interplay between behavioral firm-level processes and strategic group characteristics which ultimately brings about variations in strategic group structures (Fiegenbaum & Thomas, 1995). By simultaneously considering firm-, strategic group-, and industry-level factors and processes, our study provides an integrative perspective that overcomes the narrow theoretical and empirical scope of prior research (Bogner, Mahoney, & Thomas, 1998; McNamara et al., 2003). Further, the study introduces a continuous movement vector as its dependent variable and thereby pioneers in considering strategic group membership as a continuous rather than a binary choice (DeSarbo & Grewal, 2008; McNamara et al., 2003).

The remainder of the paper is organized as follows: First, we review extant strategic group research focused on analyzing strategic group dynamics. Subsequently, we develop hypotheses on the determinants that underlie managers' decisions to converge to or diverge from their present strategic group. We then explain our methodological design and present as well as discuss our results. We conclude with an outline of the study's limitations and implications for theory and practice.

3.2 Research on Strategic Group Dynamics

Research into strategic groups and strategic group dynamics originate from industrial organization research (Caves & Porter, 1977; Hunt, 1972; Porter, 1979), where strategic groups have been conceptualized as a middle ground between the industry- and firm-level to resolve the conflict between the s-c-p paradigm's assumption of uniform firm conduct (Bain, 1959; Mason, 1949) and the empirical evidence of performance differentials within industries (Bogner et al., 1998). Since the existence and positions of strategic groups were theoretically justified by the distribution of mobility barriers within industries (Mascarenhas & Aaker, 1989; Porter, 1980), variations in strategic groups were logically preceded by changes in mobility barriers. As to the source of such variations, various types of structural and environmental discontinuities were suggested – such as industry states or stages, technological innovation, crises, and changes in law or regulation (McGee & Thomas, 1986). These phenomena hold in common with each other that they alter a firm's opportunities and means to stabilize and defend its market position. Firms thus tend to respond to these discontinuities by adapting their strategies and practices, which translates into changes in their market positions. In turn, these changes prompt variations in the positions of strategic groups, the movements between groups, or even the number of groups present in an industry (Mascarenhas, 1989; McGee & Thomas, 1986; Zuniga-Vicente, Fuente-Sabaté, & Rodríguez-Puerta, 2004a).

Investigating the impact of such changes, scholars have studied the differences in strategic group structures between time periods that were separated by the discontinuity of interest (e.g., Downling & Ruefli, 1992; Fiegenbaum, Sudharshan, & Thomas, 1990; Hergert, 1988; Más Ruíz, 1999; Mascarenhas, 1989; Miles, Snow, & Sharfman, 1993; Zuniga-Vicente et al., 2004a). Mascarenhas (1989), for example, studied the extent of and motivation for strategic group changes during periods of economic growth, stability, and decline. He found that periods of economic decline induce higher levels of heterogeneity in firm behavior and thereby lead to more frequent repositionings between strategic groups and shifts in strategic group strategies. Others linked the life-cycle stages of industries to the number of strategic groups the industries carried. Hergert (1988) found that the number of strategic groups increases over time and conjectured that demand structures and technologies become more differentiated over time and thus offer a wider set of strategic options to potential entrants and current market incumbents. Miles et al. (1993), instead, found an opposite effect of an industry's maturity and proposed that market incumbents eventually shift their focus from the product market to production efficiency, become more similar and thereby reduce the number of strategic groups within mature industries.

Studies with a focus on industry events rather than stages oftentimes examine the history of competition in an industry by relating the evolution of strategic group structures to various historical industry events (Más Ruíz, 1999; Zuniga-Vicente et al., 2004a). Besides industry specific insights, these studies consistently showed that environmental discontinuities induce heterogeneity in the behavior of firms (e.g., Chattopadhyay, Glick, & Huber, 2001) and promote new strategic groups, firm intergroup mobility, and general shifts in the position and performance levels of groups (e.g., Zuniga-Vicente et al., 2004a).

In response to criticism on the theoretical foundation of the strategic group concept (Barney & Hoskisson, 1990; Hatten & Hatten, 1987), scholars re-evaluated the concept and shifted its theoretical base closer toward cognitive and behavioral arguments (Bogner et al., 1998). They transformed the notion of strategic groups as industry enclaves walled by mobility barriers into one of "cognitive communities" of firms that share a set of beliefs that make up a recipe for competing and doing business in an industry (Porac & Thomas, 1990; Thomas & Carroll, 1994). In this context, scholars relaxed their assumptions on how rational managers act. While IO economists considered managers as rational agents that aptly and uniformly translate stimuli from their industries into adaptive moves of firms, the new cognitive stance of strategic group research allowed for behavioral arguments (Thomas & Pollock, 1999). Scholars henceforth acknowledged that rationally bounded managers need to simplify their market environments – by grouping competitors. Strategic groups thus assumed a major role in helping managers to make sense of their environment both as cognitive references and repositories of alternative strategic practices (Fiegenbaum et al., 1996; Peteraf & Shanley, 1997; Reger & Huff, 1993).

For research on strategic group dynamics, the cognitive perspective has important implications. It not only suggests that strategic group dynamics accrue from the individual firms' strategic choices (Child, 1997; Fiegenbaum & Thomas, 1995), but it also resets the focus for empirical research from industry- to firm-level processes (Bogner et al., 1998; Cyert & March, 1963). Studies which adopt this perspective thus identified the decision-making process and its behavioral determinants, such as risk preferences of managers, and the firms' resource endowments as particularly defining for the repositionings of firms within their own and across strategic groups (Bogner et al., 1998; Bogner, Thomas, & McGee, 1996; Fiegenbaum & Thomas, 1995). They further suggest that social comparison and benchmarking with peer firms are the main reasons for managers to consider repositioning moves vis-à-vis their firm's own strategic group (Bogner, 1991; Fiegenbaum & Thomas, 1995; Greve, 1998b; Mascarenhas, 1989).

With respect to this process of strategic choice, extant research has produced several important findings. First, mobility barriers impact the repositionings of firms less than traditionally assumed (Mascarenhas & Aaker, 1989; Porter, 1980). Bogner, Thomas and McGee (1996) for example, found in their study on the U.S. pharmaceutical industry that the entry points and expansion paths of foreign entrants were more defined by the resource and competence profiles of entrants than by the mobility barriers that separated the industry's strategic groups. Also the study of Fiegenbaum and Thomas (1995) on the U.S. insurance industry attenuated the relevance of the mobility barrier concept – however on other grounds. Their analyses failed to support the basic assumption that strategic group members fortify the mobility barriers that protect their group and thus directly questioned the validity of the concept. Second, there is a reason other than mobility barriers that explains the stability of strategic group structures. Fiegenbaum and Thomas (1995) further revealed that firms continuously benchmark themselves with their own strategic group and perceive the group's strategy – i.e., the average strategy of all group members – as the initial reference point when contemplating strategic change. As a consequence, firms tend to mimic their own group's movements, keep their relative position vis-à-vis their peer firms and thus reinforce the stability of strategic groups (Fiegenbaum & Thomas, 1995).

In sum, prior research on strategic group dynamics maintains that strategic groups accommodate heterogeneous firms that differ in the degree to which they adhere to their own strategic group's strategy. These varying degrees of adherence – and thus the firms' positions within strategic groups over time – primarily lead back to managerial choices and the decision-making processes underlying these choices. These processes themselves are of behavioral character and draw on social comparison and performance benchmarking with strategic groups as major references (Ketchen, Thomas, & Snow, 1993; McNamara, Luce, & Thompson, 2002; Peteraf & Shanley, 1997; Reger & Huff, 1993).

Yet, despite a growing consent on this notion of firm and thus strategic group dynamics (Bogner et al., 1998; Fiegenbaum & Thomas, 1995), there has been no longitudinal research investigating the firm-level processes and contingencies that antecede and characterize these repositionings in a consolidated manner (Hodgkinson, 1997).

3.3 Antecedents of Strategic Convergence-Divergence

The present study empirically investigates the antecedents of strategic group dynamics at the firm level. Instead of focusing on market and environmental characteristics (Donaldson, 1985; Hannan & Freeman, 1989; Powell & DiMaggio, 1991), we consider strategic group dynamics to accrue from the individual firms' strategic choices (Child, 1997). We thus investigate how corporate decision-makers approach the repositioning of their firm and ground our reasoning on the behavioral theory of the firm (BTOF) (Audia, Locke, & Smith, 2000; Bromiley, 1991; Greve, 1998a, 2003; Miller & Chen, 1994; Miller & Chen, 2004) and research on how human decision makers simplify and approach risky decisions under uncertainty (Kahneman & Tversky, 1979, 2000; March & Shapira, 1992).

Since these works suggest that managers turn toward other firms – most notably their direct competitors (Fiegenbaum et al., 1996; Fiegenbaum & Thomas, 1993) – when contemplating change, we study the strategic repositionings of firms as the extents to which they converge to or diverge from their own strategic groups.

We argue for these movements on grounds of factors found in the individual relationships between firms and their strategic groups (Fiegenbaum & Thomas, 1995). This approach – also known as dyadic research – allows us to simultaneously consider firm and group characteristics when investigating the behavioral foundations of strategic group dynamics. Even though this approach has been extensively applied by prior research (e.g., Gulati, 1995; Lincoln, 1984; Wang & Zajac, 2007), our study differs in one aspect from most prior dyadic analyses (see Park, 2007 for an exception). Our "strategic convergence-divergence" variable directly arises from the dyadic relationship. It expresses the temporal change in the distance between a firm and its own strategic group. Since this is a new aspect to strategic group research, we provide a short definition of our dependent variable hereafter.

Strategic Convergence-Divergence

We define strategic convergence-divergence as the extent to which a firm draws closer to or further away from its own strategic group. The basic idea of this definition leans on Park (2007), who analyzes the convergence-divergence moves between firms. Instead of referring to other firms, however, we conceptualize strategic repositionings as changes in a firm's strategic profile vis-à-vis the benchmark profile of its own strategic group. Hence, a firm converges toward (diverges from) its own strategic group when its strategic profile becomes more (less) similar to that of its own strategic group. We operationalize a firm's strategic profile as a vector $X_{i,t}$ in an n-dimensional space span by the scope and resource deployment variables established for the insurance industry by Fiegenbaum and Thomas (1990, see Table 3–1). The focal firm's strategic group is characterized by a similar vector $X_{OSG(i),t}$. When firm i moved from $X_{i,t-\Delta}$ at time $t-\Delta$ to $X_{i,t}$ at time t and the strategic group's centroid has simultaneously moved from $X_{OSG(i),t-\Delta}$ to $X_{OSG(i),t}$, the distance between $X_{i,t-\Delta}$ and $X_{OSG(i),t-\Delta}$ differs from the distance between $X_{i,t}$ and $X_{OSG(i),t}$. The difference between these two distances equals the strategic distance the firm has covered vis-à-vis its own strategic group. If it is positive, the firm has converged toward its own strategic group; if it is negative, the firm has diverged from its own strategic group. Figure 3-1 illustrates our conceptualization of strategic convergence-divergence (SCD) within an exemplary space of strategic positioning with two dimensions.

Figure 3-1: Strategic Convergence-Divergence in two Dimensions

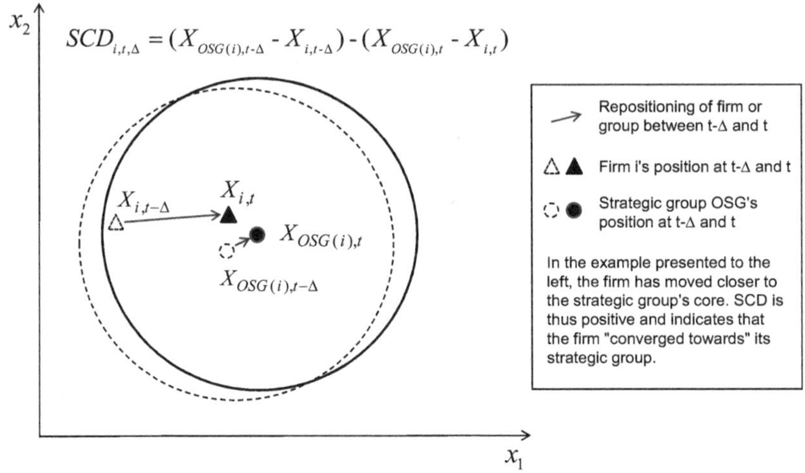

The Effects of Performance, Aspirations and Behavioral Biases

The behavioral theory of the firm holds that a firm's management's initiative for strategic change oftentimes originates from the firm's own history, with poor prior performance levels being the most important trigger (Audia & Greve, 2006; Cyert & March, 1963; Greve, 1998a, 2003; Levitt & March, 1988). Specifically, performance shortfalls were found to spark "problemistic search" processes that aim to find solutions for the performance problems at hand. While these search processes usually start in the close surrounding of the respective firm, they can become increasingly complex and far-reaching when no satisfying solution is readily found (Chang, 1996; Cool & Schendel, 1988). In other words, when managers intensify their search, they expand their search scopes and seek a new solution for the presumed problem that is more distant from the previous solution (Cyert & March, 1963). Such changes in search scope inform how firms reposition within strategic group structures. Since strategic groups function as repositories of ideas, practices and experiences (Huff, 1982) and are spatially distributed within the strategic space of the industry, managers will sequentially consult them for advice. While minor performance problems translate into less wide search efforts, more severe problems may suggest managers to consider the operational and strategic practices of adjacent strategic groups as part of potential solutions (Fiegenbaum & Thomas, 1995; Greve, 1998b; Huff, 1982). By adopting such distant practices, firms will leave their original market positions and move into the directions of adjacent groups, which will cause a divergence from their own strategic group (Mascarenhas & Aaker, 1989; Porac, Thomas, & Baden-Fuller, 1989).

In contrast, if firms perform well, their occupying positions and practices will be regarded as more attractive by others (Fiegenbaum & Thomas, 1995; Greve, 1998b). As a consequence, these other firms will try to adopt or imitate the presumably superior strategies and practices of high-performers (Greve, 1998b; Haveman, 1993; Mansfield, 1961; Park, 2007). Unless the latter succeed in compellingly deterring other firms from their plans to imitate them, the adopters will change the average strategy of the strategic group in a way that moves the high-performing firms gradually into the center of the strategic group. Besides attracting the attention of potential imitators, good performance was found to have another effect. A lack of urgency to change successful practices confirms managers in continuing their current strategies (Greve, 1998a; Miller & Friesen, 1980) and repeating the competitive actions and strategies that they attribute to past success, irrespective of whether such a causal link exists (Levitt & March, 1988; Miller & Chen, 1994; Milliken & Lant, 1991). The absence of pressures to change in combination with the bolstered confidence in the own practices narrows the attentional scope of managers of well performing firms and reduces their willingness to experiment with the operational and strategic practices of adjacent strategic groups (Miller, 1994; Walsh, 1995). Thus, the repositioning moves of such firms are less likely to be informed by adjacent strategic groups.

Taken together, the wider search scope of low-performing firms, and the higher resistance to change and the market's imitation of high-performing firms suggest that low-performing firms diverge from their own strategic group, whereas high-performing firms move into the center of their groupings. We therefore propose:

> *Hypothesis 1: A focal firm's performance is positively related to its strategic convergence-divergence vis-à-vis its own strategic group.*

Figure 3-2: Performance, Aspirations, and Strategic Convergence-Divergence

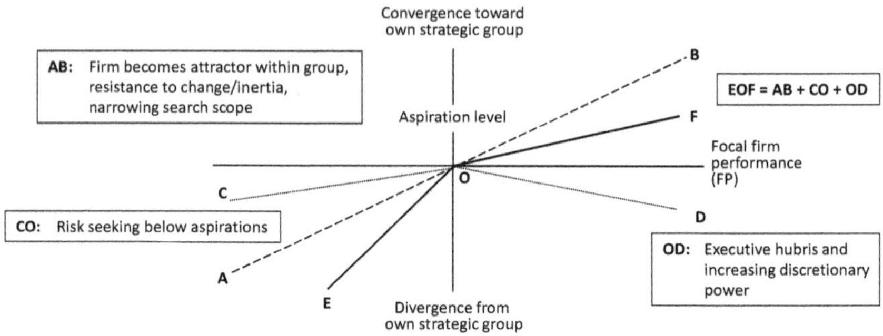

While Hypothesis 1 suggests that a firm's low financial performance is the main reason for divergence from the own strategic group and good performance moves a firm into the center of its group (see dashed line in Figure 3-2), it does not yet specify the performance level that separates convergence from divergence. The BTOF (Bromiley, 2004; March & Simon, 1958) as well as literature on performance feedback (Greve, 1998a, 2003, 2008a; Iyer & Miller, 2008) hold that firms scale up their search processes when their performance falls below a certain threshold, the aspiration level. Further, behavioral biases were found to depend on the achievement of aspirations and thereby also inform the relationship between performance and strategic convergence-divergence (Chatterjee & Hambrick, 2007; Kelley & Michela, 1980; Lopes, 1987; March & Shapira, 1987, 1992).

When firms perform below their managers' aspiration levels, prior research found that managers opt for riskier choices (Fiegenbaum, 1990; Fiegenbaum & Thomas, 1986, 1988; Lehner, 2000; Park, 2007). Though this finding could also be related to the characteristics of problemistic search processes (Cyert & March, 1963), most prior studies refer to Kahneman and Tversky's (1979) prospect theory for an explanation. Rooted in psychological research on how rationally bounded decision-makers evaluate the distributional properties of payoffs of alternative choices ("prospects") in dependence on whether they have already accrued a gain or loss (Kahneman & Tversky, 1979, 2000), prospect theory is based on more realistic assumptions on human decision makers than prior theories on risk preferences (von Neumann & Morgenstern, 1953). The theory integrates several psychological biases humans fall for and suggests that when faced with prior losses, decision-makers seek risks to overcome their loss position. Despite its origin in human psychology, the theory's implications were found to hold also for management teams and organizations as such when there is a valid substitute for the accrued gains or losses Kahnemann and Tversky had imposed on the individuals in their experiments (Bromiley, 1991; Fiegenbaum, 1990; Greve, 1998a; Lehner, 2000). Prior research suggests that a composite of historical and social performance levels offers a valid substitute toward which managerial decision-making is geared (Greve, 1998a). Particularly in the presence of strategic group structures, this proposition seems convincing: Since managers heavily engage in social comparison with their firm's direct peers, the own strategic group's average performance level represents a natural benchmark against which managers assess their firm's performance (Fiegenbaum & Thomas, 1995; Reger & Huff, 1993).

For firms that perform above their managers' aspiration level, literature also suggests behavioral biases. Most notably, it maintains that managers fall for self-serving behavior that attributes the cause of good performance outcomes to their own skills while all the same laying blame on the environment for poor outcomes (Clapham & Schwenk, 1991; Kelley & Michela, 1980). This behavioral pattern was found to boost the confidence of a firm's management when performance levels rise (Meindl, Ehrlich, & Dukerich, 1985; Staw, McKechnie, & Puffer, 1983). Positive media coverage or a natural disposition of the involved managers can further fuel the process of growing self-confidence, ultimately leading to hubris, a state of excessive confidence and presumptuousness (Chatterjee & Hambrick, 2007; Hayward & Hambrick, 1997). Such increased levels of self-confidence have important implications for the decision processes of managers. They lead to less comprehensive and faster decision-making, to lower levels of managerial attention to the firm's marketplace and competitors, and in consequence to a tendency to drop industry norms and engage in uninformed, bold experimental actions (Chatterjee & Hambrick, 2007; Hayward & Hambrick, 1997; Levinthal & March, 1993).

The presented biases impact how a firm's performance variations below and above its managers' aspiration level translate into strategic convergence-divergence vis-à-vis their firm's own strategic group (see dotted lines in Figure 3-2). For firms that perform worse than their managers had hoped, we claimed that managers seek additional risks to overcome their firm's performance problems. When contemplating which strategic direction to take, these managers will realize that convergence strategies might be easier to implement (Amburgey, Kelly, & Barnett, 1993; Fiegenbaum & Thomas, 1995; Hannan & Freeman, 1984; Spencer, 1989), but are limited in their upside potential by the practices of the own strategic group. Hence, they might seek advice from distant strategic groups even if the performance potentials of the practices common to these groups come at low odds and great risks (Bromiley, 1991; Kahneman & Tversky, 1979, 2000). Given their desire to catch up with their rival firms, managers of low-performing firms are willed to take these risks more often and thus venture further outside of their strategic groups than our initial arguments have suggested. For firms that perform better than their managers had hoped, we proposed that managers will develop higher levels of self-confidence, which may lead them to hubris and bold decision-making. These effects may convince them to follow the guidance of their own, presumably superior skills rather than their competitors' example. Thus, there are also reasons why mangers of high-performing firms may pursue divergence strategies, counteracting the inertial forces we have proposed earlier on.

Taken together, these arguments suggest that divergence strategies are more common than suggested by the arguments leading to Hypothesis 1 – regardless of whether a firm performs below or above its management's aspiration level. As for the relationship between performance and strategic convergence-divergence, this translates into a kinked-curve relationship with a structural break at the aspiration level (see solid line in Figure 3-2). Hence, we propose:

> *Hypothesis 2: A firm's performance is more strongly related to convergence-divergence when the firm performs below its management's aspiration level than if it performs above its management's aspiration level.*

The Moderating Effects of Environmental Dynamism and Munificence

The proposed relationship between a firm's performance level and managerial choice of convergence or divergence was suggested to build upon managerial search behavior, the psychological biases different levels of performance induce in the presence of clear aspirations, as well as the risk-return-profiles convergence and divergence strategies offer. Yet, if these elements work together in the proposed manner, they do so contingent upon other factors. Prior research notably identified the environmental context as an important source of contingencies for the constituting elements of the relationship at hand (Goll & Rasheed, 1997; Tosi & Slocum, 1984). Following prior research on strategic group dynamics (Fiegenbaum, Thomas, & Tang, 2001; Mascarenhas, 1989), two characteristics of environments (i.e., environmental dynamism and munificence) interfere with the main effect and the behavioral biases we have proposed.

Environmental dynamism interferes with the risk-seeking behavior we proposed for firms that perform under the aspiration level of their management. Environmental dynamism implies unpredictable change, which increases the level of uncertainty firms need to cope with (Dess & Beard, 1984; Duncan, 1972). Particularly its opaque effect on the antecedents of firm performance (Eisenhardt & Bourgeois, 1988; Gort, 1969; Hrebiniak & Joyce, 1985) questions the management's own certainty about which strategic choices would improve firm performance. The managers' increased efforts to resolve this uncertainty drains their cognitive capacity and increases the levels of stress and anxiety they experience (Tushman, 1979; Waldman, Ramirez, House, & Puranam, 2001). Faced with these challenges, the increased risk appetite of underperforming firms becomes saturated and divergence strategies less favorable.

The relationship between performance above the aspiration level and convergence-divergence experiences an opposite moderation by environmental dynamism for two reasons. The first reason relates to the role high-performing firms assume in providing cues on how performance can be maintained or improved. Similarly as within social contexts, where social referents become more important when there is a lack of "physical reality [...] to validate the opinion or belief" (Festinger, 1950: 273), environmental dynamism puts the cues firms offer on how to maintain or improve performance into higher demand (Greve, 1998b; Haunschild & Miner, 1997). Faced with a novel and largely unknown regime of performance antecedents, strategic group members will consequently increase their efforts to imitate high-performing peers. The second reason relates to the hubris bias proposed to affect managers when their firms perform high and works in the same direction. Despite their bolstered self-confidence and less reflective decision-making, self-attributing managers are prone to the effects unknown regimes of performance antecedents have on their decision-making processes. The lower predictability of the decision outcomes under conditions of increased uncertainty counteract the managers' ambitions for bold changes by making them more proactively seek social legitimacy of their decisions (Goll & Rasheed, 1997; Palmer & Wiseman, 1999). Further, internal and external stakeholders may step in and thwart venturous managers. In times of higher environmental uncertainty divergence strategies not only appear more risky (Bergh & Lawless, 1998), but also the claim of self-attributing managers that their firm's high performance results from superior foresight and abilities appears less plausible (Li & Lu, 2011; Palmer & Wiseman, 1999). As a consequence, resistance against bold strategies may arise when stakeholders withdraw their support and challenge the management's plans.

In sum, an increase in environmental dynamism is likely to weaken the effects the proposed risk-seeking and decision-making biases have on the relationship between performance relative to aspirations and convergence-divergence. In consequence, the proposed kink-like discontinuity becomes weakened and the overall tendency for repositioning moves heading outside the own strategic group reduced (see Figure 3-2).

> *Hypothesis 3a/b: For firms that perform under (over) the aspiration level of their management, environmental dynamism negatively (positively) moderates the relationship between performance and convergence-divergence.*

Compared to environmental dynamism, environmental munificence offers opportunities. Increased levels of munificence characterize situations in which the amount of slack within an organization's environment is abundant, allowing firms to expand their operations without arduously taking away business from their competitors (Aldrich, 1979; Hambrick & Finkelstein, 1987; Starbuck, 1976). Such growth opportunities also affect the strengths of the proposed risk-seeking and hubris biases in fueling ambitions to diverge.

Below their aspiration level, we proposed that risk-seeking managers are driven by their ambitions to catch up with their competitors. Faced with a less hostile environment that allows their firms to grow in old and new segments with less opposition from market incumbents, managers will consider divergence strategies as even more advantageous (Miller & Chen, 1994; Palmer & Wiseman, 1999). Consequently, the increased risk tolerance induced by their firm's performance shortfall will suggest them to sheer out further and seek pockets of particularly high performance further away than in more resource-scarce environments (Miller & Chen, 1994).

Above their aspiration level, instead, we proposed that hubris leads managers to favor bold visions and strategies. Munificent environments with high growth rates bolster these ambitions to change (Miller & Chen, 1994). With market segments growing at different rates, they fuel the visions of managers with promising strategies and practices from high-growth segments that lie outside of the markets the firm's own strategic group serves (Porter, 1980). Furthermore, munificent environments reduce the resistance of stakeholders that formerly opposed bolder strategies. The increased market size and lower level of rivalry, which come along with munificent markets, appease conservative and reluctant stakeholders by suggesting that the market environment now allows for larger strategic changes (Miller & Chen, 1994; Pettigrew & Whipp, 1991).

In sum, environmental munificence likely strengthens the effects that the risk-seeking and self-attribution biases have on the relationship between performance relative to aspirations and convergence-divergence. The proposed kink-like discontinuity in the relationship thus becomes stronger and the overall tendency for repositioning moves heading outside the own strategic group increased (see Figure 3-2). Hence, we propose:

> *Hypothesis 4a/b: For firms that perform under (over) the aspiration level of their management, environmental munificence positively (negatively) moderates the relationship between performance and convergence-divergence.*

The Moderating Role of a Firm's Within-Group Position

The relationships we proposed so far implicitly assumed that performance levels within strategic groups do not follow a systematic pattern. While this assumption appears intuitive in the light that early strategic group research thought that strategic group members were highly similar and would evenly adapt to environmental discontinuities (Caves & Porter, 1977; Porter, 1979), more recent research casts some doubt. Recent findings show that both the strategic positions as well as the performance levels of firms significantly differ within strategic groups (Cool & Schendel, 1988; Lawless, Bergh, & Wilsted, 1989; McNamara et al., 2003; Reger & Huff, 1993), raising the question of whether there is a systematic relationship between a firm's within-group position and its performance level.

There are several theoretical perspectives which support this possibility (McNamara et al., 2003). From a traditional IO perspective, one would presume that core firms recognize their interdependence more easily and profit from mobility barriers which they jointly erect around themselves (Caves & Porter, 1977; Fiegenbaum & Thomas, 1990; Stigler, 1964). Management research on the benefits of network ties of senior executives (Geletkanycz & Hambrick, 1997) similarly suggests that firms at the center of a network of firms – i.e., at the center of a strategic group – achieve higher performance levels since they have a larger number of external ties at their disposal on which they can draw to overcome major managerial challenges, such as information overload and contextual ambiguity.

On the other hand, arguments from the resource-based view of the firm (Barney, 1991; Rumelt, 1984; Wernerfelt, 1984) and the contestable markets perspective (Baumol, Panzar, & Wilig, 1982) stress that unique market positions and resource sets create value and that non-conformity with the own strategic group's strategy should lead to higher performance levels. While first empirical analyses on this subject matter indicate that the advantages from positionings at the edges of strategic groups may exceed those gained from locating at the center of the group (McNamara et al., 2003), there is no further evidence on how the strategic positions of firms within strategic groups affect their performance levels.

We conjectured that firms mainly diverge from their own strategic group because they seek more promising market positions in other groupings. However, if performance levels at the core of a strategic group are systematically higher than at its edges, firms positioned at the latter do not need to watch out for alternative groups when they seek to improve their performance levels, but can instead refer to their own strategic group's center. In this case, a strategic group's core becomes more interesting for strategic group members the closer they are located to the edges of the group. We therefore propose:

Hypothesis 5a/b: For firms that perform under (over) the aspiration level of their management, increases in strategic nonconformity negatively (positively) moderate the relationship between performance and convergence-divergence.

Alternatively, if our resource-based arguments hold, and performance levels prove lower at the core of strategic groups than at their edges, the own strategic group's center becomes less attractive. In this case, divergence strategies would be more promising for firms that seek to improve their performance. In competition with Hypothesis 5a/b, we thus also test for the following moderation effect:

Hypothesis 5c/d: For firms that perform under (over) the aspiration level of their management, increases in strategic nonconformity positively (negatively) moderate the relationship between performance and convergence-divergence.

3.4 Method[3]

Industry Setting

Mehra and Floyd assert that an industry needs to meet two requirements in order to provide sufficient "strategic space" for accommodating strategic groups: "(a) The viable positions within the industry [must] be sufficiently heterogeneous to allow for differentiation along the dimensions of group strategies and (b) [...] some or all of the resources underlying the shared strategies [must] be inimitable" (1998: 512). Our empirical analyses are set in the U.S. insurance industry, an industry that offers both a high degree of product market heterogeneity in combination with differing resource requirements for the distinct market positions. With respect to products, insurers can design their mix of service offerings by choosing from property and liability (P&L) and life insurance (Life) products. Within both product categories, various customer risks can be insured, either with focus on private or commercial customers (Grace & Barth, 1993). In total, these dimensions segment the industry into more than 40 distinct lines of business (A.M. Best, 2009). Since the risks insured in different lines of businesses vary with respect to their duration and magnitude, the legal (capital) requirements vary as well. Furthermore, the

[3] A flow diagram of all steps involved in testing our hypotheses can be found in Appendix 3.

operational processes of risk assessment, pooling, pricing, claims management and litigation differ, requiring firms to develop resources and skills tailored to their type of service. While some regulators restrict firms from combining Life and P&L products, U.S. regulators have always allowed firms to freely decide on their product mix (Berger, Cummins, & Weiss, 2000). In addition to the wide range of viable market positions, the very active market for corporate control and the vast size and non-monolithic character of the U.S. insurance industry (A.M. Best, 2009; Berger et al., 2000; Grace & Barth, 1993) provide ideal conditions for strategic group formation.

Sample and Data

Our sample covers 1,191 insurance firms over a ten year period, stretching from 1999 to 2008. While the number of sampled firms results from the overall size of the U.S. insurance market, we chose this particular ten year study period since the industry's regulatory frame remained fairly stable during that period, while the industry's natural competitive environment offered sufficient variation in our independent variables (e.g. environmental dynamism). Our comparatively extensive study period allows us to track how strategic (inter)actions among strategic group members unfold and play out (Chen et al., 1992; Nair & Filer, 2003).

Further, our study sets itself apart in terms of overall sample size. While prior studies relied on relatively small samples of less than 100 firms (Fiegenbaum & Thomas, 1990, 1995; Houthoofd & Heene, 1997; McNamara et al., 2003; Osborne, Stubbart, & Ramaprasad, 2001), we study a significant proportion of the U.S. insurance industry und thus provide a more unbiased analysis of the industry. Our sample includes the parent organizations of 76.6% of all legal insurance entities that were active in the U.S. market between 1999 and 2008 – in absolute terms, this equates to 3,736 out of 4,879 legal entities. We empirically focus on the parent organizations of these entities, consolidated at the national level, because insurance firms may legally structure themselves in numerous entities that serve different product market segments, but generally deceive their overall strategy at the level of the holding company (Fiegenbaum & Thomas, 1990). The premium income of the sampled firms exceeds 75% of the total market volume throughout all years of the study period.

Data was mainly retrieved from a proprietary database, the A.M. Best Global File statement (A.M. Best, 2009). The database represents the most comprehensive source of accounting and organizational data available for the insurance industry (Katrishen & Scordis, 1998). Since the database includes all U.S. firms that were active at one point, but not necessarily over the whole study period, some items were not available for all firms. In order to maintain a balanced panel we thus discarded 1,143 legal entities and their respective parent organizations from our analyses. Additional capital market and industry data was extracted from COMPUSTAT and Swiss Re Sigma Research (Swiss Re, 2007).

Strategic Group Identification

An accurate and reliable strategic group identification must ground on measures that are critical to the specific industry under study (Mascarenhas, 1989; Short, Ketchen, Palmer, & Hult, 2007). We chose these measures based on Fiegenbaum and Thomas (1990, 1995), who identified the strategic dimensions that cover the most important strategic choices available to firms in the U.S. insurance industry. In accord with other strategic group research, these choices fall into two broad categories: decisions on the firm's strategic scope, and decisions on the deployment of resources. Since a comprehensive reasoning for these variables can be found in Fiegenbaum and Thomas (1990, 1995), we limit ourselves in this section to a tabulated summary of the variables and to the reasoning of the few adjustments we made to the variables. After comprehensive discussions with industry experts, we made two adjustments to the variables proposed by Fiegenbaum and Thomas (1990, 1995). First, we substituted the net premiums written-component in several instances by gross premiums written, since it is the gross premiums written that marks an insurance firm's position within its product markets. The reinsurance strategy of the firms, which requires the differentiation between gross and net premiums written, is considered in a separate variable. Further, we acknowledged that not all variables have the same relevance in discriminating strategic groups (Houthoofd & Heene, 1997) and assigned variable weights. The analytical process yielding these weights is described in the following paragraph. Table 3-1 provides the definitions of the clustering variables, along with their basic meaning and the weights as applied in our cluster analyses.

Table 3-1: Variables Describing Strategy in the U.S. Insurance Industry

Variable category	Variable name	Formula	Weight[a]
Scope	Customer scope	$\frac{Personal\ gross\ premiums\ written\ (GPW)}{Personal\ GPW + Commercial\ GPW}$	2.58
	Product scope	$\frac{Property\ GPW + Liability\ GPW}{Property\ GPW + Liability\ GPW + Life\ insurance}$	3.82
	Product diversity	$H = 1 - \sum_{i=1}^{n} P_i^2$	1.86
	Firm Size	$Log(GPW)$	1.28
Resource deploy-ment	Production efficiency	$\frac{Underwriting\ expenses^b}{NPW}$	0.03
	Reinsurance strategy	$\frac{Ceded\ premiums}{GPW}$	0.31
	Financial strategy	$\frac{Total\ creditors}{Total\ liabilities}$	0.56
	Investment strategy	$\frac{Stocks}{Stocks + bonds}$	0.02

Notes: [a] The weights were calculated by the software OVW (Makarenkov & Legendre, 2001b) as described in (Makarenkov & Legendre, 2001a). The initial clusterings provided by industry experts comprised 94 firms. The weights assign a higher relevance to scope variables in the process of defining strategic groups (compare Houthoofd & Heene, 1997). [b] Net of reinsurance commissions.

Early strategic group research has been criticized for statistically deriving groups of firms that were mere analytical conveniences for researchers without theoretical substance or objective analogues in the natural environment (Barney & Hoskisson, 1990; Hatten & Hatten, 1987). Subsequent research addressed this criticism by socially re-constructing the concept in the form of cognitive strategic groups (e.g., Hodgkinson, 1997; Peteraf & Shanley, 1997; Porac et al., 1989; Reger & Huff, 1993). However, this approach was subject to other shortcomings. Since its data collection procedures were limited to interviews and surveys, sample sizes tended to be biased to specific respondents and, more critically, were oftentimes very small (for a review and critique, see Hodgkinson, 1997).

In an attempt to overcome the weaknesses of prior social constructivist research on cognitive groups as well as exploit the complementary strengths of quantitative approaches to strategic group definition, we combined the two approaches. In a first step, we thus asked industry experts to provide us with their idea on the strategic group structure of their industry, which we then used to condition a clustering algorithm so that it was able to produce an industry structure that reflected the experts' cognitive idea of the industry's strategic group structure on a much larger scale. In other words, we followed prior research's advice (Diesing, 1971; Jick, 1979) of using the qualitative interpretation of industry experts to inform subsequent quantitative research based on archival sources, particularly in the domain of strategic group research (Reger & Huff, 1993).

We conditioned the clustering algorithm by assigning weights to the clustering variables before using them in k-means clusterings, a procedure recommended in classification research (De Soete, 1986; DeSarbo, Carroll, Clark, & Green, 1984; Huh & Lim, 2009; Vichi & Kiers, 2001). From a methodological perspective, assigning such weights is an alternative to condensing clustering variables by factor analysis (e.g., Kim & Lee, 2002) which aims at reducing the “masking effect” of variables that contain only little information relevant for separating meaningful clusters (Fowlkes & Mallows, 1983). In contrast to factor analysis, however, assigning weights has one fundamental advantage. The clustering variable weights can be derived recursively from a cluster solution deemed correct, making the approach less prone to methodological criticisms than more "naïve", purely statistics driven factoring techniques which fail in various data scenarios (Milligan, 1996: 348; Sneath, 1980). We chose cognitive cluster solutions provided by industry experts as starting points for such a recursive process and thereby elicited those variable weights that were implicitly assigned by the experts when they decided on their clustering solutions. The optimization procedure we used for analytically deriving the variable weights was provided by Makarenkov and Legendre (2001b) and described in Makarenkov and Legendre (2001a). The procedure minimizes a loss function (L_P), and thereby finds weights (w) that minimize the sums of within-group squared distances to the cluster centroids (d_{ij}^2) of all clusters (k). n_k denotes the total number of firms within cluster k.

$$\min_w L_P \text{ with } L_P(w_1, w_2, \dots, w_m) = \sum_{k=1}^{K} [\sum_{i,j=1}^{n_k} d_{ij}^2(\text{w})] / n_k \text{ , while}$$

$$w_1, w_2, \dots, w_m \geq 0, \text{ and } w_1 + w_2 + \dots + w_m = 1$$

Since the validity of our strategic group structure thereby depends on the quality of the initial cluster solutions, we paid special attention to thoroughly surveying the cognitive groups. Given our research setting, we applied the full context form of the repertory grid technique, which is particularly suited to elicit similarity judgments (Fransella & Bannister, 1977; Kelly, 1955; Tan & Hunter, 2002). It demands that research participants sort a pool of elements into any number of discrete piles based on whatever similarity criteria chosen by the research participant. Following Milligan (1996), we asked four top managers of major global insurance companies to independently choose a set of 40 well known "ideal type" firms from our full sample (i.e., parent organizations they thought they could easily sort into groups) (Milligan, 1996) and to sort their samples of firms into piles of similar firms. Conforming with Reger and Huff's proposition that the idea about a "strategic group structure will be widely shared by strategists within an industry" (1993: 106), we received 12 similar cluster solutions that contained a total of 94 different firms and had varying sizes between 4 and 6 clusters. The information from these cluster solutions was then factored into separate processes for the calculation of weights as described above and the arithmetic mean values of these weights were used in the further process of this study.

We then applied cluster analysis as recommended by Ketchen and Shook (1996). Given that standard "clustering procedures provide little if any information as to the number of clusters present in the data" (Everitt, 1980; Milligan, 1996; Milligan & Cooper, 1985: 159; Sneath & Sokal, 1973), we used so called "stopping rules" to determine the number of clusters. Specifically, we used the Calinski and Harabasz (1974) pseudo-F test and Duda and Hart's (1973) Je(2)/Je(1) index because they have been found to be among the most efficient stopping rules (Milligan & Cooper, 1985). We applied these rules to the 3- to 12-cluster solutions of all years produced by a two-stage clustering process involving hierarchical (i.e., Ward's method) and non-hierarchical (i.e., k-means) clustering. Both stopping rules suggested a five cluster solution for all years, which is in line with the experts' assessment.

To further validate our clustering results, we triangulated our results with the initial clustering of our industry experts. In particular, we searched for the "ideal type" firms chosen by the industry experts and found them in the correct strategic groups. We further reviewed the clustering solutions for descriptive validity (McNamara et al., 2003; Thomas & Venkatraman, 1988). In doing so, we found that our cluster solutions cleanly discriminated between P&L and Life insurers, two naturally occurring groups within the insurance industry (Nair & Kotha, 2001), as well as between firms that focus on private or corporate customers. Based on these different types of qualitative and quantitative analyses and additional validity checks, we feel confident that the study's cluster solution closely reflects the competitive structure of the U.S. insurance industry between 1999 to 2008.

Measures

Dependent Variable

Strategic convergence-divergence. With reference to its own strategic group, a focal firm's repositioning can either take the form of convergence or divergence. Following prior research (Carroll, Pandian, & Thomas, 1994; Chen & Hambrick, 1995; Cool & Dierickx, 1993; Gimeno & Woo, 1996; Park, 2007), we operationalize a firm's degree of convergence or divergence using a distance measure which quantifies the strategic distance a firm covers during each year within the strategic space of the industry vis-à-vis its own strategic group. We calculate the distances by a Mahalanobis (1936) distance function, which is the recommended procedure when the dimensions of the space in which the distances are located exhibit correlations (i.e., are not orthogonal) or posses different ranges (Hair et al., 2009). Both characteristics apply to our clustering variables (compare Table 3-1), which span the strategic space within which we calculate all distances. Formally, the calculation of our "strategic convergence-divergence" (SCD) measure reads as:

$$SCD_{igt} = SD_{ig(t-1)} - SD_{igt} \text{ with } SD_{igt} = \sqrt{(\mathrm{x_{it}} - \mu_{\mathrm{gt}})^{\mathrm{T}} \mathrm{S}^{-1} (\mathrm{x_{it}} - \mu_{\mathrm{gt}})}.$$

Following this equation, $\mathrm{SCD_{igt}}$ expresses the strategic distance covered by firm i in year t with reference to strategic group g of which the firm was a member at $\mathrm{t-1}$. $\mathrm{x_{it}}$ is the T-sized multivariate vector holding the values of the strategic dimensions that characterize firm i at the end of year t. μ_{gt} represents the mean values of these variables as defined by the strategic group g. S denotes the covariance matrix of the variables included in the vectors. $\mathbf{SCD}_{igt}$ takes on a positive value if firm i has converged towards its own strategic group during the course of year t and a negative value if the firm has diverged from its strategic group during the course of year t.

Explanatory Variables

Performance relative to aspirations. We define performance relative to aspirations as the differential between the actual firm performance and the firm's aspiration level ($\mathbf{PRA}_{it} = \mathbf{Performance}_{it} - \mathbf{Aspiration}_{it}$). Following the suggestions of prior research (Bromiley, 1991; Cyert & March, 1963; Herriot, Levinthal, & March, 1985; Park, 2007; Wiseman & Bromiley, 1996), we operationalize the aspiration level of a firm i at the point of time t as a combination of a social and an historical aspiration level. Since a firm's strategic group acts as its cognitive reference point (e.g., Fiegenbaum et al., 1996), particularly in respect of performance (March & Shapira, 1987), we base the component of social aspirations ($SA_{i,t}$) on the average performance of the strategic group. For the historical aspiration level ($HA_{i,t}$), instead, we use the prior year's performance of the firm itself, raised by a small factor due to the upward-striving rule of Bromiley (1991). Hence, PRA_{it} reads as:

$$PRA_{it} = P_{it} - \left(I\left(P_{i,t} < SA_{i.t}\right) * SA_{i,t} + I\left(P_{i,t} > SA_{i.t}\right) * 1.05 * HA_{i,t}\right)$$

P_{it} denotes the current performance and I represents a function that takes the value 1 if its argument is true and 0 if not (Park, 2007). Similar to other research on insurance firms (e.g., BarNiv & McDonald, 1992; Elango, 2009; Oetzel & Bannerjee, 2008), we assess a company's financial performance by its return on assets (ROA) operationalized as net income before extraordinary items and preferred dividends divided by a firm's total assets. Following Park (2007), we distinguish between the effects of performance below and above the aspiration level by piecewise regression models using a linear spline function for PRA with a knot at zero. We separate the individual splines by the mkspline procedure of STATA 11. In order to provide a test for the kink in the regression line which also allows for different intercepts, we further run a switching regression in Model 4 of Table 3-4 that includes the interaction term of PRA and a dummy variable indicating whether performance is above the aspiration level.

Environmental dynamism and munificence. We study the impact the environmental context has on the strategic repositionings of firms by considering the effects of environmental dynamism and munificence, two main characteristics of environments (Aldrich, 1979; Dess & Beard, 1984). Leaning on current insurance research (Eling & Marek, 2011a, 2011b), we chose an industry specific operationalization to capture environmental dynamism within the insurance industry. By measuring the total insured catastrophe losses incurred, it quantifies the severity of market events that hit the industry and thereby provides a proxy for the uncertainties managers faced at specific points in time during the study period. For the analyzed year range, two events stand out for the U.S. insurance market. The terrorist attacks of September 11, 2001 and Hurricane Katrina in late August 2005. Both events did not only mark human tragedies of unprecedented size, but also resulted in new market regulations, market exits and bankruptcies of under-capitalized insurers (Born & Viscusi, 2006; Chen, Doerpinghaus, Lin, & Yu, 2008). They did not only offset the risk models of market incumbents, but also induced uncertainties via triggering change in the industry's governance system in an unpredictable manner (Born & Viscusi, 2006).

Similarly to prior research (Dess & Beard, 1984; Staw & Szwajkowski, 1975; Yasai-Ardekani, 1989; Zajac & Kraatz, 1993), we operationalize environmental munificence as the industry's growth rate. We measure the total market volume as the total gross premiums written within the U.S. P&L and Life markets as provided by the A.M. Best Global File Statement (A.M. Best, 2009). Our conceptualization also relates to prior research on strategic group dynamics, which has identified that periods of market growth and decline describe periods in which mobility rates between strategic groups and shifts of strategic group strategies significantly differ (Mascarenhas, 1989).

Strategic nonconformity. Not all firms identify themselves with their strategic group to the same degree. While core firms associate tightly with the average strategy of the group, others differ more from their group (e.g., DeSarbo & Grewal, 2008; McNamara et al., 2003; Peteraf & Shanley, 1997). Even though the implications of such nonconformity with the group strategy have not yet been thoroughly examined, initial results indicate that a firm's within-group positioning systematically affects its performance level (McNamara et al., 2003). Since systematic performance differences between firms at the center and at the edges of strategic groups would moderate the main relationship we propose, we consider the strategic nonconformity of strategic group members in our analyses.

Similarly to prior research, we measure strategic (non)conformity as the degree to which a firm's strategy does (not) match the average strategic profile of its competitors (Finkelstein & Hambrick, 1990). In line with our conceptualization of the strategic space of the U.S. insurance industry, we operationalize the degree of nonconformity by means of Mahalanobis (1936) distance measures. Specifically, we proxy for each firm and year the degree of nonconformity with its own strategic group as a ratio of the firm's strategic distance to its own group's center and the equivalent mean value of all strategic group members. A firm's degree of strategic nonconformity hence reads as:

$$\mathrm{SNC}_{i,t} = \frac{\mathrm{SD}_{i,t,OSG}}{\mathrm{AvgSD}_{t,OSG}},$$

with $\mathrm{SD}_{i,t,OSG}$ representing the strategic distance between the firm and its own strategic group's center, and $\mathrm{AvgSD}_{t,OSG}$ representing the average strategic distance firms within this group exhibit to the core of this strategic group.

Control Variables

Firm size. Firm size can influence organizational market power, flexibility/inertia and strategic responses to environmental concerns (Hitt, Ireland, & Hoskisson, 1995). To mitigate adverse effects of skewness in firm size, we control for the natural logarithm of gross premiums written.

Reinsurance strategy. Insurance firms can transfer parts of their business, including the associated risks, to reinsurers. Through such transfers, insurers can attract more business than their own equity base would allow. Transferring business to reinsurers changes the risk exposure of the insurance firm and has an important impact on how the firm is affected by environmental uncertainty. This in turn affects the flexibility of the firm. Consistent with prior research, we control for the risk exposure of each firm by its "ceded portion" (Augustine, 1998; Group of Thirty, 2006). This indicator is calculated as the quotient of the absolute amount of premiums transferred to reinsurers and gross premiums written.

Firm slack. Slack is a common explanatory factor for organizational behavior (Chen, Su, & Tsai, 2007; Cyert & March, 1963; Galbraith, 1973, 1974). It conveys the notion of a cushion, "which allows an organization to adapt successfully to internal pressures for adjustment or to external pressures for change in policy, as well as to initiate changes in strategy with respect to the external environment" (Bourgeois, 1981: 30). We operationalize slack by an indicator common to the insurance industry, the quick liquidity ratio. The quick liquidity ratio is calculated as quick assets divided by net liabilities plus ceded reinsurance balances payable with quick assets being cash, unaffiliated short-term investments, unaffiliated bonds maturing within one year, government bonds maturing within five years and 80% of unaffiliated common stocks (A.M. Best, 2009). By this definition, the quick liquidity ratio represents a firm's excess, uncommitted resources. Thereby it matches the concept of "unabsorbed slack", which is the type of slack that exhibits the highest level of availability.

Strength of strategic group core. One key structural feature of strategic groups is their internal structure. Past research from both economic and cognitive perspectives propose that strategic groups may exhibit internal heterogeneity in the sense that they shelter firms which identify with the strategic group in varying degrees (Ketchen et al., 1993; McNamara et al., 2003; Reger & Huff, 1993). A strong core of a strategic group can have important implications for a focal firm's motivation to converge or diverge. While institutional and oligopoly theories suggest benefits from legitimacy in the presence of a strong core, resource-based theories propose that stronger competition would discourage firms from converging to a strategic group with a strong core (McNamara et al., 2003). To control for any of these effects, we add a variable that indicates the portion of "core firms" which lie within a circle around the strategic group's centroid that has a radius equal to one third of the maximum strategic distance any firm within this group is located away from the center of the group.

Within-group rivalry. The level of rivalry between strategic group members is likely to affect a firm's tendency to converge to or diverge from its current strategic group (Cool & Dierickx, 1993). Prior research conjectured that intense rivalry positively relates to firms' abandonment of prior market positions (Hawley, 1950). We control for within-group rivalry by measuring the dispersion of firms within each strategic group. Methodologically, we divide the strategic space of each strategic group into ten equally large sub-spaces and calculate an Herfindahl index over the numbers of firms that are positioned within these sub-spaces (Cool & Dierickx, 1993; Ordover, Sykes, & Willig, 1982).

Ratio of diverging firms. Another characteristic of strategic groups which may influence firms in their repositioning is the ratio of strategic group members that have recently diverged from the strategic group. Given a lack of reliable data on the benefits of adopting new practices, such as the performance of prior adopters, managers might have to base their decisions on second best information when faced with the decision to adjust the course of their firm. In such cases, managers may consider whether others have adopted the relevant practices earlier on (Mansfield, 1961). Under the assumption that these have done so for good reason, manager may believe that the practice will also be beneficial for their own organization (Bikhchandani, Hirschleifer, & Welch, 1992; DiMaggio & Powell, 1983). We control for such mimetic behavior by a variable that measures the proportion of firms that have diverged from the strategic group in the preceding year.

Market rivalry. Even though the mobility barriers of strategic groups may shelter firms from competitive attacks from firms in other strategic groups, overall market rivalry continues to influence the repositionings of firms within strategic group structures (Porter, 1979). Similarly to prior research (Cool & Dierickx, 1993; Ordover, Sykes, & Willig, 1982), we use the industry's Herfindahl index to measure overall market rivalry. We calculate the index for each year by adding the squared value of the individual market shares of all firms in the U.S. insurance industry.

Fixed effects. Since "there is no reason, why mobility barriers should be symmetric" (Mascarenhas & Aaker, 1989: 478) within an industry, strategic groups do probably vary strongly in the level of resistance their boundaries pose to the movements of firms. We thus include strategic group dummies in our analysis to parcel out group-level characteristics. We further control for time-related factors by including year dummies.

Data Analysis

We applied a sequence of statistical analyses to test our hypotheses. In a first step, we spanned the industry's strategic space, identified and located the strategic groups within this space, and applied an ANOVA to assess the performance implications of strategic group membership. To study our main relationship between firm performance relative to aspirations and strategic convergence-divergence, we did not cross-sectionally pool data over different stable strategic time periods. We refrained from this common practice of early strategic group research (e.g., Cool & Schendel, 1987) since it hinders an uninterrupted study of firm behavior and produces statistical noise (DeSarbo et al., 2009; Fuente-Sabaté, Rodríguez-Puerta, Vicente-Lorente, & Zúñiga-Vicente, 2007).

For explaining the degree and direction of the firms' repositionings, we regressed the strategic distances they have covered vis-à-vis their own strategic groups by means of fixed effects panel regressions. We chose fixed rather than random effects models after testing for the orthogonality of the random effects and the regressors with a Hausman specification test (Hausman, 1978). The test rejected its null hypothesis of no correlation between the error term and the regressors, and thereby suggested the use of fixed effects models.

3.5 Results

Strategic Groups, Their Performance Implications and Evolutionary Paths

Table 3-2 describes the strategic groups we have identified within the U.S. insurance industry between 1999 and 2008. It provides the mean values of the clustering variables, the performance level, and the number of strategic group members for each year and strategic group. Throughout our study period, the strategic groups display significant differences in their performance levels ($p < 0.001$). Figure 3-3 illustrates these performance levels over time.

Table 3-2: Time Series of Strategic Group Attributes

Year	Group ID	Scope variables				Resource deployment				Group characteristics	
		Customer scope	Product scope	Product diversity	Firm Size	Production efficiency	Reinsurance strategy	Financial strategy	Investment strategy	Performance[a]	Number of members
1999	1	0.97	0.00	0.31	10.91	1.48	0.16	0.01	0.06	2.14	163
	2	0.13	0.02	0.40	11.94	1.11	0.18	0.03	0.08	2.02	84
	3	0.78	0.99	0.61	11.24	1.03	0.31	0.02	0.17	3.79	593
	4	0.23	1.00	0.22	9.97	0.93	0.26	0.01	0.12	6.29	214
	5	0.66	0.03	0.63	13.28	1.33	0.17	0.01	0.05	1.08	137
2000	1	0.97	0.00	0.30	11.00	1.45	0.15	0.01	0.05	2.41	166
	2	0.13	0.02	0.39	12.10	1.08	0.18	0.02	0.06	3.33	83
	3	0.77	0.99	0.61	11.36	1.04	0.32	0.02	0.16	2.63	595
	4	0.23	1.00	0.23	10.09	0.92	0.26	0.02	0.12	6.03	213
	5	0.67	0.03	0.63	13.34	1.32	0.17	0.01	0.05	0.82	134
2001	1	0.97	0.00	0.32	11.38	1.43	0.15	0.01	0.05	1.78	186
	2	0.13	0.02	0.37	11.88	1.09	0.17	0.03	0.05	1.88	82
	3	0.77	0.99	0.61	11.51	1.06	0.33	0.05	0.15	0.99	599
	4	0.23	1.00	0.24	10.30	0.93	0.26	0.04	0.11	4.06	211
	5	0.63	0.04	0.65	13.41	1.29	0.20	0.01	0.04	1.53	113
2002	1	0.96	0.00	0.32	11.59	1.32	0.17	0.01	0.04	1.73	192
	2	0.12	0.02	0.35	12.00	1.06	0.17	0.03	0.04	4.53	78
	3	0.77	0.99	0.61	11.65	1.01	0.34	0.05	0.13	1.20	598
	4	0.23	1.00	0.26	10.62	0.91	0.26	0.04	0.09	3.73	210
	5	0.62	0.04	0.65	13.39	1.28	0.17	0.01	0.04	1.06	113
2003	1	0.97	0.00	0.31	11.60	1.34	0.15	0.01	0.04	1.78	186
	2	0.13	0.01	0.36	12.04	1.04	0.15	0.03	0.04	6.32	83
	3	0.78	0.99	0.60	11.76	0.98	0.34	0.05	0.14	3.47	587
	4	0.25	0.99	0.27	10.87	0.92	0.29	0.04	0.11	4.09	223
	5	0.65	0.04	0.65	13.32	1.23	0.19	0.01	0.03	1.49	112

(continued)

Table 3-2 (continued)

Year	Group	Scope variables				Resource deployment				Group characteristics	
	ID	Customer scope	Product scope	Product diversity	Firm Size	Production efficiency	Reinsurance strategy	Financial strategy	Investment strategy	Performance[a]	Number of members
2004	**1**	0.96	0.00	0.31	11.61	1.37	0.16	0.01	0.04	1.69	199
	2	0.12	0.01	0.35	12.08	1.03	0.15	0.03	0.05	5.33	81
	3	0.78	0.99	0.60	11.84	0.95	0.33	0.05	0.14	4.91	572
	4	0.26	1.00	0.27	10.96	0.94	0.29	0.04	0.10	4.64	236
	5	0.62	0.05	0.65	13.39	1.28	0.18	0.01	0.04	1.51	103
2005	**1**	0.96	0.00	0.32	11.65	1.39	0.16	0.01	0.04	2.03	202
	2	0.13	0.01	0.36	12.03	1.01	0.15	0.03	0.04	5.62	84
	3	0.78	0.99	0.60	11.89	0.95	0.33	0.05	0.14	5.36	567
	4	0.26	0.99	0.28	11.05	0.87	0.28	0.04	0.11	5.72	243
	5	0.62	0.05	0.65	13.55	1.26	0.19	0.01	0.04	2.00	95
2006	**1**	0.96	0.00	0.31	11.76	1.41	0.17	0.01	0.04	1.92	201
	2	0.12	0.02	0.35	12.06	1.04	0.15	0.03	0.05	4.46	76
	3	0.80	0.99	0.59	11.90	0.94	0.32	0.05	0.15	5.73	528
	4	0.29	0.99	0.33	11.23	0.87	0.31	0.04	0.11	6.47	281
	5	0.62	0.05	0.65	13.36	1.29	0.19	0.01	0.04	2.29	105
2007	**1**	0.97	0.00	0.29	11.84	1.44	0.18	0.01	0.04	1.95	195
	2	0.12	0.02	0.36	12.22	1.04	0.14	0.03	0.05	4.39	77
	3	0.80	0.99	0.59	11.91	0.96	0.32	0.04	0.15	5.17	529
	4	0.28	0.99	0.33	11.24	0.94	0.32	0.04	0.12	6.29	281
	5	0.64	0.04	0.63	13.18	1.33	0.18	0.01	0.04	1.84	109
2008	**1**	0.96	0.01	0.32	11.92	1.40	0.18	0.01	0.04	1.57	222
	2	0.10	0.01	0.30	11.73	1.02	0.18	0.03	0.06	4.49	62
	3	0.80	0.99	0.59	11.89	1.01	0.32	0.04	0.11	1.91	524
	4	0.29	1.00	0.34	11.18	1.07	0.33	0.05	0.09	2.74	285
	5	0.54	0.05	0.62	13.79	1.27	0.18	0.01	0.03	1.78	98

Notes: [a] ANOVA-analysis indicates that the performance levels of the different strategic groups differs significantly in each year with $p < .001$. Performance is expressed in ROA (in %).

Figure 3-3: Strategic Group Performance Levels (ROA)

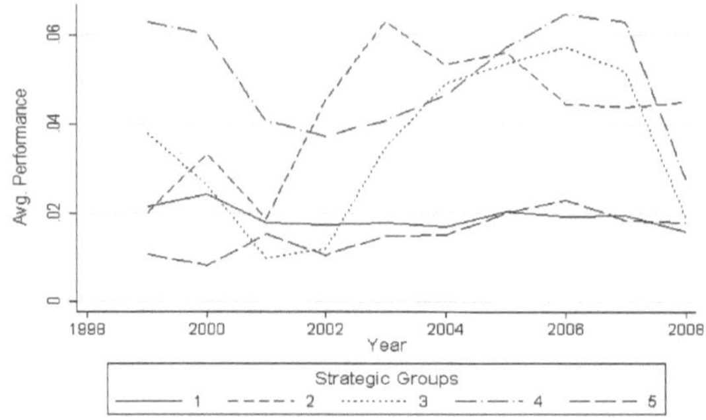

Table 3-3 holds the descriptive statistics such as means and standard deviations of the variables used in the models and the correlation matrix for all variables. The value of our dependent variable strategic convergence-divergence ranges from -4.96 to +4.90, with a mean of 0.02 and a standard deviation of 0.61. The positive value of the overall mean, 0.02, suggests that the firms within our sample slightly tend to converge to rather than diverge from their own strategic group. The high correlations between the performance relative to aspiration variables are related to the definition of the variables and do not cause problems of multicolinearity since the variables are not used in the same models.

To further examine whether multicolinearity was present, we ran respective standard OLS models with all dummies included and applied STATA's postestimation command vif to yield the variance inflation factors (VIF) for the variables in each model. Their means ranged from 1.97 to 2.53 and the individual values never exceeded 6.6. With very few values above 5 and no values above the rule-of-thumb cutoff of 10 (Neter, Wasserman, & Kutner, 1985), there seems no multicolinearity issues between our variables.

Table 3-3: Descriptive Statistics and Correlations[a]

Variable	Mean	s.d.	1	2	3	4	5	6	7	8	9	10	11	12	13	14	15
1. Strategic convergence-divergence	0.02	0.61	1														
2. Firm size	11.68	2.22	0.00	1													
3. Reinsurance strategy	0.27	0.24	-0.07*	0.11*	1												
4. Slack	0.77	0.17	0.02	-0.44*	-0.12*	1											
5. Strength of strategic group core	0.76	0.13	0.00	0.06*	0.10*	0.00	1										
6. Within-group rivalry	0.31	0.07	0.01	0.06*	0.11*	0.01	0.86*	1									
7. Ratio of diverging firms	0.48	0.08	-0.10*	-0.07*	0.04*	0.04*	-0.16*	-0.22*	1								
8. Market rivalry	43.43	1.39	0.01	0.06*	0.00	0.02*	0.49*	0.52*	-0.20*	1							
9. Environmental dynamism	0.06	1.02	0.01	0.00	0.00	0.00	-0.01	-0.17*	-0.15*	0.26*	1						
10. Environmental munificence	0.06	0.04	-0.01	-0.05*	-0.01	0.00	-0.45*	-0.44*	0.28*	-0.65*	-0.39*	1					
11. Strategic nonconformity	0.99	0.43	-0.31*	-0.10*	0.30*	-0.02*	-0.02	-0.01	0.00	-0.01	0.00	0.01	1				
12. Performance relative to aspiration	-0.01	0.05	0.05*	0.02	0.00	0.01	-0.04*	-0.08*	0.01	-0.06*	0.02*	0.09*	-0.06*	1			
13. Performance, aspiration < 0	-0.02	0.03	0.06*	0.08*	-0.01	0.00	-0.01	-0.06*	-0.01	-0.03*	0.02*	0.05*	-0.10*	0.83*	1		
14. Performance, aspiration ≥ 0	0.01	0.03	0.01	-0.06*	0.02	0.02*	-0.05*	-0.06*	0.04*	-0.08*	0.01	0.09*	0.02*	0.71*	0.20*	1	
15. Performance ≥ aspiration	0.31	0.46	0.02*	-0.09*	0.01	0.09*	-0.07*	-0.10*	0.02*	-0.03*	0.04*	0.06*	-0.01	0.59*	0.36*	0.58*	1

Notes: [a] The correlations were calculated over all years present in our sample. Each observation therefore represents one firm-year-combination. Since there are 1,191 firms that moved during nine years between 1999 and 2008, N equals 10,719. * $p < .05$ or lower.

Table 3-4: Panel Regressions Estimating Strategic Convergence-Divergence

Variables	Model 1		Model 2		Model 3		Model 4		Model 5		Model 6		Model 7	
	Coef.	SE	Coef.	SE	Coef.	SE	Coef.	SE	Coef.	SE	Coef.	SE	Coef.	SE
Constant	0.32*	(0.14)	0.30*	(0.14)	0.33*	(0.14)	0.32*	(0.14)	0.33*	(0.14)	0.32*	(0.14)	0.34*	(0.14)
Firm size	-0.02	(0.03)	-0.02	(0.03)	-0.01	(0.03)	-0.01	(0.03)	-0.01	(0.03)	-0.01	(0.03)	-0.01	(0.03)
Reinsurance strategy	-0.19	(0.12)	-0.18	(0.12)	-0.20	(0.12)	-0.20	(0.12)	-0.20	(0.12)	-0.20	(0.12)	-0.21†	(0.12)
Slack	0.05	(0.18)	0.09	(0.18)	0.05	(0.18)	0.06	(0.19)	0.06	(0.19)	0.05	(0.18)	0.03	(0.18)
Strength of strategic group core	0.32**	(0.12)	0.30**	(0.12)	0.32**	(0.12)	0.32**	(0.12)	0.32**	(0.12)	0.34**	(0.12)	0.31**	(0.12)
Within-group rivalry	-0.60*	(0.25)	-0.57*	(0.25)	-0.60*	(0.25)	-0.61*	(0.25)	-0.60*	(0.25)	-0.60*	(0.25)	-0.58*	(0.24)
Ratio of diverging firms	-0.74***	(0.08)	-0.73***	(0.08)	-0.73***	(0.08)	-0.72***	(0.08)	-0.73***	(0.08)	-0.73***	(0.08)	-0.72***	(0.08)
Market rivalry	-0.00	(0.01)	0.00	(0.01)	-0.00	(0.01)	-0.00	(0.01)	-0.00	(0.01)	-0.00	(0.01)	-0.00	(0.01)
Environmental dynamism	0.01	(0.01)	0.01	(0.01)	0.01	(0.01)	0.01	(0.01)	-0.01	(0.01)	0.01	(0.01)	0.01	(0.01)
Environmental munificence	-0.18	(0.22)	-0.21	(0.22)	-0.21	(0.22)	-0.22	(0.22)	-0.15	(0.22)	0.56*	(0.27)	-0.17	(0.22)
Strategic nonconformity	1.73***	(0.05)	1.74***	(0.05)	1.74***	(0.05)	1.73***	(0.05)	1.74***	(0.05)	1.73***	(0.05)	1.61***	(0.06)
$I(P < A)$							-0.06**	(0.02)						
Performance relative to aspiration (PRA)			0.60*	(0.25)			1.84***	(0.40)						
Performance, aspiration < 0 ($PRA-$)					1.85***	(0.43)			1.84***	(0.42)	1.70***	(0.42)	2.56***	(0.40)
Performance, aspiration ≥ 0 ($PRA+$)					-0.30	(0.30)			-0.31	(0.30)	0.00	(0.30)	-0.65*	(0.26)
I(Performance ≥ Aspiration) × PRA							-1.53**	(0.56)						
Environmental dynamism × $PRA-$									-0.53†	(0.28)				
Environmental dynamism × $PRA+$									0.73*	(0.31)				
Environmental munificence × $PRA-$											25.60*	(11.61)		
Environmental munificence × $PRA+$											-24.63***	(7.59)		
Strategic nonconformity × $PRA-$													-4.74***	(1.20)
Strategic nonconformity × $PRA+$													2.83***	(0.87)
Observations	8,337		8,337		8,337		8,337		8,337		8,337		8,337	
Number of firms	1,191		1,191		1,191		1,191		1,191		1,191		1,191	
R^2	0.392		0.394		0.397		0.398		0.399		0.400		0.406	
F-statistic	86.05***		80.52***		76.23***		72.2***		68.95***		68.32***		71.49***	

Notes: [a] Strategic group and year dummies are not reported; all explanatory and control variables lagged by one year; robust/white-corrected standard errors in parentheses; $^{\dagger} < .10$; $^{*} p < .05$; $^{**} p < .01$; $^{***} p < .001$

Table 3-4 shows the results of our regression analyses. Model 1 is the control model and indicates that increases in within-group rivalry ($p < 0.05$) and the ratio of diverging firms in the preceding year ($p < 0.001$) negatively relate to a firm's strategic convergence toward its present strategic group. In contrast, we find a positive effect of both the strength of the group's core ($p < 0.01$) and a firm's strategic nonconformity ($p < 0.001$).

Hypothesis 1 predicted that a focal firm's financial performance is positively related to its extent of convergence-divergence vis-à-vis its own strategic group. As shown in Model 2, the coefficient of the firm performance variable – i.e., the performance relative to aspiration (PRA) variable – is positive and significant ($p < 0.05$), providing support for Hypothesis 1.

Hypothesis 2 suggested that performance increases below the aspiration level lead to greater increases in strategic convergence-divergence than performance increases above the aspiration level. Model 3 presents the results of a piecewise regression that breaks the regression line of the PRA variable from Model 2 at the aspiration level into two separate regression splines. We find that the coefficient of the performance below the aspirations variable (PRA –) is positive and significant ($p < 0.001$). The size of the coefficient is also significantly larger than for the PRA variable in Model 2, providing support for the proposition that firms that perform below the aspiration levels of their managers tend to diverge the most from their strategic groups. The coefficient of the performance above aspirations variable, instead, is not significant, which questions whether there is a clear effect of performance on the direction firms take when they perform well. Model 4 confirms the kink-like discontinuity expressed by Model 3 by providing consonant results from a switching model, which, in contrast to the piecewise regression, allows the intercepts of the two splines to change at the time of the regression line's structural break (McGee & Carleton, 1970; Williams, 2010).

Hypothesis 3a/b proposed that environmental dynamism negatively (positively) moderates the relationship between a firm's performance and its convergence-divergence under (above) the aspiration level of its managers. With the coefficients in Model 5 bearing the corresponding signs and being significant ($p < 0.10$ and $p < 0.05$), we find this proposition supported. Hypothesis 4a/b proposed an opposing effect for environmental munificence. The coefficients shown in Model 6 provide clear support for this effect ($p < 0.05$ and $p < 0.001$). Taken together, our results suggest that adverse developments in the environment dampen both the risk-taking behavior of managers from low-performing firms and the bold ambitions of managers within high-performing firms. Positive scenarios, which are subsumed under increases of the environmental munificence variable, in contrast, spur both behavioral biases.

Model 7 tested how a firm's initial strategic position within its strategic group, expressed as strategic nonconformity, moderates the relationship between its PRA and strategic convergence-divergence. Given conflicting arguments from prior research, we tested competing hypotheses (Hypothesis 5a/b vs. 5c/d). We find support for our reasoning based on collusion and mobility barriers (Hypothesis 5a/b, $p < 0.001$ and $p < 0.001$) – i.e., a significant negative sign for the interaction term combining the strategic nonconformity variable with the negative spline of the PRA variable, and a positive sign for the respective interaction term for firms above the aspiration level. This shows that the further away a firm is located from the center of its strategic group, the lower the influence of negative performance feedback in prompting its managers to pursue strategies that make the firm diverge from its strategic group.

3.6 Discussion

The strategic group concept has been a central element within strategic management research for a long time (DeSarbo et al., 2009; Fiegenbaum & Thomas, 1990; Hunt, 1972). It has been enthusiastically contested and defended more than most other concepts. From this process, a consensus emerged that strategic groups do not merely arise from the existence of mobility barriers, but that they also, and probably even more importantly, arise because managers structure their industry by identifying their core competitors (Reger & Huff, 1993). The purpose of our study was to extend the reach of the behavioral foundation of the strategic group concept into the sub-field of strategic group dynamics research. Consequently, our study focused on the firm-level drivers of strategic repositionings and explored how managers decide upon whether they adopt or reject practices of their own strategic group.

The study's main result is that a firm's performance strongly affects the extent and direction of its strategic change, framed as convergence and divergence vis-à-vis its own strategic group. Our results on this relationship provide initial empirical evidence on how strategic group membership affects the managerial decision-making processes when contemplating strategic change. We find prior research's argument, that dissatisfaction with the own firm's performance provides strong incentives to innovate and change (Cyert & March, 1963; Huff, 1982), confirmed by our finding that lower levels of firm performance raise a firm's tendency to diverge from its own strategic group. Yet, consonant with performance feedback theory (Greve, 1998a), we find this relationship dependent on whether a firm performs below or above its management's aspiration level. While performance decreases below the aspiration level clearly translate into divergence, performance changes above the aspiration level have no clear/significant implication on a firm's strategic convergence-divergence choice.

The study also provides an important record for the benchmarking role strategic groups assume for firms. Following the argument that firms constantly compare themselves with their direct competitors (e.g., Bogner, 1991; Fiegenbaum & Thomas, 1995), we derive the aspiration level of a firm's management not only from the firm's past performance level, but also from the average performance its peer firms achieve. Our findings suggest that this peer benchmark represents the average performance of the strategic group the focal firm is part of and thus underline the role of a firm's own strategic group as its major reference point. As a consequence, managerial aspirations, and thereby the hurdle for organizational change and innovation, are tied to the firm's own strategic group and its performance level (e.g., Fiegenbaum & Thomas, 1993; Greve, 1998a).

By considering behavioral biases in the managerial decision process, our results further characterize the relationship between performance relative to aspiration and strategic convergence-divergence. Biases below and above the aspiration level add to, or respectively counteract, the main relationship we had proposed for particularly low and high performance levels. Under the aspiration level, we find support for prior research's claim (Greve, 1998a; Kahneman & Tversky, 1979) that managers may seek further risks to catch up with their competitors. Above the aspiration level, effects from managerial hubris (Chatterjee

& Hambrick, 2007) counteract our initial proposition that high-performing firms are moved to the center of their own strategic groups by the mimetic actions of their fellow group members (Haveman, 1993; Park, 2007). These effects jointly produce the kinked-curve relationship illustrated in Figure 3-2. Both statistical models testing this kink suggest that the individual regression splines below and above the aspiration level have significantly different slopes, what provides support for the behavioral biases proposed.

The study further acknowledges factors that prior research suggests as moderators of the proposed relationship. First, it considers that the repositioning moves of firms not only take place within a strategic group structure but also within the broader context of the environment. Informed by prior research (Goll & Rasheed, 1997), we find that environmental dynamism and munificence moderate how strongly the proposed biases impact the directions firms take when they reposition. We find that dynamic environments dampen both the risk-seeking behavior of managers from underperforming firms and the bold ambitions of successful managers whereas munificent environments spur these ambitions. These results are consistent with similar research on the moderating effects of environmental munificence and dynamism in other contexts (e.g., Ensley, Pearce, & Hmieleski, 2006; Goll & Rasheed, 2004; Li & Simerly, 1998). Second, we test for moderation effects that result from the internal structure of strategic groups (McNamara et al., 2003). Following arguments that performance levels may systematically differ within strategic groups, we find that the forces suggesting divergence work less strongly for firms that are located at the edges of their group than for members that are located at the core of their group. Positionings characterized by strategic nonconformity with group strategies therefore appear as transitory states which firms try to end preferentially by moving toward their own group's core (Fiegenbaum & Thomas, 1995).

The study also makes important methodological contributions. Most notably, it introduces a more accurate dependent variable to analyze strategic group dynamics. This is crucial since prior research's practice of analyzing the discrete events when firms move between two groups (Mascarenhas, 1989) is highly contestable. Given that the clustering approach suffers from the criticism of producing statistical artifacts (Barney & Hoskisson, 1990), it seems arbitrary to study when an algorithm assigns a firm to a group different from its previous one. In contrast, our continuous dependent variable, which periodically measures the distance between a firm and the relatively stable statistical centroid of its own strategic group, is less prone to this methodological criticism. Further, advancing the empirical validity of our results, our clustering approach blends the previously separated analytical (e.g., Fiegenbaum & Thomas, 1990) and cognitive approaches (e.g., Reger & Huff, 1993) of defining strategic group structures. By analytically applying the mental model of industry experts to the full sample of firms, we avoid two issues of prior research: First, we lessen the problems associated with the researcher's discretion in selecting and weighting the clustering variables. Second, we circumvent the problem of purely statistical approaches (i.e., factor analysis for reducing the dimensionality of the clustering problem), which oftentimes fail to facilitate the discovery of meaningful clusters (Chang, 1983; Yeung & Ruzzo, 2001).

3.7 Implications and Limitations

Our results indicate that there is a substantial need for strategic group research at the firm-level. The behavioral arguments of prior research stand in conflict with empirical research designs that have remained disconnected from the behavioral factors underlying the studies' phenomena of interest. Our study not only provides the first counterexample, but also offers two methodological advancements that seem capable of reconnecting strategic group dynamics with organizational behavior. We invite future research to adopt our contributions as a starting point for explicating the behavioral foundations of strategic group dynamics.

One fruitful avenue for future research is to analyze the directions firms take when they diverge from their group. Our study only differentiates between movements away or toward the own strategic group and thereby does not yet exploit the full dimensionality of the strategic space. It would be interesting to analyze how adjacent strategic groups guide firms that have decided to diverge from their own groupings. Following prior research (Chang, 1996; Fiegenbaum et al., 1996; Huff, 1982), adjacent strategic groups offer helpful landmarks to firms when they reposition. Studying which factors, such as strategic distance or performance differentials, spur or hamper firms in moving closer to these groups would be of utmost importance for progressing our understanding of strategic group dynamics (Fiegenbaum & Thomas, 1993, 1995; McNamara et al., 2003).

As with all research, our study comes with limitations. Concerning our empirical setting, we have studied insurance fleets and aggregated the legal entities that operate under common ownership within the U.S. market. While this level of analysis clearly exhibits a well-defined industry structure (Fiegenbaum & Thomas, 1990, 1995), there are also arguments advocating separate studies for the P&L and Life sectors (Ferguson, Deephouse, & Ferguson, 2000). With the different delays in the final settlement of P&L and Life products, both sectors are subject to distinct market rules and could also be considered as individual industries. In this setting, ROA may represent the smallest common denominator of practically applied performance indicators, yet, both sectors offer more specific ones. In order to improve the practical relevance of our findings, future research could thus conduct sector studies with more specific variables. With respect to the general validity of our findings, there is a need for future research to confirm our findings in industries other than insurance.

4 From Crisis to Opportunity: How Market Shocks Impact Interfirm Rivalry

4.1 Introduction

Since its inception in the mid 1980s, competitive dynamics research has been concerned with the causes and consequences of interfirm rivalry (Bettis & Weeks, 1987; MacMillan et al., 1985; Smith et al., 2001b). In their analyses, competitive dynamics scholars have adopted the idea that interfirm rivalry is reflected in the ongoing interchange of competitive actions between individual competitors (Chen & MacMillan, 1992; Ferrier, 2001) – an idea rooted in Schumpeterian and Austrian economics (Schumpeter, 1934; Young et al., 1996). This notion of rivalry had an important impact on the empirical approach of competitive dynamics research in that it geared the scholarly focus toward the real competitive actions exchanged between pairs (dyads) of firms (Baum & Korn, 1999; Chen & MacMillan, 1992; Chen et al., 1992; Chen, Su, & Tsai, 2007).

Despite its various contributions to our understanding of interfirm rivalry, dyad-based research suffers from a strong assumption inherent in its empirical approach that weakens the validity of its findings in important market settings (Hsieh & Chen, 2010). Dyadic analyses consider each competitive action as a clear-cut reaction to the preceding action of the rival firm it was matched to in the dyad. In this vein, scholars also presumed that the motivation for each competitive action largely rests in the prior rival action and the distinct relationship with this rival. While such a clear-cut action-reaction-mechanism may hold in markets that are dominated by pairs of rivals – such as the markets for commercial aircrafts or soft drinks – it seems excessively restrictive for competitive markets with a more "perfect" internal structure holding a large number of rivals (Hsieh & Chen, 2010; Zuchhini & Kretschmer, 2011).

In response to this criticism, scholars pioneered to search for antecedents of competitive actions beyond the mere firm dyad (Hsieh & Chen, 2010; Zuchhini & Kretschmer, 2011). With these efforts, however, they did not yet take full advantage of the range of factors available to them at the higher level of abstraction they argue upon. Instead, these scholars abided by the extant argument that a firm's competitive behavior is largely a function of its rivals' actions (Chen et al., 2007; Smith et al., 2001b) and sought reason for a firm's competitive actions only in the collective rival actions the firm has recently faced. They found that rivals collectively build up competitive pressure on firms, to which the latter respond with own actions – with the response speed somewhat dependent on distributional properties of the total rival actions (Hsieh & Chen, 2010). While this finding provides an important first element of a theory on antecedents of interfirm rivalry in competitive markets, it does not complement the theory yet.

There are further factors that need to be considered when expanding the focus beyond the firm dyad; above all, the environmental market context, which hosts the actors and their actions (Ghemawat & Cassiman, 2007). In comparison to seminal work on competitive strategy (Porter, 1980; Tosi & Slocum, 1984), competitive dynamics research has assigned little relevance to the environment when it reasoned about the competitive behaviors of firms. So far, it limited its arguments to strictly contextual aspects, such as industry growth, or how much buffer distinct industries provide against fierce competition (Ferrier, 2001; Miller & Chen, 1994, 1996a). However, more and more erratic market environments ask for a new perspective on the environment's role in the competitive game (Angbazo & Narayanan, 1996; Calvo, Izquierdo, & Talvi, 2006; D'Aveni, 1994). Recent experiences from market shocks – ranging from market bubbles to man-made catastrophes – suggest that the environment assumes a much more active role in driving interfirm rivalry. When market shocks abruptly disrupt the economic growth trajectories of economies, the same should hold for the rivalrous process among firms, which is inherently connected to the higher level economic aggregates (Schumpeter, 1934, 1943).

Drawing on research on competitive dynamics, environmental disruptions, and organizational change (Hsieh & Chen, 2010; McGrath et al., 1998; Meyer, 1982; Meyer, Brooks, & Goes, 1990; Quinn, 1980; Zuchhini & Kretschmer, 2011), we argue that market shocks have two distinct effects on the competitive behavior of firms. First, a direct effect on a firm's inclination to take competitive action. And second, an indirect effect on the mechanisms that govern the competitive choices of firms (Hsieh & Chen, 2010; Lieberman & Asaba, 2006). We argue for these effects as follows: Market shocks abruptly confront firms with fundamentally new sets of opportunities. Firms thus need to adjust swiftly in order to preempt their rivals in taking advantage of the new situation (McGrath et al., 1998; Meyer et al., 1990). The indirect effect, instead, leads back to the circumstance that market shocks discount the effectiveness of past decisions and actions. Since this also applies to the competitive actions of rival firms, market shocks weaken both the extant level of competitive tension that has been build up by prior rival actions (Zuchhini & Kretschmer, 2011), and the relevance of prior rival actions in advising the competitive decision-making in the focal firm (Lieberman & Asaba, 2006).

Our study incorporates the effects of market shocks into current efforts of developing a theory of interfirm rivalry in competitive market environments (Hsieh & Chen, 2010; Zuchhini & Kretschmer, 2011). We thus challenge the continuous character prior research associates with the competitive interplay between firms. Our research suggests that market shocks punctuate interfirm rivalry and temporarily suspend the regime of behavioral mechanisms that typically drive competitive choices. Since we find these propositions largely confirmed, our study contributes an innovative angle on and novel answers to two of the most central questions of competitive dynamics research (Chen et al., 1992; Smith, Grimm, Chen, & Gannon, 1989): What factors trigger competitive actions? What factors prompt managers to choose a distinct competitive action type?

The remainder of this study is organized as follows: First, we trace recent developments toward a theory of interfirm rivalry in competitive markets, and discuss the treatment of environmental effects in extant competitive dynamics research. We then derive hypotheses on the behavioral mechanisms that govern a firm's competitive behavior, both with respect to its inclination to take new competitive action and its distinct choice of action. From this baseline, we introduce the external environmental context to the discussion and test the stability of the behavioral mechanisms governing the firms' competitive behavior. We proceed with our methodological design, and present and discuss our results. The paper concludes with the study's limitations and implications for future research.

4.2 Competitive Dynamics Research and the Environment

Competitive dynamics research (Bettis & Weeks, 1987; MacMillan et al., 1985), with its unique focus on competitive actions, has produced valuable insights into the competitive behavior of firms. Particularly the behavioral interdependences between competing firms and their action-response patterns (e.g., Chen, 1996; Chen et al., 2007; Yu & Cannella, 2007) helped in identifying antecedents of firm actions (Chen et al., 1992; Smith et al., 1989). Yet, dyadic analyses have recently been criticized for being mostly appropriate and valid for studying the interactions within highly concentrated markets (Hsieh & Chen, 2010). Scholars argue that within more competitive settings with a multitude of rivals and weak one-to-one interfirm dependencies, managers might not be able to individually perceive and interpret every rival's competitive action in isolation and respond to it. Also within such settings, it seems too restrictive to presume that competitive actions target one competitor only (Hsieh & Chen, 2010). In response to these limitations of prior dyadic work, scholars have reached beyond the dyad-level and found that managers also derive their competitive decisions on grounds of overall market conditions (Hsieh & Chen, 2010; Zuchhini & Kretschmer, 2011). The major antecedent of interfirm rivalry in competitive markets these scholars have identified is the overall rivalry firms face – expressed as the volume of total rival actions and further characterized by the distributional properties of the actions (Hsieh & Chen, 2010; Zuchhini & Kretschmer, 2011). As of today, however, the overall market conditions remain characterized by this very single variable, missing out on other factors from the external environment that co-determine the competitive behavior of firms.

With its focus on the characteristics of the actors and their actions (see Smith et al., 2001b), the dyadic tradition of competitive dynamics research accommodates only very few studies that consider market characteristics in their analyses. Those that do conceptualize the environment in terms of industry characteristics, such as market growth, industry concentration, or the height of the barriers of entry that protect a specific market segment (Chen et al., 2009; Ferrier, 2001; Miller & Chen, 1996a; Schomburg, Grimm, & Smith, 1994; Smith, Young, Becerra, & Grimm, 1996). Market growth has been associated with environmental munificence and was found to induce complacency in firms which again reduces the variety of the competitive actions they employ (Miller & Chen, 1996a). Further, market growth has also been found to increase the proportion of long-term/strategic actions in a firm's action portfolio (Miller & Chen, 1994). Environmental uncertainty and dynamism, on the other hand, were proposed as "variety mechanisms" that expand the "array of entrepreneurial actions" of firms (Koka, Madhavan, & Prescott, 2006:

726). Recent research on rivalry in hypercompetitive environments, however, could not support this notion (Chen et al., 2009). Instead, industry concentration as a classical economic determinant of rivalry (Scherer & Ross, 1990) was found to reduce the competitive activity between industry incumbents (Young et al., 1996).

Even though all of these findings suggest that the external market context assumes an important role in determining interfirm rivalry, prior competitive dynamics research – both at the level of the firm-dyad and at the market level – has assigned a literally contextual role to it. While this contrasts with the relevance strategy research generally attributes to the environmental context (Lieberman & Montgomery, 1998; Porter, 1980; Tosi & Slocum, 1984), it is also the assumption of a gradual evolution of environmental characteristics that concerns. Variations in market growth or concentration indices seem little apt to fully describe the character of markets that are as erratic as the ones we have been experiencing in the most recent decades (Angbazo & Narayanan, 1996; Calvo et al., 2006; D'Aveni, 1994). To overcome this shortcoming, we propose a theoretical consideration of market shocks that sheds light on how sudden discontinuities punctuate interfirm rivalry.

4.3 Hypotheses

Mechanisms Driving Rivalry in Competitive Markets

Before theorizing on the effects of market shocks, we first need to understand the regime of behavioral mechanisms that typically governs interfirm rivalry. This leads us back to research on the individual relationships between competing firms (Baum & Korn, 1999; Chen & Miller, 1994; Chen et al., 1992), where scholars found that three broad behavioral categories of factors determine the competitive behavior of firms. These categories describe the awareness, motivation, and capability of firms to exchange competitive moves (Chen & MacMillan, 1992; Chen et al., 2007; Ferrier, 2001; Smith et al., 2001b). Integrating these dimensions, scholars conceived the concept of competitive tension (Chen et al., 2007), which expresses the behavioral strain between a focal firm and a given rival that builds up over time until it releases itself in rivalrous activity.

As for the antecedents of competitive tension, scholars have investigated various factors related to the characteristics of the involved firms and the actions these firms exchanged. Among other results, they found – from a defending firm's perspective – that highly visible actions increase the awareness to react (Chen & Miller, 1994), or that attacks of core markets or high attack volumes particularly fuel the managerial motivation to respond (Chen & MacMillan, 1992; Ferrier, 2001; Gimeno, 1999). Since these findings originate from research on firm-dyads, there is ample reason for doubts on whether the findings can be directly applied to competitive market settings where large numbers of rival relationships question the strong relational assumptions underlying dyadic analyses.

First efforts that go beyond the level of firm-dyads have adopted the general behavioral triad expressed in the awareness-motivation-capability framework – with one adjustment. Instead of presuming that managers focus on the competitive actions of an individual rival, scholars suggest that managers consider the overall market conditions when they decide on their firm's competitive moves (Hsieh & Chen, 2010). Prior research has perceived these market conditions as largely characterized by the collective competitive actions undertaken by the focal firm's rivals. The findings from this research suggest a similar mechanism at play in competitive markets as within firm-dyads: Higher levels of total rival actions increase the pressure on a focal firm to take action. Since interpreting the collective rival behavior in an integrative manner poses a major managerial challenge, Hsieh and Chen (2010) have complemented this basic finding by identifying distributional properties of the rivals' actions (i.e., actions are more concentrated in terms of actors, time, or geographic space) that ease their interpretation and increase the likelihood of a competitive response by the focal firm.

Despite us agreeing with the idea that the overall rival activity impacts a firm's inclination to take new competitive action, we elaborate on this mechanism by differentiating between the effect of all rival actions – independent of their type – and the effect originating from trends within the composition of rival actions. With respect to the total number of rival actions, we parallel prior research's arguments. Larger volumes of rival actions change the market status quo (Ferrier, 2001; Ferrier et al., 1999; Young et al., 1996) and build up pressure to respond (Chen et al., 2007; Zuchhini & Kretschmer, 2011), which eventually pulls the static relationship between a firm and its rivals into a dynamic interplay of rivalry (Chen et al., 2007).

We further suggest that compositional changes in the body of rival actions impact a firm's competitive choices. When faced with uncertainty about the benefits of distinct action types, we suggest that managers seek advice from their rivals, and, more importantly, from their rivals' past competitive actions. We do so for two reasons. First, research suggests that managers tend to assume that rivals ground their competitive choices on superior information, and thus conclude that imitating these rivals might also benefit their own organization (Lieberman & Asaba, 2006). And second, managers are prone to fears of falling behind. One proven means to overcome this fear is to imitate rivals for the mere sake of maintaining competitive parity (Bikhchandani et al., 1992; Chen et al., 1992; DiMaggio & Powell, 1983). With respect to the competitive behavior of firms, prior research thus concludes that "rivalry-based imitation often proceeds for many rounds where firms repeatedly match each other's moves" (Lieberman & Asaba, 2006: 28).

Based on these arguments, we propose two antecedents to a focal firm's decision to take new competitive action. First, we propose that a firm's inclination to take new competitive action increases with the competitive pressure exerted by rivals – defined as the recent total action volume. And second, the inclination to take new competitive action is bolstered if rivals have recently engaged more often in the same action type as the one the firm is engaging in. Hence, we propose:

Hypothesis 1: Higher degrees of competitive pressure increase a firm's inclination to take new competitive action.

Hypothesis 2: A trend of rivals to pursue a distinct competitive action type increases a firm's inclination to take new competitive action of this type.

Market Shocks as Antecedents to Competitive Actions

One of the central tenets of strategic management and organization literature is that firms achieve higher performance levels when their strategies and actions are aligned with both the external environment and the firm's internal resources and activities (Lawrence & Lorsch, 1967; Porter, 1980; Siggelkow, 2001). Presuming that firms continuously aim at maintaining external and internal fit, unanticipated environmental change requires adjustments in strategies and organizational behavior that eventually transform organizations (Chattopadhyay et al., 2001;

Hannan & Freeman, 1989; Meyer et al., 1990; Pennings, 1987; Staw, Sandelands, & Dutton, 1981). How important such adjustments are subsequent to external change was found to largely depend on the change's magnitude (Miller & Friesen, 1980; Quinn, 1980). While incremental change might be addressed with piecemeal adjustments in strategy or even be ignored for a while, disruptive change fundamentally unhinges a firm's fit with its environment and does not allow for momentum or inertia (Miller & Friesen, 1980). Instead, it was suggested that disruptive change demands for a period of "unlearning yesterday" and "inventing tomorrow" (Hedberg, Nystrom, & Starbuck, 1976; Miller & Friesen, 1980: 594).

Market shocks present prime examples of disruptive change that significantly impact interfirm rivalry through several mechanisms. First, market shocks significantly increase the level of environmental complexity and uncertainty in markets. Prior cause and effect relationships with respect to performance outcomes become obsolete and firms lack proven strategies in navigating the new situation (Pfeffer & Salancik, 1978). They are thus led astray as to the shock's implications and the future course of the industry. With respect to their competitive behavior, firms were found to take advantage of such situations by deviating from the current state of mutual forbearance with the intention to enhance their own sphere of influence (McGrath et al., 1998). In the case of market shocks, this tendency of firms might be further buffered by the heterogeneous conditions in which rivals will find themselves after the shock. Due to idiosyncratic resource endowments and strategic postures, firms have different, partly opposing exposures and will therefore be impacted in different ways by the event. As a consequence, some firms will be consumed with restoring their businesses, whereas others can actively take advantage of the situation and seize market shares from ailing competitors (Amit & Schoemaker, 1993; Chattopadhyay et al., 2001; Hitt & Tyler, 1991; Simon, 1972).

The presented arguments jointly suggest that in the aftermath of market shocks, mutual forbearance equilibriums more likely fail because firms will experience an enormous temptation to act opportunistically under the cover of increased environmental complexity and allured by the rich menu of newly created competitive opportunities (McGrath et al., 1998). Accordingly, we propose that market shocks generally stimulate competitive actions and thus raise a firm's inclination to take new competitive action:

Hypothesis 3: Market shocks increase a firm's inclination to take new competitive action.

Changing the Mechanisms of Rivalry: On the Moderating Effects of Market Shocks

Besides suggesting that market shocks serve as direct catalysts for interfirm rivalry, our arguments also maintain that disruptive events unhinge the mechanisms that generally drive the competitive decision-making of firms. Similarly to extant research (Hsieh & Chen, 2010; Lieberman & Asaba, 2006), we proposed that two key outcomes of competitive decision-making, the decision to engage in competitive actions as well as the choices for specific action types, are informed by the historic competitive actions of rivals (Chen & MacMillan, 1992; Chen et al., 1992; Smith et al., 1989). We argued for this backward-looking bias within competitive decision-making by referring to the competitive tension concept (Chen et al., 2007; Hsieh & Chen, 2010), its industry-level variant competitive pressure (Zuchhini & Kretschmer, 2011), and the managerial tendency to imitate rivals' actions when faced with uncertainty (Lieberman & Asaba, 2006).

Yet, when environmental contexts fundamentally change in an instance, most arguments favoring such a backward-looking bias in decision-making lose appeal. By tossing industries into disarray, market shocks create novel contexts with a fundamentally different set of competitive opportunities (Fiegenbaum & Thomas, 1995; Meyer et al., 1990; Wan & Yiu, 2009). In hindsight, these new contexts deny managers in the pre-shock environment the ability to make valid assumptions about the future or to conceive competitive actions effective in the post-shock environment. This has two important implications impacting the drivers of competitive behavior. First, it discounts the impact pre-shock competitive actions effectively have (Miller & Friesen, 1980). And second, it depreciates the value of the information on performance antecedents and competitive opportunities embedded in pre-shock rival actions (Kreps, 1990; Meyer et al., 1990).

The discounted impact and efficiency of the rivals' pre-shock actions counteract their compounding to competitive pressure and thereby reduce the influence past rival actions have in initiating new competitive actions at the focal firm (Chen et al., 2007; Hsieh & Chen, 2010; Zuchhini & Kretschmer, 2011). Similarly, their role in advising the focal firm's action choices is impeded. Under stable contextual conditions – such as during periods of continuous change (Watzlawick, Weakland, & Fisch, 1974) – managers seek for cues on performance antecedents and competitive opportunities in prior rival actions when contemplating their own moves (Bogner, 1991; Lieberman & Asaba, 2006). After market shocks, however, it will dawn on managers that also rivals have conceived their past actions based on scenarios that did not become reality, and that imitating these actions will not help them in developing competitive advantages. In consequence, managers will no longer base their decisions on prior rival actions until a new history of competitive moves, valid in the new environmental context, has been established.

There is another reason why managers might not turn toward rival actions when they seek guidance in the aftermath of market shocks. Despite their tendency to cluster in groups of similar firms within their industry (Fiegenbaum & Thomas, 1995), firms remain unique in various ways, e.g., in terms of the regional markets they serve, or their distinct resource endowments. These individual profiles entail different exposures to market shocks, as well as different degrees of preparedness to respond (Amit & Schoemaker, 1993). Market shocks thus affect each firm in a unique manner. This reinforces the existing differences between firms and advises their managers to pursue competitive actions that, most importantly, consider their own firm's unique profile (Chattopadhyay et al., 2001; Pfeffer & Salancik, 1978).

With respect to the basic mechanisms driving a firm's competitive behavior, the presented arguments on market shocks are twofold: Market shocks first discount the prevailing level of competitive pressure and thus negatively moderate how the latter relates to a firm's inclination to take new competitive action. And further, market shocks devalue the informational content of prior rival actions and advise managers to focus on their own firm's profile rather than prior rival actions when contemplating competitive actions. Hence, we propose the following two moderating effects:

> *Hypothesis 4: Market shocks negatively moderate the relationship between competitive pressure and a firm's inclination to take new competitive action.*

> *Hypothesis 5: Market shocks negatively moderate the relationship between the trend of rivals to pursue a distinct competitive action type and a firm's inclination to engage in this competitive action type.*

4.4 Method

Research Setting

Our research is set in the global insurance industry and studies the competitive moves of the world's leading 37 P&L insurance firms between 2001 and 2007. We chose this empirical setting for several reasons. First, the global P&L insurance industry is characterized by a manageable set of multinational firms that perceive each other as core competitors. Second, the global scale of operations of the sampled firms as well as their international community of investors requires the firms' managers to adhere to high disclosure standards and thus to release information on important corporate decisions (Grace & Barth, 1993). Third and finally, despite their differing regional market focus, the global integration of insurance markets exposes these firms to a common risk environment, what makes their competitive behaviors subject to the same market events (Angbazo & Narayanan, 1996; Chen et al., 2008). Particularly within P&L markets, market shocks, such as catastrophic losses, disrupt business cycles and may change the competitive conditions in an instance. Oftentimes, market shocks significantly reduce the capital base of insurers and shift back the short-run supply curve. If the initial capital endowment cannot be restored at low cost, insurance firms will either face increased risks of bankruptcy or are forced to change their pricing strategy (Cummings, Harrington, & Klein, 1991; Harrington & Niehaus, 1999).

We start our study period – which is recorded on a daily basis – on September 11, 2001 and end with the year 2007. Choosing this period allows us to test our hypotheses on the two most severe market shocks that have ever hit the global P&L insurance industry. We focus on these two market shocks since they provide natural experiments of disruptive change that allow to uncover the implications of market shocks on an amplified scale (Chen et al., 2008; Goll & Rasheed, 2009; Meyer, 1982; Pettigrew, 1990; Wan & Yiu, 2009). Our data record starts on September 11, 2001 when terrorists attacked the World Trade Center in New York City and the Pentagon in Arlington (9/11) with hijacked airplanes and killed almost 3,000 people. Besides of transforming the world in the years thereafter, the attacks also had immediate effects which thrust the global insurance industry into disarray. With 20.7 billion USD, they led to a volume of claims only reached until then by

Hurricane Andrew in 1992. Further, the attacks instantaneously altered the demand and supply structure of the industry, sent stock markets into dive and considerably increased the environmental uncertainty, fears of war and levels of future directions. In the medium-term, 9/11 decreased the firms' capacities to supply catastrophe insurance, brought a new risk class into being (Chen et al., 2008) and triggered far-reaching regulatory processes that ultimately turned terrorism insurance into a product (Cabantous & Gond, 2009). The second high-impact event that hit the insurance industry during the study period was Hurricane Katrina in 2005. The tropical storm caused tremendous death and devastation in New Orleans and at the U.S. Gulf Coast. Its death toll amounted to 1,836 and the total insured property damage to 45.5 billion USD, more than double as much as any other prior market event ever cost. Katrina drove several insurance firms out of the coastal markets and even led to the bankruptcy of a major insurance firm (Born & Viscusi, 2006).

Sample and Data

The data of this study describes the competitive actions of the 37 largest global P&L insurance firms, the insurance firms themselves, as well as their environmental context. It covers the period from 2001 to 2007. We identified this sample of firms from the Dow Jones Global Insurance Index, which lists 81 insurers of global reach. We excluded four broker firms that focus on the retail of insurance policies and have no significant insurance operations, and 14 firms for which either no financial data or no competitive actions were available. Further, we discarded 26 insurance firms that solely provided life insurance or reinsurance products and were thus not or substantially differently affected by the studied market shocks.

We captured the competitive behaviors of the sampled firms by systematically identifying their competitive moves and allocating them in time (e.g., Bresser, 2008; Chen & Hambrick, 1995; Yu & Cannella, 2007). As for the source of these moves, we chose the press release archives available on the corporate websites of the studied firms (see Duriau, Reger, & Ndofor, 2000 for a discussion on this data source). Since high disclosure standards in the industry require firms to release relevant corporate decisions in a timely and complete manner, we considered corporate press releases superior to periodicals or other third party articles oftentimes analyzed by prior research (Bresser, 2008; Chen & Hambrick, 1995;

Uotila et al., 2009; Yu & Cannella, 2007). To collect and characterize the competitive actions of the sampled firms, we applied several steps that made the press releases accessible, identified their announcement dates and analyzed their content by a structured content analysis (see Fetch Technologies, 2011 for a similar approach; Jauch, Osborn, & Martin, 1980; Shapiro & Markoff, 1997).

Specifically, we downloaded the press release archives of the firms with an open source download manager (Maier, Parodi, & Verna, 2008) and collected 9,613 individual HTML files, each representing a corporate press release. Using VBA, we then cleaned all files from unnecessary information (such as navigation elements) and compiled the text strings of the press releases within a database. Next, we identified the announcement dates of the press releases by searching for regular expressions (Friedl, 2006; see Appendix 4 for details). To ensure correct dates, we steered the identification by providing information on the firm specific syntax for dates and the most probable location of the announcement date within the press releases of each firm by an extensive review of the results. We highlighted all press releases that included a total of more than one date and found in a random sample of 200 of these press releases that all announcement dates were correctly identified.

Firm-level data was retrieved from two sources. We used the A.M. Best Global File statement, the most comprehensive source of accounting and organizational data for the insurance industry (Katrishen & Scordis, 1998) and COMPUSTAT as sources for data describing the sampled firms. Information on the environmental context, notably on the occurrence and severity of market shocks, was collected from the online portal of Swiss Re Sigma Research (Swiss Re, 2007).

Identification of Competitive Moves

In order to categorize the press releases and classify the competitive moves of the sampled firms, we applied a structured content analysis on the downloaded press release texts (Hilliard et al., 2006; Lowe, 2003). Since the collection and identification of competitive moves poses a major challenge in competitive dynamics research (Bresser, 2008; Chen et al., 1992), we paid particular attention to the definition of our categorization procedure and defined it according to the advice of prior categorization research (King & Lowe, 2003). Our categorization procedure consists of a categorization scheme that combines action categories with keyword lists and a classification algorithm programmed in VBA.

For defining the categorization scheme, we first screened a sub-sample of press releases and reviewed similar research on competitive dynamics (Bettis & Weeks, 1987; Bresser, 2008; Gimeno & Woo, 1996; Rindova et al., 2010; Young et al., 1996; Yu & Cannella, 2007) and strategic change (Lant, Milliken, & Batra, 1992). This yielded an initial categorization scheme. We then let the data and algorithm further inform our categorization scheme in a step-wise manner. We iteratively brought in changes in our categories and keyword-lists and reviewed the impact of these changes on the matching results (Lowe, 2003). We applied numerous iterations since prior research found that the quality of automatized categorization schemes is critical for achieving results comparable to the ones human coders produce (King & Lowe, 2003).

We eventually settled for the seven competitive action types described in Table 4-1 and discarded those filtering categories mentioned below the table. In total, the algorithm successfully assigned 85% of all downloaded press releases and achieved an inter-rater reliability with a human coder, assessed by Cohen's (1960) kappa, of 0.64 ($p < 0.01$) (based on a random sample of 100 press releases).

Table 4-1: Categorization Scheme - Action Types and Keyword Lists

Action type	Keywords/word stems
Acquisition	acqui, merge, buy
Divestiture	divest, spin-off, carve-out, sale of, sharpen, focus, downsize
Alliances & Joint Ventures	collaborat, cooperat, co-operate, interfirm, inter-industry, inter-organization, joint venture, network, partnership, outsourcing, alliance
Corporate Restructuring	restruct, bankruptcy, co-insurance, reorganization, divest, downsize, efficiency gain, failure, distress, reorientation, revitalization, turnaround, reposit, radical, change
Market expansion	market expansion, market entry, new dependence, entrepr, start-up, first mover, enters, market, introduce
Product expansion	product, innovation, introduction, launch, first, innovat, introd
Managerial change	appoint, leave, join, director, board

Notes: We further searched for and discarded announcements for annual and quarterly reports, directors' dealings, credit ratings and refinancing decisions such as bond issuances.

Methodologically, the classification algorithm identified the competitive action type of each press release by counting the occurrences of words or word stems. It thus took advantage of the unique distributional properties of words within texts (Mandelbrot, 1968; Zipf, 1932) that allow for an accurate categorization of the latter (Lowe, 2003). Our algorithm assigned to each press release one action category by comparing the cumulative word counts of the words representing the different categories (Lowe, 2003). Since the different press releases vary in length and since less specific words occur in many contexts, we took two measures. First, we normalized the count measures – pertaining to the different action categories – of a press release by the length of the press release, and second, we corrected the count measures by benchmark values expressing the mean frequencies with which the respective categories' keywords appeared in the full sample of press releases.

Measures

Dependent Variable

Inclination to take new action. We follow recent competitive dynamics studies (Hsieh & Chen, 2010; Yu & Cannella, 2007) and operationalize the competitive behaviors of firms as the firms' inclinations to take new competitive actions. Based on our sample of competitive moves, we measure these inclinations to act as the instantaneous probabilities for the occurrences of different competitive actions at any given moment of time during our study period. With this conceptualization and the notion of firms as conscious actors, the dependent variable gives answer to the question of when a firm will take again competitive action after having implemented its most recent competitive move. Hence, the variable directly relates to the timing of competitive actions.

Explanatory Variables

Competitive pressure. Competitive pressure is a relatively new concept within competitive dynamics research. It refers to the aggregate number of actions taken by a firm's rivals and expresses the pressure rivals jointly exert on a firm to engage in competitive actions (Hsieh & Chen, 2010; Zuchhini & Kretschmer, 2011). However, extant research disagrees on whether the full range of a firm's rivals' moves (Yu & Cannella, 2007) or only actions of the same type as the response (Hsieh & Chen, 2010) trigger responses. While we integrate both aspects in our analyses, we believe that competitive pressure is generally exerted by the overall body of all action types competitors engage in. Hence, our first independent variable sums the number of all actions rival firms have undertaken during the 30 days preceding the focal action (since we apply an event history analysis, the focal action marks the last day of the spell/duration time analyzed). In order to test the robustness of our analyses, we also explored alternative moving windows of 10 to 100 days. We found that even though the effects were similar for all windows between 20 and 70 days, effect sizes were strongest for windows of 30 and 40 days.

Trend of rivals to pursue a distinct competitive action type. While our competitive pressure variable captures the pressure the joint competitive actions of rivals exert on a focal firm to take any new competitive action, this variable acknowledges that also the choice for a distinct action type may be informed by the rivals' actions. Prior competitive dynamics research suggests such an effect by presuming that actions and reactions are of the same action type (e.g., Hsieh & Chen, 2010). We capture such mimetic behavior, also dubbed as response imitation (Smith et al., 1991), by a measure that quantifies the recent popularity of the action category to which the focal action belongs. We calculate this measure as the difference between the actual and the expected portion of the respective action type during the 30 days preceding the focal action. At this, the expected portion represents the total number of moves of this action type divided by all competitive actions over the full observation period.

Market shock. To capture the effect of market shocks on the competitive behaviors of firms, we acknowledge that their impact eventually declines after the disruptive event has taken place (Meyer et al., 1990). We account for this temporal dynamism of the impact by a clock variable that counts the weeks elapsed since the disruptive event has unfolded. We invert this clock variable so that the values of the variable match the proposed logic that the event's impact declines over time. To validate our results, we also applied alternative operationalizations in which we replaced the clock variable by its logarithm to the base of ten, or measured the time elapsed in months instead of weeks. Since our results remained fairly stable, we settled for the simplest operationalization, 1/(week since market shock).

Control Variables

Size. While prior research also found that a firm's size breeds simplicity in its competitive actions (Miller & Chen, 1996a), it all the same found that size positively relates to a firm's overall action volume (Yu, 2003; Yu & Cannella, 2007). Scholars argued for two different levers driving this effect. First, size may relate to slack, which itself is considered a driver of and necessity for taking actions (Ferrier, 2001; Young et al., 1996) and second, size equates into reputation, which again requires firms to take more bold action when being threatened by competitors (Chen & Hambrick, 1995; Clark & Montgomery, 1998). We control for size by the natural logarithm of the total gross written premiums of firms.

Business scope. Even though all firms in our sample are engaged in P&L markets, they do so at different degrees. Market shocks that mostly impact P&L businesses thus affect the sampled firms differently. We control for these varying degrees of exposure by a variable that expresses the split of the total business between P&L and Life businesses. The variable divides the gross written premiums from P&L markets by the total gross written premiums.

Diversification level. An important empirical fact within the global P&L insurance industry is the long-term coexistence of firms that follow a conglomeration strategy and firms that follow a focused strategy (Berger et al., 2000). Within our study, the diversification level may have an important impact on the competitive behaviors of firms: After market shocks, a broader revenue base might reduce the vulnerability to specific market segments and thus allow the focal firm to better exploit opportunities in the shock's aftermath. We control for the diversification level of our sampled firms by a Herfindahl index over the gross premiums written in the different lines of business each firm operates in.

Reinsurance strategy. Despite the global reach of the market shocks we studied, they may still impact firms at different levels of intensity. The major measure for insurance firms to hedge themselves against risks is to transfer business to reinsurance firms. Similarly to prior research (Augustine, 1998; Group of Thirty, 2006), we control for these hedging strategies by the "ceded portion", a ratio that divides the absolute amount of premiums transferred to reinsurers by the total gross premiums written.

Financial leverage. Financing risk plays an important role within the insurance industry. It is a major determinant of the risk taking capacity of firms and as such, has an important bearing on their business capacity (Doherty, 1980; Haugen, 1971). Within the context of turbulent markets, high levels of leverage pose a behavioral constraint on firms: As a fixed obligation, debt consumes a fixed portion of a firm's cash flows, irrespective of the situational needs. Further, debt oftentimes bears covenants that further restrict firms in engaging in competitive moves. Similarly as prior research within this industry, we thus control for the capital structure of firms measured by a firm's long term liabilities over total assets (Chen et al., 2008; Fiegenbaum et al., 1990).

Investment strategy. Likewise to financial leverage, a firm's investment strategy has an important bearing on its opportunity set (Fiegenbaum & Thomas, 1995). With large amounts of financial assets on their balance sheets, insurance firms are exposed to various risk factors. Since the two broadest asset classes, equity and fixed income, are affected in different manners by market shocks, we need to control for the firms' investment strategies in order to capture their different financial postures following such disruptions. We thus control for a firm's investment strategy by a ratio of its equity holdings over its total investments consisting of equity and fixed income investments (Fiegenbaum et al., 1990).

Past performance. Despite being a classic outcome variable, performance has also been discussed as an antecedent of firm actions (Thompson, 1967). Discrepancies between organizational goals and actual performance levels were found to predict organizational change: Success has been portrayed as a factor that creates complacency and inhibits competitive activity, whereas performance shortfalls were found to prompt change and competitive actions (Ferrier, 2001; Fiegenbaum & Thomas, 1986, 1988; Greve, 1998a). We control for a firm's financial performance by its return on assets operationalized as net income before extraordinary items and preferred dividends divided by its total assets.

Slack resources/liquidity. Besides a firm's awareness of its rivals and its motivation to act, Chen and Miller (1994) found that a firm's ability to act is a major determinant of a firm's competitive activity. Similarly, McGrath, Chen and MacMillan state that "no matter what a firm's intentions, if it is not able to launch a meaningful response because of a lack of resources or competing claims on limited resources, it is unlikely to take action" (1998: 727). To control for differing levels in the firms' capabilities to take competitive actions, we control for slack in terms of the quick liquidity ratio. The quick liquidity ratio is calculated as quick assets divided by net liabilities plus ceded reinsurance balances payable with quick assets being cash, unaffiliated short-term investments, unaffiliated bonds maturing within one year, government bonds maturing within five years and 80% of unaffiliated common stocks (A.M. Best, 2009).

Data Analysis

The examination of our hypotheses requires dynamic analyses. We want to study when and why companies choose to take new competitive action after they have announced their previous move. Hence, we are concerned with predicting a firm's inclination to take new competitive action contingent upon its previous actions, the state of the actor, its rivals and the market at any given time during our study period. The analytical technique appropriate for this type of analysis is event history analysis, also called duration models (Coleman, 1981; Kiefer, 1988).

The method requires us to prepare the data for each firm in a specific format. Specifically, we generate for each firm a series of "spells" (durations in days between competitive actions) that stretches across the study's observation period.

The first spell of each firm begins with the first competitive action the firm has taken after September 11, 2001 and ends with the competitive action that succeeds its first move. The next spell begins after the second competitive action and ends with the third action of the firm. Following this logic for all competitive moves undertaken by the firms, we structured our data in a multiple record per-subject pattern with unconditional ordering (Box-Steffensmeier & Zorn, 2002; Cleves, 1999) and added all explanatory variables, including a clock-style variable for the effect of market shocks, as of the beginning of each spell.

We then applied Cox models (Cox, 1972) to validate the mechanisms we have proposed to drive a firm's inclination to take new competitive action (see Yu & Cannella, 2007 for a similar application). Cox proportional hazard models derive a hazard function – expressing a conditional probability of event occurrence (i.e., a firm's inclination to take new competitive action) – from the empirically observed durations of spells and the time-varying states of the explanatory variables. The analytical form of the models reads as follows (Box-Steffensmeier & Jones, 2004):

$$h(t) = h_0(t) \cdot e^{X\beta}$$

In this equation, $h(t)$ denotes the hazard function which expresses the probabilities that an event occurs conditional upon that it has not occurred until time t. $h_0(t)$ represents a baseline hazard rate which is common to all units, and to which $h(t)$ relates proportionally. $e^{X\beta}$ is an exponential function of the explanatory factors X, which adjusts the baseline hazard up or down.

4.5 Results

Table 4-2 provides the means, standard deviations, and correlations for all variables used. In order to determine the degree of multicolinearity in our independent variables, we ran for each of our models a respective standard OLS model and applied STATA's postestimation command vif to produce the variance inflation factors (VIF) for the model's independent variables. Their mean values across the models ranged from 1.56 to 1.79 and the individual values never exceeded 2.51. Since all values are very low, far below the most commonly applied critical values (e.g., the rule-of-thumb cutoff of 10 by Neter et al., 1985), there seems to be no multicolinearity issue between our variables (Allison, 1999).

Table 4-2: Descriptive Statistics and Correlations

Variables		Mean	s.d.	1	2	3	4	5	6	7	8	9	10	11
1.	Firm size	16.52	11.43	1										
2.	Business scope	0.71	0.33	-0.23*	1									
3.	Diversification level	0.44	0.21	0.01	-0.18*	1								
4.	Reinsurance strategy	0.19	0.20	0.25*	0.56*	-0.28*	1							
5.	Firm leverage	0.05	0.03	-0.21*	0.16*	-0.28*	0.16*	1						
6.	Investment strategy	0.19	0.16	-0.46*	-0.24*	0.33*	-0.48*	-0.11*	1					
7.	Performance	0.03	0.03	-0.16*	0.43*	0.24*	0.05*	-0.13*	-0.00	1				
8.	Slack	0.09	0.08	-0.45*	0.09*	-0.16*	0.07*	0.05*	0.26*	-0.04*	1			
9.	Competitive pressure	88.12	23.00	0.06*	-0.07*	0.09*	-0.04*	-0.23*	-0.03	0.23*	0.11*	1		
10.	Trend towards action type	0.10	5.41	-0.00	0.01	0.01	-0.03*	-0.02	0.04	0.05*	-0.02	-0.01	1	
11.	Market shock	0.03	0.06	0.01	0.03	0.07*	0.01	0.01	0.01	0.05*	0.02	-0.02	-0.03	1

Notes: N = 2,467. * $p < .05$ or lower.

Table 4-3: Cox Models of Action Rate[a]

Variables	Model 1		Model 2		Model 3		Model 4		Model 5		Model 6		Model 7	
	Coef.	SE	Coef.	SE	Coef.	SE	Coef.	SE	Coef.	SE	Coef.	SE	Coef.	SE
Firm size	0.13†	(0.07)	0.13†	(0.07)	0.13†	(0.07)	0.12†	(0.07)	0.12†	(0.07)	0.12†	(0.07)	0.12†	(0.07)
Business scope	-0.20	(0.29)	-0.17	(0.29)	-0.17	(0.29)	-0.18	(0.29)	-0.18	(0.29)	-0.19	(0.29)	-0.19	(0.29)
Diversification level	0.34	(0.33)	0.35	(0.33)	0.35	(0.33)	0.34	(0.33)	0.34	(0.33)	0.33	(0.33)	0.33	(0.33)
Reinsurance strategy	-0.10	(0.39)	-0.09	(0.39)	-0.08	(0.40)	-0.07	(0.40)	-0.07	(0.40)	-0.06	(0.39)	-0.06	(0.40)
Financial leverage	1.73	(1.86)	2.04	(1.91)	2.04	(1.91)	2.00	(1.91)	2.00	(1.91)	2.04	(1.90)	2.04	(1.90)
Investment strategy	0.51	(0.42)	0.56	(0.44)	0.57	(0.44)	0.57	(0.44)	0.57	(0.44)	0.57	(0.44)	0.57	(0.44)
Past performance	1.50	(1.68)	0.96	(1.69)	0.96	(1.70)	0.92	(1.71)	0.91	(1.72)	0.95	(1.69)	0.94	(1.70)
Slack	3.07***	(0.68)	2.95***	(0.68)	2.96***	(0.68)	2.91***	(0.69)	2.92***	(0.69)	2.93***	(0.69)	2.94***	(0.69)
Competitive pressure			0.003*	(0.002)	0.003*	(0.002)	0.003*	(0.002)	0.003*	(0.002)	0.003*	(0.002)	0.003*	(0.002)
Tendency towards action type					0.007*	(0.003)	0.007*	(0.003)	0.007*	(0.003)	0.007*	(0.003)	0.007*	(0.003)
Market shock							0.75*	(0.33)	0.74*	(0.34)	0.71*	(0.31)	0.71*	(0.31)
Market shock × Competitive pressure									-0.01	(0.03)			-0.01	(0.03)
Market shock × Tendency towards action type											-0.16**	(0.06)	-0.16**	(0.06)
Observations	2,467		2,467		2,467		2,467		2,467		2,467		2,467	
Log-likelihood	-16831.52		-16826.30		-16825.89		-16823.41		-16823.33		-16819.65		-16819.61	
Chi-square	26.79***		32.58***		36.68***		35.41***		36.65***		66.18***		69.66***	

Notes: [a] The dependent variable represents the hazard of taking a new competitive action (termed here as inclination to take new action). The reported values for the independent variables indicate whether the variables increase (positive sign) or decrease (negative sign) a firm's inclination to take a competitive action. They reflect how much the hazard ratios of each independent variable differ from 1 (Box-Steffensmeier & Jones, 2004). $^{\dagger}p < .10$; $^{*}p < .05$; $^{**}p < .01$; $^{***}p < .001$.

Table 4-3 presents the results of our analyses. Model 1 provides the control model. Model 2 to 4 add independent variables, whereas Model 5 and 6 add interaction terms. Model 7 is the full model including all variables and interaction terms. All coefficients in Table 4-3 represent percentage changes in the hazard rate for a one-unit increase in the respective independent variable. While negative values indicate a decrease in the independent variable, positive values indicate increases in a firm's inclination to take competitive action.

Model 2 and 3 provide support for Hypotheses 1 and 2 that lay out the basic mechanisms that drive the number and types of competitive actions within competitive markets ($p < 0.05$). Specifically, we find that higher numbers of total rivals' actions increase a firm's inclination to take new competitive action. We also find that the choice for a distinct type of competitive action is significantly affected by the competitive choices competitors have made in the recent past.

Starting from this baseline, we predicted that market shocks will impact the competitive behaviors of firms. Hypothesis 3 theorized that shocks will increase a firm's inclination to take new competitive action. We find support for this hypothesis in Model 4 ($p < 0.05$).

Further, we investigated if market shocks not only directly trigger competitive actions, but also moderate the mechanisms that generally govern the number and types of competitive actions within competitive markets. While we find no support for our proposition that market shocks attenuate the relevance of competitive pressure for a firm's inclination to take competitive action (Hypothesis 4, Model 5), we did find evidence for a moderating effect on the competitive choices firms make (Hypothesis 5, Model 6). Market shocks negatively moderate the relationship between the rivals' trend to pursue a distinct competitive action type and a firm's inclination to engage in the very same action type ($p < 0.01$).

Aside from the hypothesized effects, our control variables reveal two further interesting insights with regard to firm characteristics that stimulate competitive actions. First, larger firms seem to be more active in taking competitive action ($p < 0.10$) and second, slack resources clearly function as a very important precondition for taking competitive actions ($p < 0.001$). Our results remain consistent throughout all models.

4.6 Discussion

This paper contributes to recent developments within competitive dynamics research. It connects to and extends prior efforts of establishing a novel perspective on the mechanisms driving interfirm rivalry within competitive markets (Hsieh & Chen, 2010; Zuchhini & Kretschmer, 2011). The need for such a perspective was identified by Hsieh and Chen (2010), who found that earlier findings from dyadic research were limited in their reach to oligopolistic market settings with clear interdependencies between firms.

With our hypotheses on the general mechanisms driving rivalry during stable periods, we complement their argument that "the build-up of rivals' actions eventually presses a firm to take a new action in response to the mounting competitive tension" (Hsieh & Chen, 2010: 24). Based on the wider range of competitive actions present in our sample, we show that not only the decision to take new competitive action is informed by the recent competitive activity of rivals, but also the distinct choice of competitive response for which firms opt. Our findings confirm prior research in that firms pick up trends in rival actions and tend to imitate rivals in their choice of competitive action (Lieberman & Asaba, 2006).

From this ground, we introduce the environment as an important factor impacting the competitive behavior of firms. We find that not only a firm's inclination to take new competitive action changes in the aftermath of environmental shocks, but also how the mechanisms work that govern the competitive decision-making of firms. We argue that market shocks temporarily offset these mechanisms and find our proposition confirmed for the distinct competitive choices firms make. While the action types rivals engage in seem to inform the competitive choices firms make during stable times, this relationship does not hold after market shocks. After shocks, firms seem to decide on their competitive choices irrespective of the actions their rivals have recently pursued.

Taken together, these findings suggest that the external environment and its disruptions play a more important and active role than previously thought (Chen et al., 2007; Smith et al., 2001b). Considering the various profound shocks that have unsettled markets during recent decades (Angbazo & Narayanan, 1996; Calvo et al., 2006; D'Aveni, 1994), the study fills an important research gap. It not only unravels another important antecedent of interfirm rivalry, but also illustrates how environmental disruptions impact the managerial decision-making processes that drive interfirm rivalry. With this innovative perspective, the study provides a foundation to explore which competitive strategies firms may use to take advantage of the competitive opportunities arising from market shocks.

Besides of these theoretical contributions, the study offers innovative methodological ideas to future research. It is the first large scale event history analysis that investigates the temporal dynamics of competitive actions with exact daily records in a non-dyadic setting. This type of record allows for a more granular and accurate application of the event history analysis technique (Box-Steffensmeier & Jones, 2004). Based on this level of accuracy, questions on the timing and sequencing of individual actions could be addressed more directly than if the data was aggregated with the longer intervals (e.g., monthly) that were common in prior research (Hsieh & Chen, 2010).

4.7 Avenues for Future Research and Limitations

Our study draws attention to the relationship between interfirm rivalry and the external environmental context. While our analyses suggest a strong influence of the environmental context on the competitive choices of firms, we find this relationship largely neglected by prior competitive dynamics research (Lieberman & Montgomery, 1998; Smith et al., 2001b). So far, scholars have only briefly touched upon the topic while focusing on actor and action characteristics. Also, their interest related to aspects that gradually evolve on a year to year basis, such as market growth. Given our findings, we advise future studies to adopt a more granular perspective with respect to contextual influences and study how the timely occurrence and characteristics of market events affect the interplay between firms.

Relating to market shocks in particular, studying interaction effects of firm and shock characteristics could provide further insights on the organizational response mechanisms that drive the competitive choices in disrupted markets. We further ask future research to elaborate on the characteristics of response behavior that are affected by market shocks. While our study focused on whether a firm's inclination to take new competitive action and its mimicking behavior are impacted, our arguments may be equally valid for other dimensions of competitive behavior –

such as its aggressiveness or the mix between internally or externally oriented competitive actions (Chen & Hambrick, 1995; Chen & MacMillan, 1992; Ferrier, 2001; Ferrier et al., 1999; Young, Smith, Grimm, & Simon, 2000).

The present study then leaves some questions open. With its focus on the two most outstanding market shocks of the past decades, it circumvents the valid question of how severe a market disruption needs to be in order to impact interfirm rivalry in the proposed manner. The same applies to other characteristics of market shocks. Even though individual analyses of the both sampled events yielded results closely similar to the ones of the joint analysis, the question which characteristics give rise to the competitive relevance of an event remains unanswered. While 9/11 and Hurricane Katrina had very similar impacts on the amount of interfirm rivalry and the managerial mechanisms driving competitive choices, other market shocks may display differing effects. Alternative study designs that categorize disruptive market events by their type, strength, or other relevant characteristics may offer clarification on this issue. Another aspect of this study which warrants discussion is the generalizability of its findings based on data from a single industry. Since competitive reaction patterns to shocks may vary across industries, our results need to be validated in alternative empirical settings.

5 Performance Effects of Corporate Divestiture Programs

5.1 Introduction

Even though acquisitions have generally taken a much more prominent place in strategic management research, divestitures have attracted more and more research attention recently (Brauer, 2006; Johnson, 1996). The term divestiture stands for a group of vehicles through which a firm adjusts its ownership structure and reduces its business portfolio scope. The most prominent vehicles which are commonly captured under the umbrella term divestiture are sell-offs, spin-offs or equity carveouts. Over the past few decades, scholars have contributed considerably to our knowledge of the antecedents of divestitures and offered further insights into divestiture performance (Berger & Ofek, 1999; Bergh & Lim, 2008; Haynes, Thompson, & Wright, 2002, 2003; Hite, Owers, & Rogers, 1987; John & Ofek, 1995; Lang, Poulsen, & Stulz, 1995; Montgomery, Thomas, & Kamath, 1984). But still, many ambiguities and gaps remain in our understanding of divestitures.

In particular, there is still much debate about the stock market responses to divestitures. While there is a general agreement on positive shareholder wealth effects from divestiture announcements, researchers are less unanimous about why these effects come about. Various differing explanations for the sources of divestiture gains have been explored but none of these were found to be equally valid in a larger number of studies and transaction contexts (Brauer, 2006; John & Ofek, 1995; Kaiser & Stouratis, 2001). This study proposes that one potential explanation for the inconsistent findings is that divestitures were never studied as strategically interrelated events (Bergh & Lim, 2008; Haynes et al., 2002). Constrained by a lack of information on which divestitures jointly implement distinct portfolio changes and thereby relate to each other, many scholars have been bound to adopt the notion of divestitures as isolated, self-contained events. This view on divestitures as isolated corporate events conflicts with recent developments in acquisition research (Chatterjee, 2009; Laamanen & Keil, 2008) and does not reflect current business practice, where it has been recognized that "selling businesses is rarely a one-off activity" (Mankins, Harding, & Weddigen, 2008: 99) but a sequential, recurring task that is oftentimes guided by the business logic of a corporate divestiture program.

The purpose of this study is to address this shortcoming. Specifically, we adopt a novel program-based perspective on divestitures and analyze the performance of program divestitures in comparison to single "stand-alone" divestitures. We define divestiture programs as groups of (unit) divestitures that adjust the corporate focus of a firm according to an explicitly announced strategic logic. Given such change in a firm's focus, we use the terms "divestiture program" and "refocusing program" synonymously. By adopting this view, we acknowledge that firms engage in transaction sequences rather than in single transactions to implement their corporate strategies (Haynes et al., 2002; Laamanen & Keil, 2008; Schipper & Thompson, 1983).

Our empirical analyses of the global insurance industry indicate that program divestitures generate higher abnormal returns than stand-alone divestitures. We further study the sources for the greater abnormal returns of program divestitures. Specifically, we study the influence of experience transfer and timing. Learning theory suggests that improved divestiture performance may originate from specific and general experience transfer (Bergh & Lim, 2008; Haleblian & Finkelstein, 1999). Consequently, we test whether specific experience transfer between divestitures of the same program and general experience transfer between prior divestitures and program divestitures influence abnormal returns. However, neither specific nor general experience seems to influence abnormal returns. Instead, we find that the scheduling of program divestitures significantly influences abnormal returns. Firms that allow for sufficient time between divestitures generate higher announcement returns than firms that schedule their divestitures too tightly and thus may become subject to time compression diseconomies (Dierickx & Cool, 1989).

The remainder of the paper is organized as follows: First, we review prior research on the impact of divestitures on a firm's market performance. Based on acquisition research, we identify a set of explanatory factors that relate to the presence and scheduling of divestiture programs, which might account for the inconclusive findings of extant literature on the determinants of divestiture success. Subsequently, we explain our methodological design and present and discuss our results. We conclude with an outline of the study's limitations and implications for theory and practice.

5.2 Extant Research on Sources of Divestiture Gains

Extant research on the financial performance implications of divestitures agrees upon the following: The stock price of a firm that announces a divestiture rises on the days surrounding the announcement. Though on average positive, however, these announcement returns have been found to vary quite substantially. Table 5-1 highlights the range of effect sizes that were found by studies analyzing cumulative average abnormal returns caused by divestiture announcements.

Table 5-1: Shareholder Wealth Effects (Sell-Side) of Prior Studies

Author [Orientation/Focus[a]]	Period	Sample size	Country	Event window (days)	Model[b]	CAAR (%)
Miles & Rosenfeld (1983) [F]	1962-80	55	US	1	MA	0.2
Schipper & Smith (1983) [F]	1963-81	93	US	2	MM	2.8
Alexander, Benson & Kampmeyer (1984) [F]	1964-73	53	US	2	MA	1.3
Hearth & Zaima (1984) [F]	1979-81	58	US	11	MM	3.6
Rosenfeld (1984) [F]	1969-81	62	US	2	MA	2.3
Jain (1985) [F]	1976-78	1064	US	1	MM	0.1
Klein (1986) [F]	1970-79	202	US	3	MM	1.1
Hite, Owers & Rogers (1987) [F]	1963-81	55	US	2	MM	1.7
Sicherman & Pettway (1987) [F]	1981-87	278	US	2	MM	0.9
Denning (1988) [F]	1970-82	133	US	13	MV	n/a
Afshar, Taffler & Sudarsanam (1992) [F]	1985-86	178	UK	1	MM	0.9
Markides (1992) [SM]	1980-88	45	US	2	MM	1.7
John & Ofek (1995) [F]	1986-89	231	US	3	MM	1.5
Lang, Poulsen & Stulz (1995)[F]	1984-89	93	US	2	MM	1.4
Lasfer, Sudarsanam & Taffler (1996) [F]	1985-86	142	UK	2	MA	0.8
Wright & Ferris (1997) [SM][c]	1984-90	116	US	1	MM	-25
Krishnaswami et al. (1999) [F]	1979-93	118	US	2	MM	3.2
Kaiser & Stouratis (2001) [F]	1984-94	590	UK	2	MM	1.2
Schill et al.(2001) [F]	2000	11	US	3	MM	11.3

Notes: [a] Strategic Management (SM), Finance (F). [b] Market Model (MM), Mean Adjusted Return Model (MA), Mean & Variance of Return Model (MV). [c] Special case of involuntary divestitures following public pressure. N.B.: Montgomery, Thomas, Kamath (1984) are excluded as their event window stretches over 24 months.

The relatively broad range of abnormal returns also raises the question about the sources of divestiture gains. Scholars in both finance and strategy have studied various aspects of divestitures and their transaction contexts to identify explanations for the observed stock price effects. Based on a review of previous research in strategy and finance, we derived five major hypotheses on the sources of positive divestiture announcement returns.

Refocusing Hypothesis

Overdiversification has been found to be one of the most prominent antecedents of divestitures (Brauer, 2006). Consequently, divestiture gains have been related to positive effects of a reversal of such overdiversification. Specifically, it has been argued that capital markets receive divestitures positively because refocusing is expected to reduce managerial (i.e. owner-manager conflict of interest; influence costs) and operational inefficiencies – predominantly in regards to financial resource allocation (Afshar et al., 1992; Hite et al., 1987; John & Ofek, 1995; Schipper & Smith, 1983). Essentially, this hypothesis builds upon previous empirical research which shows that highly diversified firms earn greater announcement returns and that divestitures of units which belong to different industry sectors than the parent firm are more positively received by capital markets than divestitures of businesses which belong to the firm's core (e.g., Comment & Jarrell, 1995; Daley, Mehrota, & Sivakumar, 1997; Desai & Jain, 1999; John & Ofek, 1995). Markides (1992) ascribes this relationship between the diversification level of firms and the abnormal return sizes of focus-enhancing divestitures to diminishing returns from specializing a firm's management in an ever narrower range of operations. Similarly, research in corporate finance suggests that divestiture stock market returns positively relate to the number of business segments before the divestiture (Vijh, 1999). Consistently, a firm's refocusing from two business segments to one business segment has been theorized to generate different returns than a reduction from eight to seven business segments (Dittmar & Shivdasani, 2003; Lang & Schulz, 1994).

Pure Play Hypothesis

Closely related to the refocusing hypothesis is the pure play hypothesis. The pure play hypothesis – often also called complexity or undervaluation hypothesis –

argues that value in divestitures is created through the separation of unlike parent and subsidiary assets into independently traded units, which helps markets, respectively analysts, to gain a better understanding of their true value (e.g., Krishnaswami & Subramaniam, 1999; Schipper & Smith, 1986; Vijh, 1999; Zuckermann, 2000). Zuckerman (2000) argues that capital markets will reward the effort of firms to make their stock more easily understood for financial analysts who usually specialize by industry-use to compare assets and thus have difficulties with firms that straddle multiple industries. Also, capital markets are expected to respond positively to such a separation due to the fact that the new stand-alone company has to supply audited periodic financial reports. Another performance enhancing effect may also result from the fact that the pure play might not only serve analysts but also investors. By creating a pure play, different investor clienteles for the two separated stocks might emerge and the attractiveness of pure play stocks to these different clienteles may lead to positive announcement returns (Vijh, 2002). Essentially, capital markets thus award a premium to the parent firm for offering a novel investment alternative to equity investors (Hakansson, 1982; Miles & Rosenfeld, 1983).

Information Asymmetry Hypothesis

The information asymmetry hypothesis is based on empirical evidence that has shown that the abnormal returns for sell-offs, equity carveouts and spin-offs differ. Several authors propose that rational managers would only issue stock when they have private information that their stock is likely to be overvalued at the specific point in time (Myers & Majluf, 1984; Nanda, 1991; Nanda & Narayanan, 1999; Slovin, Sushka, & Ferraro, 1991; Vijh, 2002; Welch, 1989). Investors would thus lower the stock price on the announcement of an issuance of stock for a unit by the parent. But this explanation only holds for divestiture modes which are share-for-cash transactions such as equity carveouts or sell-offs, but not for spin-offs. This explanation for the source of divestiture abnormal returns is further complicated by the fact that the non-issuance of parent stock also conveys information. The non-issuance of parent stock suggests that the management issues subsidiary stock because it sees the parent's assets undervalued and the subsidiary's assets overvalued. In turn, this piece of positive information might dominate the negative information and thus actually lead to a divestiture gain (see Myers & Majluf, 1984 for a discussion). Other studies, however, have greatly questioned whether the type of exit mode may explain varying divestiture gains by showing that in many instances investors are unable to distinguish the different divestiture modes and, for example, often confuse carveouts with spin-offs (Hand & Skantz, 1997).

Financing Hypothesis

The financing hypothesis is based on divestiture studies in corporate finance which found that market returns are on average more positive if the proceeds are used to repay the parent's or the subsidiary's debt (Allen & McConnell, 1998; Lang *et al.*, 1995). Further, it is argued that the parent firm benefits from the fact that through a divestiture separate financing for the divested unit's investment projects is obtained (Schipper & Smith, 1983).

Managerial Incentive Hypothesis

The managerial incentive hypothesis suggests that the positive market returns to divestiture announcements might originate from more efficient compensation contracts for the subsidiary's managers (Schipper & Smith, 1986). This explanation of divestiture gains, however, only applies to spin-offs and carveouts where the divested unit functions as an independent entity after divestiture. In these instances, managers who receive stock based compensation have indeed been found to create firm value by better exploiting investment opportunities (Aron, 1991; Krishnaswami & Subramaniam, 1999; Larraza-Kintana, Wiseman, Gomez-Mejia, & Welbourne, 2000; Vijh, 2002).

The aforementioned hypotheses from finance and management research illustrate that divestitures were predominantly studied with an emphasis on financial rather than strategic rationales underlying the individual transactions. It is further striking to observe that compared with acquisition research, in which learning and experience effects have become major explanatory factors (e.g., Barkema & Schijven, 2008a; Barkema & Schijven, 2008b; see Haleblian, Devers, McNamara, Carpenter, & Davison, 2009 for a review; Haleblian & Finkelstein, 1999; Hayward, 2002), these effects have been left unconsidered in divestiture research. The consequences of this neglect of divestitures' joint underlying strategic rationales and the neglect of the role of learning and experience effects in prior studies set the stage for our analyses.

5.3 Hypotheses

Implementing a change in corporate strategy typically requires firms to adjust their business portfolios. If a company strives to change its business configuration more than incrementally, it will often launch a transaction program to transition from the current to the envisioned business portfolio. The more radical the envisioned changes are, the more important a well-designed transaction program becomes. To implement corporate growth strategies, firms often devise acquisition programs (Asquit, Bruner, & Mullins, 1983; Barkema & Schijven, 2008a; Laamanen & Keil, 2008; Schipper & Thompson, 1983). In the context of corporate restructuring strategies, divestiture programs are of major importance to adjust a firm's business portfolio (Berger & Ofek, 1999; Brauer, 2006; Dranikoff, Koller, & Schneider, 2002). During the most recent financial market crisis (so called "subprime" crisis starting 2007), examples of such divestiture programs have been abundant. For instance, Alcoa, a major player in the steel industry, announced a divestiture program which shed non-core businesses with more than 22.000 employees (Alcoa, 2009). Similarly, in the economic downturn that ended in 2003, companies such as Thyssen-Krupp or Tyco International used divestiture programs to respond to challenges in their respective economic contexts. Thyssen-Krupp and Tyco International trimmed their business portfolio by divesting more than 33 respectively more than 50 businesses at this time (Tyco, 2003).

While the performance implications of transaction programs or series have been studied in acquisition research (Asquit et al., 1983; Laamanen & Keil, 2008; Schipper & Thompson, 1983; Voss & Müller-Stewens, 2006), research on divestitures has so far ignored their widespread use. Instead, divestitures have been analyzed as independent, unrelated events (Chang, 1996; Dess, Gupta, Hennart, & Hill, 1995). Since divestitures are not mere reverse images of acquisitions but complex strategic moves of their own (Brauer, 2006; Johnson, 1996) and given the fact that divestitures substantially differ from acquisitions both in terms of their determinants and their overall effect on firm market and accounting performance, findings on acquisition programs cannot be easily transferred to divestitures, which deserve independent study.

While researchers have conjectured that divestitures which "are part of clearly identified strategies should create more value than divestitures that take place in a reactional or piecemeal manner" (Montgomery et al., 1984: 831), only recent practitioner-oriented research has acknowledged the interrelation between multiple divestitures by the same firm and sought to qualitatively discriminate between well-planned series of divestitures and reactive divestitures (Dranikoff et al., 2002). Divestiture programs have thus been proposed as a major source and determinant of divestiture gains. The increased value creation potential of program divestitures compared to non-program divestitures may theoretically be argued to build upon the so-called principle of internal consistency, which claims that decisions in a series of choices that are taken in close alignment with each other and in reference to relevant external correspondences are superior (Johnson, Scholes, & Whittington, 2005; Sen, 1993). Based on this notion we suggest that program divestitures that by definition aim at collectively implementing a corporate strategy or are driven by a core business logic generate higher market returns than "stand-alone" divestitures.

Besides the internal consistency attributed to program divestitures, it is the strategic relevance of program divestitures which suggests higher market returns. Prior research found out that divestitures which "impact the way the firm does business" (Montgomery et al., 1984: 833) receive higher abnormal returns and argued that such transactions have a more important role with a greater impact on future earnings. Since such a change in the way a firm does business is much less likely to materialize from a single divestiture, but rather from a coordinated series of divestitures as part of a firm's divestiture program (Berger & Ofek, 1999; Brauer, 2006; Dranikoff et al., 2002), investors are likely to perceive program divestitures more positively than "stand-alone" divestitures. Given that most firms divest when they are confronted with poor financial performance, program divestitures may benefit more from being perceived as proactive and concerted steps that are not an outcome of compromised opportunities and market pressures (Dranikoff et al., 2002). Following these lines of reasoning and taking the capital market's perspective, divestiture programs should be awarded with a premium. We therefore propose:

Hypothesis 1: Program divestitures are associated with greater abnormal returns than "stand-alone" divestitures.

As mentioned above, the strategic consistency and relevance attributed to program divestitures may lead to above average positive market returns for program divestitures. However, prior studies on serial acquirers further argued that above average abnormal returns may result also from positive experience effects (Barkema & Schijven, 2008a; Laamanen & Keil, 2008; Schipper & Thompson, 1983). Research on learning and experience effects in acquisitions, however, has produced very mixed results (see Barkema & Schijven, 2008b for a review). Experience from prior acquisitions has been found to affect the performance of the focal acquisition in positive (Bruton, Oviatt, & White, 1994; Fowler & Schmidt, 1989; Pennings, Barkema, & Douma, 1994), concave (Haleblian & Finkelstein, 1999), neutral (Hayward, 2002; Zollo & Singh, 2004) and negative manners (Kusewitt, 1985). Given these equivocal findings, acquisition researchers have introduced more fine-grained notions of experience. Haleblian and Finkelstein (1999), for instance, proposed that only the transfer of specific acquisition experience – that is the transfer of experience between acquisitions which are similar in type and nature – is beneficial to acquisition performance while the transfer of general acquisition experience may even have a detrimental effect on acquisition outcome.

While experience effects have been documented for acquisitions, little research has been done on divestitures, let alone on divestiture programs. So far, only Bergh & Lim (2008) produced evidence for experience effects in restructuring actions. They found that experience in sell-offs and spin-offs affect a firm's propensity to further engage in these actions. As concerns performance implications of experience, they found that experience in restructuring actions increases post restructuring performance in terms of ROA. The argument for positive experience effects on divestiture performance and the distinction between general and specific experience transfer, however, has not yet been brought up but seems to be of great relevance from a divestiture program perspective. Valuable, organizational learning is particularly attributed to events which resemble each other in such a way that routines can be developed (Cohen & Levinthal, 1990). Since transactions within divestiture programs are often of the same type, involve units with similar characteristics (e.g. in term of unit performance, relatedness, size, age), and are usually implemented by the same management team, experience transfer between program divestitures not only becomes more probable than between "stand-alone" divestitures but is also likely to be more specific and thus more value-enhancing (Bergh & Lim, 2008; Singh & Zollo, 1998; Zollo & Winter, 2002). Also, smaller temporal intervals between the implementation of program divestitures, as promoted by the usually limited time horizon of a divestiture program, may amplify the positive effects of experience transfer on financial outcome of program divestitures. Long time intervals between divestitures lower managerial expectations that activities will repeat in the near future, increase reluctance to codify experiences, and therewith render inferences unavailable or inapplicable (Argote, Beckman, & Epple, 1990; Ellis, 1965; Hayward, 2002; Zollo & Singh, 2004). In line with this argument, Hayward (2002) found that firms only benefit from recent but not distant acquisition experience. Overall, this suggests that experience transfer from one program divestiture to the other is more likely to be performance-enhancing. Thus, program divestitures which occur later in a program of divestitures should generate higher announcement returns.

> *Hypothesis 2: The amount of prior specific experience from divestitures which are part of the same divestiture program is positively related to the abnormal returns of the focal program divestiture.*

In comparison, we propose a positive, albeit weaker, experience effect for the overall dealflow. Since non-program divestitures share fewer similarities with program divestitures, the experience transfer between non-program and program divestitures is likely to have less positive effects and is less likely to be perceived as beneficial by capital markets. Hence, we propose:

> *Hypothesis 3: Prior general divestiture experience positively influences program divestitures' abnormal returns. This effect is weaker than for specific experience transfer between program divestitures.*

As mentioned above, the ability to benefit from learning effects seems also to depend on how the company schedules its divestitures. Insights from acquisition research suggest that a rather tight scheduling of divestitures seems to benefit experience transfer (Hayward, 2002). However, a tight scheduling of divestitures may also be detrimental to divestiture performance. While such timing effects have remained unexplored for divestitures, acquisition research suggests that scheduling acquisitions too tightly (Gary, 2005; Hill & Hoskisson, 1987) or departing from established rhythms of deal making, defined as the standard deviation of the yearly number of transactions (Laamanen & Keil, 2008; Vermeulen & Barkema, 2002), may negatively affect acquisition financial performance. The negative implications of a tight scheduling of multiple acquisitions can be explained by organizational frictions that arise at the acquirer's side: The acquisition and integration of target firms temporarily absorbs large portions of the acquiring firm's scarce management capacity (Cohen & Levinthal, 1990), which cannot be easily expanded for two reasons. First, the current management's cognitive capacity is naturally constrained and not scalable (Cyert & March, 1963; Greve, 2003; Simon, 1959); and second, the labor market is imperfect and cannot be expected to quickly provide managers who possess the required skill-sets and experiences (Dierickx & Cool, 1989). Hence, overloading a firm's management by scheduling acquisitions too tightly may create severe problems in the post-merger integration phase and other areas of the firm's operations (Gary, 2005; Hill & Hoskisson, 1987); both effects compromise transaction and overall firm performance.

Similarly, the issue of appropriate scheduling is of central concern in divestiture programs. The issue seems particularly acute in divestiture programs because divestiture programs usually follow a predetermined time schedule which specifies by what time (usually year) a firm wants to have its divestiture program completed. In 2000, for example, the chemical firm Degussa announced a divestiture program worth 6.5 billion Euros in sales which was set out to be completed by 2002. Similarly, in 1998 the German electronics company Siemens defined a divestiture program worth 8 billion Euros which was scheduled to be completed by 2000. Moreover, the studies by Nees (1978, 1981) and Brauer (2009) suggest that divestitures are associated with complex decision-making and implementation processes that span multiple levels in the organization and require considerable management capacity during each phase. In the initiation stage, the top management of the divesting firm has to analyze and weigh alternative options and to overcome internal resistance before agreeing on the decision to divest. Thereafter, a time-consuming process of developing and implementing a transaction plan follows, which is largely constrained to the top management due to confidentiality reasons (Brauer, 2009). Once announced, divestitures also draw on the capacities of middle-managers to implement the divestiture which involves the detaching from customers and the disentangling of the firm's resource portfolio (Brauer, 2009; Nees, 1978, 1981; Penrose, 1959). Similar to acquisitions, the available management capacity is thus likely to limit the number of divestitures a firm can handle effectively within a short span of time (Cohen & Levinthal, 1990; Dierickx & Cool, 1989). Thus, we propose the following relationship:

Hypothesis 4: The time elapsed since the last divestiture of a firm is positively related to the abnormal return of a firm's divestiture.

5.4 Method

Sample and Data

In contrast to previous studies on acquisition programs (Laamanen & Keil, 2008), we opted for a single-industry study so that all firms were exposed to the same environment. While this consideration hampers generalizability, it also naturally reduces the number of required control variables that may be critical in explaining relationships among the studied variables (Hansen & Hill, 1991). Also, our approach of conceptualizing programs on the basis of the firms' divestiture announcements demands similar disclosure and reporting practices from each of the studied firms, which could not be so easily secured when studying different industries. Due to its regulated character, disclosure and reporting practices are fairly uniform in the insurance industry and the high disclosure standards allow us to perform our analyses on an extensive, longitudinal set of press releases. A focus on the insurance industry is not uncommon. For instance, in strategic management research, the insurance industry has been used as a setting in research on competitive dynamics (Greve, 2008b). Moreover, the focus on a service industry is an interesting change to prior divestiture studies which exclusively focused on manufacturing industries (Brauer, 2006). Our choice of industry is thus responsive to prior requests in divestiture research that future studies should include knowledge-based service firms in their analyses (Brauer, 2006). This focus on a service industry seems also particularly apt given that recent studies by the Organization for Economic Cooperation and Development (OECD) (2003) displayed that in the European business service sector, both entry and exit rates have been much higher than in manufacturing industries throughout the mid-1990s to late 1990s. Similarly, figures for the United States show that the business service sector belongs to the most actively divesting industries (Thomson Media, 2001).

We derived our firm sample from the Dow Jones Global Stoxx Insurance Index. However, the composition of the index and the availability of information on the firms required us to discard the following groups of firms: First, broker firms which focus solely on the retail of financial products; second, firms for which either no financial or no consistent transaction data was available. Our ultimate sample of firms consists of 31 companies listed on the Global Insurance Index throughout the study period from 1998 to 2007. Data availability restricted the analysis of years prior to 1998. The wake of the major global financial crisis starting in August 2007 advised us to choose 2007 as the upper bound for our empirical analysis. These 31 firms undertook a total of 160 divestitures within this time span. Given our single industry setting, this sample size can be considered high compared with prior multi-industry divestiture studies (compare Table 5-1).

To allow for an in-depth analysis of individual transactions, we identified and collected the press releases the firms had issued with their divestiture decisions. We proceeded as follows: In an initial step, we fully retrieved the press release archives of the sampled firms for the stated year range. This resulted in 7,445 saved web pages. Using automated procedures coded in Visual Basic, we isolated the plain texts of the press releases and identified their announcement dates. Next, we compiled the firm names, text strings and dates in an Excel database. Then, we identified the different types of portfolio transactions by means of structured content analysis based on keyword lists (Chen & Hambrick, 1995). Following these steps, we generated the sample of divestitures in two further steps: First, we matched the consolidated database by the date as key with the respective data on divestitures from the Thomson One Deal Module, which yielded – after a manual review of the matched press releases – 85 divestitures. Since our arguments rest on business unit sales, a manual review was needed to exclude other sales such as share sales or sales of minority holdings. Second, we reviewed the remaining press releases, which we had classified as divestiture announcements, and identified 83 more divestitures. To rule out stock market effects from confounding events, we dropped any divestiture within three days of any other strategic move of the same firm

(McWilliams & Siegel, 1997). This process resulted in a transaction total of 160. The accounting data for our sample firms was retrieved from Worldscope database.

Measures

Dependent Variable

Divestiture market returns. We used cumulative abnormal returns (CAR) as proxies for the total shareholder value created or destroyed by each divestiture. To calculate abnormal returns, we applied event study methodology. For the regression analysis, we chose to cumulate the abnormal returns over an event window of three days, as this length is assumed to capture the significant stock price effects while being short enough to minimize the number of events with overlapping event windows (Berger & Ofek, 1999; McWilliams & Siegel, 1997). Specifically, we enclosed the day before the announcement to factor in information leakage and the day after the announcement to cover the case that the divestiture news was released on the announcement day after the trading hours of the respective stock exchange. To ensure the robustness of our results, we aggregated the abnormal returns for further event-window lengths ranging from an asymmetric two day window (-1, 0) to a symmetric window of a total length of eleven days surrounding the event date (-5, +5).

Independent Variables

Program divestiture. For analyzing the differences between program and non-program divestitures, we needed to classify these two groups of transactions. In acquisition research, two approaches have been used to distinguish program from non-program acquisitions. The first is to denote all transactions in the years following an initial program announcement (Bhabra, Bhabra, & Boyle, 1999; Schipper & Thompson, 1983) as program transactions; the second approach is to take all transactions that form an acquisition cluster within time and label them as program acquisitions (Conn, Cosh, Guest, & Hughes, 2004; Laamanen & Keil, 2008). However, since both approaches only allow for uninterrupted sequences of program divestitures, they risk mislabeling opportunistic divestitures as programmatic. Since our research aims at investigating whether the market awards the implementation of a strategically coherent divestiture sequence with a premium rests on an unequivocal separation of the two divestiture types, neither of the two approaches is suitable. Identifying program divestitures on the basis of divestiture announcements also seems favorable because divestiture announcements are most influential in shaping the perceptions of capital markets about a divestiture (Kaiser & Stouratis, 2001; Tetlock, Saar-Tsechansky, & Macskassy, 2008). The determination of programs based on statistical clustering in contrast occurs in hindsight. It is thus highly doubtful that capital markets will in fact associate a divestiture with a program since it has no information that suggests so.

In our approach resting on text analysis, two raters read through the press releases of the 160 divestitures in our sample. Each divestiture was coded as "program divestiture" if the press release explicitly stated that the divestiture belonged to a "restructuring, refocusing, divestiture or downscoping program" or when the press release stated that the divestiture transaction "was part of a wider strategy to restructure, refocus or downscope". The coding was carried out in two steps. First, each of the raters categorized the transactions independently. Raters' assessment matched for all but four press releases. This translates into an inter-rater reliability assessed by Cohen's (1960) kappa of 0.94 ($p < 0.01$). Second, the four inconsistently rated press releases were discussed and categorized in mutual agreement between the two raters. Raters' codings were then translated into a binary variable with the value "1" if the transaction was part of a program and with the value "0" ($n = 104$), if not. In our sample, approximately one third of the corporations' divestitures were identified as program divestitures ($n = 56$). Though managers may rationalize clusters of divestiture activity as divestiture programs (Burgelman, 1996), this seems unlikely in our case. The firms only denoted a plausible share of the firms' divestitures as programmatic – roughly one third – and they did so in advance and not in hindsight. Ex post rationalization by the corporate management thereby becomes implausible.

Specific divestiture experience. In research on acquisitions (Haleblian & Finkelstein, 1999; Ingram & Baum, 1997), experience is normally captured with a count measure – the number of divestitures a firm has undertaken prior to the focal divestiture. Similarly, we use a count measure to capture potential experience transfer effects between divestitures which are part of the same program. But to distinguish specific from general divestiture experience, specific divestiture experience is measured only as the *number of program divestitures* that took place prior to the focal program divestiture. Essentially, the variable expresses the specific experience that was accrued within the specific program up to each divestiture.

General divestiture experience. In line with the operationalization for specific divestiture experience, we also use a count measure to capture general divestiture experience. Specifically, we operationalize general divestiture experience determining the position of each divestiture in the firm's full sequence of divestitures. The position values are assigned in ascending order throughout the time-span of the study, starting with "1" for the earliest divestiture undertaken by the firm.

Elapsed time since last divestiture of the firm. This variable is a clock variable which counts the number of days elapsed between the firm's last and focal divestiture announcement. Constructed like this, the variable is not a substitute to rate or rank variables, which focus on cumulated experience effects, but expresses the recency of the preceding divestiture and therefore captures potential time compression effects. For keeping the cumulated abnormal returns of our sampled divestitures unbiased, we discard those that have overlapping event windows with any other material firm event, including other divestitures (Afshar et al., 1992; McWilliams & Siegel, 1997).

Control Variables

Firm performance. Poor and well performing firms divest for different reasons which may also affect divestiture market returns. Previous research suggested that poor firm performance not only raises a firm's propensity to divest (Haynes et al., 2003), but that poor performing firms surprisingly earn higher abnormal returns than well performing firms (Dranikoff et al., 2002; Duhaime & Grant, 1984; John & Ofek, 1995; Johnson, 1996; Ravenscraft & Scherer, 1991). We control for firm performance by averaging firms' return on assets (ROA) over the three years preceding the focal divestiture.

Firm size. Prior studies found that a firm's size positively relates to its propensity to divest (Bergh, 1997; Duhaime & Grant, 1984; John, Lang, & Netter, 1992; John & Ofek, 1995; Sanders, 2001). While this conflicts with the interests of managers, who personally benefit from operating larger firms (Rhoades, 1983) and (at least short-term) usually do not benefit from rendering operations more profitable by refocusing (Haynes, Thompson, & Wright, 2007), it conforms with the arguments of the refocusing hypothesis mentioned earlier. We control for effects from firm size by using the natural logarithm of a firm's total sales in the year preceding the focal divestiture.

Degree of diversification. The degree of a firm's diversification at the time of divestiture has been found to be strongly associated with its decision to divest and to influence stock market returns upon the divestiture's announcement (Dittmar & Shivdasani, 2003; Lang & Schulz, 1994; Markides, 1992). The scope of diversification serves the capital market as an indicator for control problems associated with the management of complex organizations and thereby as a proxy for the efficiency gains that can be realized by the divestiture (Haynes et al., 2003). Following John and Ofek (1995), we measure firm diversification with a sales-based Herfindahl index. For each divestiture, we chose the index value from the end of the year which precedes the divestiture.

Debt-to-equity ratio. Since debt reduces a management's ability to invest its firm's free cash flow and raises costs for further external funding, it also makes divestitures a more attractive source of financing (Jensen, 1986, 1989; Weston & Chung, 1990). Consistently, prior research found debt to increase a firm's propensity to divest (Haynes et al., 2003). Yet, literature suggests confounding effects of debt on the abnormal returns generated by divestiture announcements. Proposing a positive effect, Lasfer, Sudarsanam and Taffler (1996) interpret divestitures as strategies that ameliorate the financial situation of the divestor. Finding a negative effect, others (Hearth & Zaima, 1984; Sicherman & Pettway, 1987) consider debt to reduce the divestor's negotiating power, ultimately leading to lower transaction prices. We control for divestor financial condition (Chatterjee & Wernerfelt, 1991; Vermeulen & Barkema, 2002) by calculating the firm specific debt-to-equity ratio ((long term debt/(common equity + policyholder's equity))*100) as of the end of the year preceding each divestiture.

Data Analysis

To test the aforementioned hypotheses, we apply an event study analysis and run a regression on the cumulative returns of the announcements. For the calculation of the cumulative returns, we follow the procedures described by MacKinlay (1997). Specifically, we calculate the cumulative abnormal return (*CAR*) for each announcement (*i*) and each event window length $(t_2 - t_1)$ as $CAR_i(t_1, t_2) = \sum_{t=t_1}^{t_2} AR_{it}$ with $AR_{it} = R_{it} - (a_i + b_i R_{mt})$, where a_i and b_i are the ordinary least squares parameter estimates from the regression of R_{it} (actual return of the stock on day *t*) on R_{mt} (actual market return on day *t*) over an estimation window with the length of 120 trading days before of the announcement. Because we study a set of international firms, an issue with differences in operating hours of the different stock markets arises (Park, 2004). We resolve this issue by using the respective home market index (*m*) for each company as its reference index and systematically exclude the local non-trading days from the respective calculations. According to finance theory (Ashley, 1962; Ball & Brown, 1968; Fama, Fisher, Jensen, & Roll, 1969), $CAR_i(t_1, t_2)$ represents the net present value of all future cash flows to the shareholders that the specific firm event (*i*) gives rise to and which are capitalized in between the days t_1 and t_2. To calculate the wealth effect of a day (*t*) between t_1 and t_2 (AR_{it}), the formula stated above calculates the difference between the actual returns (R_{it}) surrounding the event and the "normal" returns ($a_i + b_i R_{mt}$) which the stock would have exhibited if the event would not have occurred. While the actual returns can be calculated from the actual stock prices, the expected returns need to be estimated. This is done by calculating the firm's stock's historical correlation (b_i) with the market and using this relationship to project the hypothetic stock returns based on the actual market returns.

For a meaningful application of the event study methodology, several requirements must be considered (Bromiley, Govekar, & Marcus, 1988; McWilliams & Siegel, 1997; Oler, Harrison, & Allen, 2008). First, the events under study need to be of substantial relevance for the company and its shareholders (Brown & Warner, 1980), as well as understandable for the capital market participants, so they can properly estimate and price performance implications (Oler et al., 2008). Second, the events must release information that is new to the stock market. And third, the stock markets on which the divesting firms are listed, need to exhibit a level of information efficiency that allows for a timely capitalization process (Bromiley *et al.*, 1988; Fama *et al.*, 1969). For research based on press releases, information efficient stock markets require the press release to be the initial source of information and thereby demand that the sampled firms practice efficient financial market communication. Peterson (1989) further points out that the stocks must be actively traded in a sufficient volume to prevent distortions in the price effects.

In our study, all of these requirements are met. First, divestitures are critical events that attract considerable shareholder attention (Jensen & Ruback, 1983; Klein, 1986). All the same, while showing complexity during the decision stage (Nees, 1978, 1981), divestitures induce only minor ambiguity as soon as they are decided and announced. Herein, they differ from acquisitions, which come with a much more challenging implementation phase and a high level of inherent uncertainty about the ultimate performance outcome (Oler et al., 2008). Second, each divestiture releases new information to the capital markets. This also applies for program divestitures. Instead of pre-releasing an initial statement on their programs, revealing the units for sale and thereby compromising bargaining power, the sampled firms used the occasion of each program divestiture to relate the transaction to prior ones that followed the same rationale and, in most of the cases, explained how the firm is progressing in achieving this rationale. Since the details of the divestiture programs thereby materialized from the individual divestitures, the stock markets were less likely to capitalize the program transactions at once (Schipper & Thompson, 1983) but rather one by one (Afshar et al., 1992). Third, also the stock market requirements are met. The analyzed firms were all listed on well-developed stock exchanges during the full study period and were obliged to operate professional financial market communication by their regulators. Further, distortions from thinly traded stocks can be excluded as the free-float ratios of all securities in the DJ Stoxx Global Insurance Index (2008) were constantly high (> 75%) throughout the study period.

Since we regressed the abnormal stock returns on several independent variables, these also must conform to the method's assumptions and closely reflect the information the capital markets have absorbed and capitalized. We consider the use of official corporate press releases superior to other sources, such as newspaper articles or annual reports. The official corporate press releases have the advantage that they are published in an ad hoc fashion since the firms are legally bound to publish stock-price relevant events such as divestitures in an immediate fashion. So they are timely very accurate. Also, in terms of content, these releases can be assumed to be highly accurate as firms may otherwise by charged with providing misleading stock-market information. In contrast, newspaper articles, especially when they are drawn from various sources, may indicate wrong event dates (Afshar *et al.*, 1992; Peterson, 1989) or include other information than those released on the event dates (Haynes *et al.*, 2002; Peterson, 1989). Both effects obviously can distort the calculation of announcement returns. Given recent findings on which information stock markets consider (John & Ofek, 1995; Oler et al., 2008; Tetlock, 2007; Tetlock et al., 2008), we can expect our regression to yield valid relationships. We run a cross-sectional regression on the cumulative abnormal returns centering on the announcement dates of the sampled divestitures.

5.5 Results

Table 5-2 reports the means, standard deviations and correlation coefficients for the variables used in our regression models.

Table 5-2: Descriptive Statistics and Correlations

Variable	Mean	s.d.	1	2	3	4	5	6	7	8
1. CAR (-1, 1)	0.07	2.88	1.00							
2. Firm performance	1.01	1.05	0.17*	1.00						
3. Firm size[a]	4.46	0.56	-0.04	0.14	1.00					
4. Degree of diversification	0.50	0.18	-0.01	-0.05	-0.14	1.00				
5. Debt-to-equity ratio	259	398	0.03	0.33*	0.45	0.15	1.00			
6. Program divestiture	0.35	0.48	0.13	-0.13	-0.07	-0.13	-0.15	1.00		
7. Specific divestiture experience	4.61	4.26	-0.09	-0.25	0.45*	-0.21	-0.07	n/a	1.00	
8. General divestiture Experience	7.46	7.27	-0.11	-0.09	0.51	-0.23*	0.26*	0.13	0.59*	1.00
9. Elapsed time[b]	286	441	0.22*	-0.01	-0.19*	0.00	-0.01	-0.10	-0.33*	-0.33*

Notes: [a] Logarithm. [b] Elapsed time (in days) since the last divestiture of the firm. * $p < .05$ or lower.

The average three day cumulative abnormal return (CAAR) in our sample is slightly positive. This is in line with prior studies which consistently found positive cumulative abnormal returns for divestiture announcements. Table 5-2 also indicates that the time elapsed between divestitures is significantly positively correlated with divestiture market returns. The significant correlation of this time variable with the experience variables does not cause any problems of multicolinearity as these variables are not used in the same models. The positive correlation is, however, plausible as a greater number divestitures is likely to require tighter scheduling.

Table 5-3 further details the abnormal returns found in our analysis. It compares the shareholder wealth effects of the full sample with the ones generated by the two sub-samples (program vs. non-program divestitures) and gives the t-statistics for the comparison between the two divestiture types.

Table 5-3: Shareholder Wealth Effects (CAAR) for Different Event Windows

	Overall		Program		Non-program		t
Event window	CAAR	Positive	CAAR	Positive	CAAR	Positive	
0	0.28	54.38	0.57	58.93	0.13	51.43	-1.35*
-1 to 0	0.08	53.75	0.50	58.93	-0.14	50.48	-1.63*
-1 to 1	0.07	51.25	0.59	53.57	-0.22	49.52	-1.68**
-2 to 2	0.09	53.13	0.27	50.00	-0.00	54.29	-0.54
-5 to 5	-0.38	51.88	0.26	58.93	-0.73	47.62	-1.26

Notes: Cumulative average abnormal returns (CAARs) are calculated over selected intervals for a sample of 160 divestitures during the period 1998 to 2007. Abnormal returns are calculated using the market model parameters estimated over a 120-(trading) day period prior to the announcement date. The percentage positive is the ratio of the number of transactions with positive cumulative abnormal returns to the total number of transactions. Both sets of figures are individually provided for the full sample and the sub-samples of program (N=56) and non-program (N=104) divestitures. All figures, except of the t-statistics, are percentages. Conservative two tailed test comparing program and non-program divestitures. * $p < .10$; ** $p < .05$.

We find positive abnormal returns around the announcement date for all event windows with lengths up to five days. However, this effect largely leads back to divestitures from corporate programs. For non-program divestitures, the average abnormal returns are negative for event windows with lengths from two to eleven days. Thus, Table 5-3 lends initial support to our first hypothesis and indicates less positive shareholder wealth effects for non-program divestitures. However, these results do not consider contingency factors. To control for these and to test whether further factors related to the program perspective affect divestiture performance, we run a cross-sectional regression on the cumulative abnormal returns (-1, +1). Table 5-4 presents the results of our regression analysis.

Table 5-4: Results of OLS Regression Models for CAR (-1, +1)

	Models				
Variable	**1**	**2**	**3**	**4**	**5**
Constant	1.08 (2.29)	0.41 (2.29)	-0.32 (2.35)	4.40 (5.44)	-1.00 (2.62)
Program divestiture		0.94** (0.48)	1.05** (0.48)	n/a	1.07** (0.51)
Specific divestiture experience			-0.05 (0.04)		
General divestiture experience				-0.06 (0.11)	
Elapsed time between divestitures[a]					0.0015*** (0.0006)
Firm performance	0.48** (0.23)	0.52** (0.23)	0.45* (0.23)	0.53 (0.50)	0.55 (0.26)
Firm size[b]	-0.31 (0.47)	-0.28 (0.47)	0.01 (0.51)	-0.34 (1.06)	-0.09 (0.52)
Diversification level	-0.23 (1.29)	0.08 (1.29)	-0.30 (1.32)	-4.11 (2.70)	0.10 (1.41)
Debt-to-equity ratio	0.00 (0.00)	0.00 (0.00)	0.00 (0.00)	-0.001* (0.00)	0.00 (0.00)
N	160	160	160	56	129
R^2	0.03	0.05	0.06	0.16	0.10
Adjusted R^2	0.01	0.02	0.03	0.07	0.07

Notes: [a] Elapsed time (in days) since the last divestiture of the firm. [b] Logarithm. * $p < .10$; ** $p < .05$; *** $p < .01$. Conservative two tailed test. Standard errors are reported in parentheses.

Our regression results support our initial findings from the calculation of abnormal returns. Program divestitures generate, on average, significantly higher abnormal returns of approximately 1% in all models ($p < 0.05$). Thus, Hypothesis 1 is supported. Our regression results in Models 2 and 3, however, do not support our hypotheses related to specific and general experience effects (Hypothesis 2 and 3). Program divestitures that occur late in a divestiture program do not seem to generate higher abnormal returns than program divestitures that take place at the outset of a program. Model 3 also does not reveal any general positive experience transfer effects from prior divestiture activity.

Hypothesis 4 suggests that firms may benefit from not scheduling their divestiture too tightly since time compression diseconomies may exist in too tightly scheduled sequences. This hypothesis is supported by our empirical analysis ($p < 0.01$). We find a significant positive relationship between the days elapsed since a firm announced its previous divestiture and the abnormal return of the focal divestiture.

5.6 Discussion

The purpose of this study was to further our understanding of the sources of divestiture gains. While prior research on divestiture gains has treated divestitures as isolated events, we direct our attention toward the analysis of divestiture programs. This is in line with the most recent developments in acquisition research and, in fact, business practice. However, our study deviates from acquisition research by applying a potentially more accurate way of identifying and operationalizing divestiture programs. Instead of applying statistical clustering to determine divestiture programs, we ground our empirical analysis on the detailed text analysis of corporate press releases to identify those divestitures that are explicitly mentioned to be part of a divestiture or refocusing program and thus follow a joint explicit strategic rationale or business logic.

In doing so, our empirical results advance extant knowledge on divestiture gains. Findings for the global insurance industry suggest that program divestitures generate significantly higher market returns than “stand-alone” divestitures. The neglect of prior research to differentiate between program and non-program divestitures may thus partly account for the range of results on divestiture gains. As indicated, the higher market returns could result from the fact that capital markets may consider program divestitures as being more strategically relevant and reward them for greater strategic consistency. Prior research on corporate finance additionally suggests that this above average positive market return of program divestitures may also be due to the explicit link to corporate strategy and the delivery of a strategic motive for the transaction. Firms that provide a sound strategic motivation for their divestitures have been found to benefit from greater positive announcement returns compared to firms which provide no such motivation (e.g., Allen & McConnell, 1998; Lang et al., 1995; Vijh, 2002).

In an effort to further explore and detail the sources for the above average positive effects of program divestitures, our hypotheses 2 to 4 set out to investigate the influence of specific and general divestiture experience as well as the influence of divestiture timing on divestiture market returns. While transaction experience is one of the most studied performance determinants in acquisition research (Barkema & Vermeulen, 1998; Bergh & Lim, 2008; Haleblian & Finkelstein, 1999; Vermeulen & Barkema, 2001), little research has been done on the impact of divestiture experience on divestiture gains. Despite the practically intuitive arguments in learning theory that suggest a positive influence of experience on divestiture outcome, our findings do not show any support for a significant impact of experience on divestiture market returns. Our insignificant findings, however, should not be easily discarded as an indication for the irrelevance of experience transfer in divestitures. Given the fact that firms have generally far less routinized divestiture processes than they have acquisition processes (Dranikoff *et al.*, 2002; Mankins *et al.*, 2008), these findings may simply reflect that firms are usually less accustomed with divestitures and have not yet installed the same kind of learning and routinization processes that they may have installed for acquisitions.

Besides experience, timing is another potential source for higher returns of program divestitures. Timing is a general element of divestiture programs since these are usually assigned a certain deadline by which the units should be divested. Our results for hypothesis 4 propose significantly higher performance of moderately paced divestitures, suggesting that too tightly scheduled divestitures may experience time compression diseconomies (Dierickx & Cool, 1989). This result is in line with prior findings from acquisition research (Gary, 2005; Haunschild, Davis-Blake, & Fichman, 1994; Hill & Hoskisson, 1987).

Our study also makes two methodological contributions. First, it departs from the practice of assuming that transaction clusters in time automatically constitute transaction programs (Conn et al., 2004; Laamanen & Keil, 2008). While prior research on acquisition programs suffered from being "unable to link [their phenomena of interest] with explicitly defined acquisition programs and their characteristics" (Laamanen & Keil, 2008: 670), our conceptualization of programs is based on a thorough review of the information the firms have disclosed with their divestitures. By adopting our approach, future research on divestiture and acquisition programs could ensure to base their empirical analyses on the same information the capital markets have absorbed. The statistical clustering of transactions to identify programs seems also highly questionable given the fact that these patterns only emerge ex post. At the time of an acquisition or a divestiture announcement, the capital market which operates in real time cannot process this information. The link to market returns at the time of announcement thus seems flimsy based on such an approach. Second, our study is one of the first to analyze divestiture abnormal returns in a service industry. Prior studies have usually been set in manufacturing industries.

Our findings also bear implications for business practice. First and foremost, capital markets seem to reward divestitures that are guided by an explicit strategic rationale. Divestitures that are not tied to a firm's overarching corporate strategy by means of an explicit divestiture program generate, on average, inferior returns. In such cases, shareholders may see their future earning potentials at risk by shortsighted action. Consistent with this notion, we also find that firms are penalized for implementing their divestitures too quickly. Higher abnormal returns were attributed to moderately paced divestiture series.

5.7 Avenues for Future Research and Limitations

Our results imply that research on divestiture gains could benefit from a greater incorporation of process issues. Specifically, this study drew attention to the interrelation between divestitures in form of divestiture programs as well as the importance of the temporal dynamics of divestitures. So far, researchers have treated divestitures as isolated events and thereby might have overlooked an important explanatory factor responsible for the limited reach of extant explanations for the announcement returns of divestitures. We suggest that future studies should adopt a program perspective and try to elaborate on the characteristics of these programs and the conditions under which these programs enhance divestiture market performance. Of particular interest are the interaction effects of divestiture program characteristics with additional covariates, such as firm or governance characteristics, which could provide further insights on the capital market's divestiture pricing mechanics. To extent upon this line of research, it would also be valuable to not only look at process characteristics but also link these to process outcome measures. Announcement returns are unquestionably the most widely used performance measure and can be deemed to be superior to accounting measures for several reasons (see Haleblian et al., 2009 for a discussion). However, announcement returns only capture changes in market expectations about the future firm performance. Alternative study designs, such as the one applied by Haynes, Thompson and Wright (2002), may focus on the long-run implications and thereby analyze whether the predictions made by the announcement returns also translate into differences in long-term profitability or become overlapped by other factors. Last but not least, future studies are needed to test for the wider generalizability of our findings across different industry settings. Our more accurate but also more restrictive approach to identify divestiture programs based on text analysis of firm press releases instead of grounding our analysis purely in readily available secondary data from SDC Platinum constrained our overall sample size and suggested a single-industry set-up.

5.8 Conclusion

In general, our study emphasizes the need for moving beyond the analysis of divestitures as isolated events. We propose to stress the analysis of causal and temporal interrelationships in firms' divestiture behavior. Both are shown to significantly influence divestiture market returns. In the face of the current financial crisis, as firms across industries restructure their business portfolios, these findings may be particularly useful. Managers are advised to refrain from piecemeal divestiture behavior lacking clear strategic focus. Instead, they are encouraged to bundle their divestitures as part of a divestiture program with a clear strategic intent and shared business logic. At the same time, they are advised to stage these divestitures in a careful manner. Too tightly scheduled "fire sales" are likely to diminish returns from divestitures.

6 Discussion and Conclusion

With this dissertation, we focused on interfirm rivalry within the competitive dynamics branch of strategic management research. The scope of our research was set by the desire to mitigate two general issues of competitive dynamics research and its sub-fields (Ketchen et al., 2004). These issues being first, a prevailing paucity of dynamic theories and longitudinal analyses (Daems & Thomas, 1994; Miller & Chen, 1994), and second, narrow theoretical roots (Smith et al., 2001b). With this overall intention in mind, we reviewed extant literature on competition and rivalry and derived a research agenda that advances recent developments within competitive dynamics research (chapter 2). Relying on our broad empirical strategy, we then conducted three quantitative studies in different sub-fields of competitive dynamics research. In chapter 3, we investigated why some firms leave their own strategic group whereas others converge toward it. In chapter 4, we integrated the external environmental context of firms into an action-based theory of interfirm rivalry within competitive markets (Hsieh & Chen, 2010). And in chapter 5, we highlighted – within the research context of divestitures – that competitive actions are oftentimes interrelated and should be studied in a manner that takes the relationships between such actions into account.

In this last chapter, we summarize the results of the distinct studies (6.1), discuss their theoretical and practical implications (6.2), identify the limitations of our research (6.3) and outline potential future research avenues (6.4). We end with a conclusion for the overall dissertation (6.5).

6.1 Summary of the Results

In chapter 3, we developed theory behind the factors that precede the repositioning choices of firms vis-à-vis their own strategic groups. Our theory grounds on the BTOF (Bromiley, 2004; March & Simon, 1958) and related fields such as performance feedback theory (Greve, 1998a) and literature on behavioral biases (Kahneman & Tversky, 1979; Kelley & Michela, 1980). Based on theoretical arguments from these perspectives, we derived the hypotheses enlisted in Table 6-1.

Table 6-1: Results of Chapter 3

Hypothesis	Predicted Effect	Result
H1	A focal firm's performance is positively related to its strategic convergence-divergence vis-à-vis its own strategic group.	Supported
H2	A firm's performance is more strongly related to convergence-divergence when the firm performs below its management's aspiration level than if it performs above its management's aspiration level.	Supported
H3a/b	For firms that perform under (over) the aspiration level of their management, environmental dynamism negatively (positively) moderates the relationship between performance and convergence-divergence.	Supported
H4a/b	For firms that perform under (over) the aspiration level of their management, environmental munificence positively (negatively) moderates the relationship between performance and convergence-divergence.	Supported
H5a/b	For firms that perform under (over) the aspiration level of their management, increases in strategic nonconformity negatively (positively) moderate the relationship between performance and convergence-divergence.	Supported
H5c/d	For firms that perform under (over) the aspiration level of their management, increases in strategic nonconformity positively (negatively) moderate the relationship between performance and convergence-divergence.	Not supported

Taken together, our results draw quite an intuitive picture on when a firm moves closer to or further away from its own strategic group: Firms tend to diverge from their own strategic groups when their performance levels do not meet the aspiration levels of their managements – which are defined by a benchmarking process with the firms' peers. In this case, the management engages in problemistic search processes, is willing to take additional risks and has a higher tendency to adopt promising business practices that are uncommon to its firm's own strategic group. Conversely, if a firm performs well, its management will have little motivation to strike a risky new course. Instead, other firms might be inclined to mimic the high-performing firm, which would move it closer to the center of its strategic group (Hypothesis 1). Since particularly high and particularly low performance levels are presumed to trigger behavioral biases that induce risk-taking behaviors (Kahneman & Tversky, 1979; Kelley & Michela, 1980), we tested by means of piecewise and switching regression models for a kink-like discontinuity in the relationship proposed by Hypothesis 1 at the aspiration level (Hypothesis 2). Given the clear presence of this discontinuity in the regression line, we further explored whether external factors that relate to risk affect the two splines of the piecewise regression in opposing manners (Hypothesis 3a/b to Hypothesis 5c/d). As suggested by the theory, we find that environmental dynamism dampens the risk-seeking induced by deviations from the average performance level and thereby negatively (positively) moderates the relationship between performance and convergence-divergence for firms that perform under (over) the aspiration level of their management (Hypothesis 3). We find the exact opposite effect for environmental munificence (Hypothesis 4). With respect to the internal structure of strategic groups, we find that for firms positioned at the edges of strategic groups, the proposed behavioral biases work less strongly, suggesting that within strategic groups, performance levels are higher at the core (Hypothesis 5a/b).

In chapter 4, we developed an action-based theory of interfirm rivalry within competitive markets that explains how shocks in the external environmental context change the competitive game. It largely draws on recent action-response research about competitive markets (Hsieh & Chen, 2010; Zuchhini & Kretschmer, 2011), on research into behavioral decision-making (Bikhchandani et al., 1992; Lieberman & Asaba, 2006), and on research into the environment and environmental shocks (Chattopadhyay et al., 2001). Table 6-2 provides an overview of the hypotheses of this study.

Table 6-2: Results of Chapter 4

Hypothesis	Predicted Effect	Result
H1	Higher degrees of competitive pressure increase a firm's inclination to take new competitive action.	Supported
H2	A trend of rivals to pursue a distinct competitive action type increases a firm's inclination to take new competitive action of this type.	Supported
H3	Market shocks increase a firm's inclination to take new competitive action.	Supported
H4	Market shocks negatively moderate the relationship between competitive pressure and a firm's inclination to take new competitive action.	Not supported
H5	Market shocks negatively moderate the relationship between the trend of rivals to pursue a distinct competitive action type and a firm's inclination to engage in this competitive action type.	Supported

With our first result, we confirmed prior research's conjecture that competitive tension not only builds up within firm dyads, but also at a higher level of abstraction (Hypothesis 1) (Chen et al., 2007; Hsieh & Chen, 2010). We found that increased levels of total rivals' actions raise a firm's inclination to take new competitive action. Further, our findings suggest that the distinct choices of competitive actions are also related to the types of actions rivals have recently performed (Hypothesis 2). With respect to the role of the external environmental context, our analyses yielded two important results. First, we initially identified market shocks as an important antecedent of competitive activity (Hypothesis 3). Second, we found that such disruptions also systematically impact the decision process of managers when contemplating their next competitive move. Instead of turning to past rival actions for guidance, in the aftermath of market shocks, managers derive their firm's competitive moves mainly on the grounds of the novel context they are faced with (Hypothesis 5).

In chapter 5, we focused on a distinct competitive action type, divestitures, and explored whether divestitures that follow a joint strategic rationale received more favorable stock market responses than isolated "stand-alone" transactions. Our arguments are based on divestiture and restructuring literature (Bergh & Lim, 2008; Brauer, 2006), related acquisition research (Barkema & Schijven, 2008a; Laamanen, 2007; Schipper & Thompson, 1983), studies on learning (Greve, 2003; Pennings et al., 1994; Zollo & Winter, 2002), and research into time compression diseconomies (Dierickx & Cool, 1989). Table 6-3 lists our hypotheses and the results of our analyses.

Table 6-3: Results of Chapter 5

Hypothesis	Predicted Effect	Result
H1	Program divestitures are associated with greater abnormal returns than "stand alone" divestitures.	Supported
H2	The amount of prior specific experience from divestitures which are part of the same divestiture program is positively related to the abnormal returns of the focal program divestiture.	Not supported
H3	Prior general divestiture experience positively influences program divestitures' abnormal returns. This effect is weaker for specific experience transfer between program divestitures.	Not supported
H4	The time elapsed since the last divestiture of a firm is positively related to the abnormal return of a firm's divestiture.	Supported

With our first analysis, we found that divestitures that adjust the corporate focus of a firm according to an explicitly announced strategic logic (i.e., a divestiture program) achieve more favorable stock market responses than isolated divestitures (Hypothesis 1). Besides the value created by the more explicit strategic motivation of these divestitures, we consider additional potential sources for the greater stock market responses of program divestitures. Specifically, we study the influence of experience transfer and timing. While our results show no support for a significant impact of experience transfer on divestiture market returns (Hypothesis 2 and 3), they indicate that moderately paced divestitures receive a more favorable vote from the capital markets (Hypothesis 4).

6.2 Summary of the Theoretical Contributions

The contributions of this dissertation are closely related to those its three empirical studies make to their respective theoretical discussions. Since we have elaborated on these contributions in great detail within the individual studies, we limit ourselves in this chapter to an overview of the most important contributions. The overview is also limited to contributions made to competitive dynamics research and excludes several insights relevant for other areas of research – this caveat particularly relates to some findings of our third study. Figure 6-1 provides a short summary of the dissertation's major contributions and links them to the research gaps we had described earlier on (see chapter "Toward a Research Agenda", particularly Figure 2-2).

Figure 6-1: Contributions to Competitive Dynamics Research

Research gap	Contribution
Interplay between behavioral firm-level processes and SG structure	We pioneer a behavioral theory on how firms reposition themselves vis-à-vis their own strategic group. Our theory connects firm, strategic group, and environmental characteristics and describes how they jointly drive the managerial decision process of repositioning the firm.
Integration of the external environmental context	We advance an emergent action-based theory of rivalry in competitive markets by integrating the different effects market shocks have on the competitive behavior of firms.
Implications of relationships between competitive moves	Within the context of divestitures, we show that relationships between competitive actions matter. We provide theory and empirical evidence on why well-conceived and strategically linked competitive actions receive better stock market responses than isolated actions.

The first study of this dissertation represents an important step toward a behavioral theory of strategic group dynamics that explains how firms navigate within strategic group structures given behavioral biases of the acting management, stimuli from the external market environment, and the existence of intra-group structures. (DeSarbo et al., 2009; Mascarenhas, 1989; McNamara et al., 2003). While our theory adopts the idea that firms identify with their strategic groups and refer to them as reference points when contemplating strategic change (Fiegenbaum et al., 1996; Reger & Huff, 1993), it also focuses on the circumstances under which firms diverge from their own strategic groups. In contrast to prior efforts, we directly consider the behavioral decision-making processes at the firm-level and combine arguments from performance feedback theory (Greve, 2003) with insights on behavioral biases (Clapham & Schwenk, 1991; Kahneman & Tversky, 1979; Kelley & Michela, 1980). With our distinct focus on firm-level mechanisms, we provide a novel theoretical depth in linking the repositionings of firms with firm and strategic group characteristics, performance variables and major environmental variables. Given access to granular data at the firm- and industry-level, we can test this comprehensive theory and validate key substantive claims that have been underlying the cognitive theory of strategic groups ever since (Porac et al., 1989; Reger & Huff, 1993), but which have eluded empirical scrutiny so far (Hodgkinson, 1997). From this perspective, our work not only contributes by improving our theoretical understanding of strategic group dynamics, but also by filling some empirical gaps on theoretical claims left open by earlier research.

Our second study adds to competitive dynamics research concerned with interfirm rivalry in market environments that are characterized by a large number of competitors. It joins recent efforts in developing a theory of interfirm rivalry more valid in competitive markets (Hsieh & Chen, 2010; Zuchhini & Kretschmer, 2011) than the propositions made by research focusing on firm dyads (Baum & Korn, 1999; Chen et al., 1992). The study's main theoretical contribution to this theory building lies in introducing abrupt variations in the external environmental context (i.e., market shocks) as an important determinant of the competitive behavior of firms – which seems particularly relevant in light of today's erratic economic environments (Vassolo, Sanchez, & Mesquita, 2010). The study further relates to work on whether mutual forbearance equilibriums are sensitive to the ambiguity that surrounds competitive environments (McGrath et al., 1998). Our findings concur with the idea that environmental uncertainty and complexity in conjunction with bounded rationality at the decision makers creates incentives for firms to foray into the spheres of influence of rivals (Axelrod & Dion, 1988; Bendor, Kramer, & Stout, 1991; McGrath et al., 1998). The study, however, further contributes to our understanding of how the external environmental context impacts competitive behaviors with another, more intriguing finding. It tests whether the behavioral mechanisms that have previously been proposed to guide the competitive choices of managers (Hsieh & Chen, 2010; Lieberman & Asaba, 2006) always hold. We challenge this presumption of prior research by exposing these mechanisms to market shocks and find that market shocks partially abandon them for some time. This sheds new light on extant knowledge on how managers decide upon their firms' competitive actions (Chen & MacMillan, 1992; Chen et al., 2007) and stresses the importance to further contextualize existing and future theories on interfirm rivalry. At a more abstract level, the study exposes the need to study underlying mechanisms within research on action-response patterns rather than abstract empirical correlates (Miller & Tsang, 2011).

Our third study contributes to two different fields of research at once. It adds to divestiture research (Brauer, 2006), as well as to the strand of competitive dynamics research concerned with the stock market responses to competitive actions (Bettis & Weeks, 1987; Ferrier & Lee, 2002; Lee, Smith, Grimm, & Schomburg, 2000). With respect to the latter field of research, our study highlights that the performance implications of competitive actions may strongly vary with differences in the causal and temporal interrelationships between individual actions. It thus strongly discourages the study of competitive actions in isolation, but recommends to analyze streams of competitive actions under consideration of the various interrelationships among their constituting actions.

The theoretical contribution of the dissertation as a whole and its distinct composition refers back to the theoretical and epistemological diversity that can be found in competitive dynamics research (Ketchen et al., 2004). This dissertation explores different levels of competitive dynamics and thence supports earlier efforts to promote an understanding of interfirm rivalry as a phenomenon with outcomes at multiple levels of analysis and aggregation (Gnyawali & Madhavan, 2001).

6.3 Practical Implications

This dissertation holds several findings that are important for managers. With its first study on strategic group dynamics, the dissertation provides managers interested in the U.S. insurance market with a comprehensive model of the industry's internal structure over the full study period. It maps how different market positions have related to firm performance at different points in time and invites the use of this information for various purposes. For example, business analysts may link it with market events and gain a deeper understanding on how sensitive firm performance is to external influences in different sectors of the industry. Alternatively, firms may use the historic map of groups and performance levels as an instrument in their own benchmarking analysis that may yield periods of relative success and failure. As a more future oriented application, corporate analysts might adopt our clustering method to monitor their industry or to identify prospective M&A targets that ideally fit their own repositioning ambitions.

The dissertation's second study exposes the need for managers to adopt a perspective on competitive actions and interfirm rivalry that goes beyond the notion of a continuous competitive process. While our results confirm the basic going-concern presumption and its implication to keep a steady eye on prior rivals' actions, they also prompt managers to prepare for sudden twists in the competitive game. Recently, market shocks have struck markets more and more frequently and heralded completely different competitive situations than prior rivalry would have suggested (Vassolo, Sanchez, & Mesquita, 2010). In order to benefit from such twists, managers need to quickly draw their attention from their rivals' past actions to the competitive opportunities newly created by the market shock. Further, they must actively take advantage of prevailing uncertainties and the heterogenic states of rivals in the aftermath of market shocks. This does not only require sufficient organizational resources, but also calls for managers to perceive market shocks as breaking points in an otherwise continuous competitive process. Embracing this mindset and deriving the corresponding actions from it may allow managers to help their firms leap-frog their rivals at the competitive cross-roads market shocks create.

Finally, the study at the level of individual competitive actions conveys a lesson that echoes one of the most fundamental tenets of strategic management. It underlines the need for strategic consistency and coordination between individual actions within larger sequences of moves. Specifically, within its area of investigation (i.e., divestitures), the study advises managers to refrain from piecemeal behavior that lacks strategic focus, and instead encourages them to create coherent divestiture programs that better "sell" the strategic intent of the individual transactions to the capital markets. While this advice might not be equally valid and important for all types of competitive actions, it should hold for those types that are not intended to act in the dark but also work as signals.

With these three studies and the comprehensive theoretical review at the beginning, the dissertation provides a comprehensive and multifaceted view on competition and interfirm rivalry to managers that might help them gain some valuable insight on the ambiguity that generally surrounds these concepts.

6.4 Limitations

The research design of this dissertation presents several limitations that may confine the validity of its results. First and foremost, all studies in this dissertation share an empirical foundation that is constrained to a distinct industry and time period. Specifically, all studies are set in the insurance industry – either with a focus on U.S. firms or with a focus on the major global P&L insurance groups – and investigate the time period between 1999 and 2008. It is thus possible that our results reflect factors that are specific to either the industry or the time period under study. To rule out this possibility, future research would need to replicate our results in empirical settings that are different from the one of this dissertation.

Second, we used accounting data to calculate the control and independent variables of our research – in our first study, this also applies to the dependent variable. Even though accounting data is one of the most common sources of data in business research, we want to acknowledge that such data is subject to managerial choices about accounting procedures and thus may counteract the validity of our results (Fields, Lys, & Vincent, 2001). Since preferences for accounting procedures differ across countries (Alford, Jones, Leftwich, & Zmijewski, 1993; Ball, Kothari, & Robin, 2000), this caveat is particularly relevant for our second and third studies that treat international samples of firms.

Third, when analyzing the competitive actions of firms, our studies only considered those competitive actions that could be retrieved from the corporate press release archives of the sampled firms. Since these archives may not keep a complete record of competitive actions, there is some risk that our results may prove misleading. This risk also differs for the two studies of this dissertation that investigate competitive actions. It mainly exists for the study on interfirm rivalry that draws on the full range of competitive actions. In comparison to similar research (Bresser, 2008; Yu, 2003), ours may suffer from blind spots with respect to pricing or marketing actions. For our study on divestitures, instead, no such issues exist. Since divestitures are corporate events of significant importance for shareholders (Jensen & Ruback, 1983; Klein, 1986), firms are legally obliged to disclose them to their investors in a timely fashion. The firms' press releases thus provide a complete and accurate record of their divestitures.

6.5 Future Research Avenues

Similarly to the dissertation's contributions and practical implications, its implications for future research largely follow from the individual studies it is comprised of. Having outlined these in detail at the end of the individual studies, we proceed by highlighting some broad directions which we consider as particularly promising to follow.

With respect to research on strategic group dynamics, we see the greatest potential in complementing our analysis with further research on how adjacent strategic groups guide firms in their repositioning. While we deliberately reduced the dimensionality of a firm's repositioning to the convergence-divergence vis-à-vis its own strategic group in order to focus on the role of its own strategic group, divergence could also be studied by analyzing the explicit movement vectors of a firm toward all the other strategic groups that are present in the industry (see Appendix 3 for the marginal adjustment this would imply for the empirical workflow of our study). In combination with the insights gained on when firms diverge from their own group, such research would considerably add to our understanding of how firms navigate strategic group structures.

Referring to our second study, the early stage of development in which the theory of interfirm rivalry within competitive markets still is, creates various research opportunities. With a focus on the integration of the external environmental context into this emergent theory, we ask future research to complement our findings on how market shocks impact a firm's competitive behavior. While we focused on the impact market shocks have on a firm's inclination to take new competitive action and its mimicking behavior, our arguments may be equally valid for other dimensions of competitive behavior – such as its aggressiveness or the mix between internally or externally oriented competitive actions (Chen & Hambrick, 1995; Chen & MacMillan, 1992; Ferrier, 2001; Ferrier et al., 1999; Young, Smith, Grimm, & Simon, 2000). Furthermore, it seems promising to investigate whether different types of market shocks have varying effects on interfirm rivalry. We largely circumvented this question by studying the impact of two very severe market shocks, but we presume that shocks of lower severity also have effects on the competitive behaviors of firms. Therefore, further research is required to fully explain the role of market shocks.

Concerning research on competitive actions and their interrelationships, our third study hints at a single broad new field of future research. Similar to prior research, it stresses that competitive actions are rarely isolated events, but instead part of longer sequences of moves that are consciously conceived to advance the firm's own foray, to counter a rival's attack or to pursue a strategy for its own sake (Chen & MacMillan, 1992; Ferrier, 2001; McGrath et al., 1998). Assuming that a lack of descriptive data might have impeded prior research into how competitive actions are interlinked with each other, our study provides with its approach of tapping the press release archives of firms a methodological solution to this empirical problem and invites future research to investigate the plethora of possible interrelationships between competitive actions.

With respect to the challenge of writing a sequence of papers on competitive dynamics, we want to highlight the importance of conducting synergistic research. With its characteristic focus, the field poses unique empirical challenges that warrant a comprehensive research strategy emphasizing a sound empirical basis from which ideally several studies can draw. Similarly to Chen (2009b), we further advise future research to start with very broad questions and to narrow down the theoretical focus through building an expansive review of the academic field.

6.6 Conclusion

Competition and rivalry are ubiquitous concepts, particularly in economics and strategic management research. George Stigler once aptly remarked that "competition may be the spice of life, but in economics, it has been more nearly the main dish" (Stigler, 1968: 181). Luckily, the dish has always been served in varied ways and well-seasoned with various assumptions from a wide range of theories.

Strategic management's competitive dynamics perspective has contributed its fair share to this variety, and merits credit for many of the most recent advancements in our understanding of the determinants and implications of the dynamic, action-based process of interfirm rivalry. Despite the caveat that the Austrian and Schumpeterian economists (Hayek, 1968; Schumpeter, 1934) have pioneered this notion of competition, it was competitive dynamics scholars that put it to an empirical test (Bettis & Weeks, 1987; MacMillan et al., 1985) and created the academic momentum that not only produced many tangible results, but also revived the interest in interfirm rivalry and related discussions (Bresser, 2008; Chen, 2009b; Ferrier et al., 1999; Ketchen et al., 2004; Smith et al., 1992).

With its three empirical studies, this dissertation adds to the scholarly pursuit of competitive dynamics research through three related discussions (Ketchen et al., 2004). It progresses our understanding of strategic group dynamics, interfirm rivalry in competitive markets, and the performance implications of interrelationships between competitive actions. The dissertation built on an innovative research strategy, which allowed for conceptual and methodological flexibility throughout the whole research process. Thanks to this flexibility, we could design our studies to bridge important research gaps while also innovating dynamic considerations and new theoretical views. With the latter contributions, we answer prior research's call for novel dynamic theories and research strategies, as well as more multilectic thinking in competitive dynamics research (Baldwin, 1995; Chen, 2009a; Daems & Thomas, 1994). Each of our studies thus also provides valuable methodological and theoretical cues for future research.

Overall, it is our hope that this dissertation helps to mitigate current issues of competitive dynamics research and stimulates further research in this exciting field.

References

A.M. Best. 2009. **Global File Statement - Version 2009.3**: A.M. Best.

Afshar, K. A., Taffler, R. J., & Sudarsanam, P. S. 1992. The effect of corporate divestments on shareholder wealth: The UK experience. **Journal of Banking and Finance**, 16: 115-135.

Aiken, L. S. & West, S. G. 1991. **Multiple regression**. Newbury Park, CA: Sage.

Alcoa. 2009. **Alcoa Taking Decisive Action to Address Economic Downturn**; http://www.businesswire.com/portal/site/alcoa/?ndmViewId=news_view&newsId=20090106006407&newsLang=en; 02 October 2009.

Aldrich, H. E. 1979. **Organizations and environments**. Englewood Cliffs, NJ: Prentice-Hall.

Alexander, G. J., Benson, P. G., & Kampmeyer, J. M. 1984. Investigating the valuation effects of announcements of voluntary corporate selloffs. **The Journal of Finance**, 39: 503-517.

Alford, A., Jones, J., Leftwich, R., & Zmijewski, M. 1993. The relative informativeness of accounting disclosure in different countries. **Journal of Accounting Research**, 31(S): 183-223.

Allen, J. W. & McConnell, J. J. 1998. Equity carve-outs and managerial discretion. **Journal of Finance**, 53(1): 163-186.

Allison, P. 1999. **Multiple Regression: A Primer**. Thousand Oaks, CA: Pine Forge Press.

A.M. Best. 2009. **Global File Statement - Version 2009.3**: A.M. Best.

Amburgey, T. L., Kelly, D., & Barnett, W. P. 1993. Resetting the clock: The dynamics of organizational change and failure. **Administrative Science Quarterly**, 38: 51-73.

Amit, R. & Schoemaker, P. J. H. 1993. Strategic Assets and Organizational Rent. **Strategic Management Journal**, 14(1): 33-46.

Angbazo, L. A. & Narayanan, R. 1996. Catastrophic shocks in the property-liability insurance industry: Evidence on regulatory and contagion effects. **Journal of Risk and Insurance**, 63(4): 619-637.

Argote, L., Beckman, S., & Epple, D. 1990. The persistence and transfer of learning in industrial settings. **Management Science**, 36: 140-154.

Aron, D. 1991. Using the capital market as a monitor: corporate spin-offs in an agency framework. **RAND Journal of Economics**, 22: 505-518.

Ashley, J. 1962. Stock prices and changes in earnings and dividends: Some empirical results. **Journal of Political Economy**, 70: 82-85.

Asquit, P., Bruner, R. F., & Mullins, D. W. 1983. The gains to bidding firms from merger. **Journal of Financial Economics**, 11: 121-139.

Audia, P. G., Locke, E. A., & Smith, K. G. 2000. The paradox of success: An archival and laboratory study of strategic persistence following radical environmental change. **Academy of Management Journal**, 42(5): 837-853.

Audia, P. G. & Greve, H. R. 2006. Less likely to fail? Low performance, firm size, and factory expansion in the shipbuilding industry. **Management Science**, 52: 83-94.

Augustine, L. V. 1998. Catastrophe risk mitigation: A survey of methods. **Casualty Actuarial Society Forum Casualty Actuarial Society**: 323-342.

Axelrod, R. & Dion, D. 1988. The further evolution of cooperation. **Science**, 242(4884): 1385-1390.

Bain, J. S. 1956. **Barriers to new competition**. Cambridge: Harvard University Press.

Bain, J. S. 1959. **Industrial Organization**. New York: Wiley.

Baldwin, J. 1995. **The dynamics of industrial competition**. Cambridge: Cambridge University Press.

Ball, R. & Brown, P. 1968. An empirical evaluation of accounting income numbers. **Journal of Accounting Research**, 6: 159-178.

Ball, R., Kothari, S. P., & Robin, A. 2000. The effect of international institutional factors on properties of accounting earnings. **Journal of Accounting and Economics**, 29(1): 1-51.

Baltagi, B. H. 2005. **Econometric analysis of panel data** (3 ed.). Chichester: John Wiley & Sons.

Barkema, H. & Schijven, M. 2008a. Toward unlocking the full potential of acquisitions: The role of organizational restructuring. **Academy of Management Journal**, 51: 696-722.

Barkema, H. G. & Vermeulen, F. 1998. International experience through start-up or acquisition: A learning perspective. **Academy of Management Journal**, 41(1): 7-26.

Barkema, H. G. & Schijven, M. 2008b. How do firms learn to make acquisitions? A review of past research and an agenda for the future. **Journal of Management**, 34(3): 594-634.

Barney, J. B. & Hoskisson, R. E. 1990. Strategic groups: Untested assertions and research proposals. **Managerial and Decision Economics**, 11(3): 187-198.

Barney, J. B. 1991. Firm resources and sustained competitive advantage. **Journal of Management**, 17(2): 151-166.

BarNiv, R. & McDonald, J. B. 1992. Identifying financial distress in the insurance industry: A synthesis of methodological and empirical issues. **Journal of Risk and Insurance**, 59(4): 542-574.

Baum, J. A. & Lant, T. K. 1995. Cognitive sources of socially constrained and competitive groups: Examples from the Manhattan hotel industry. In W. T. Scott & S. Christensen (Eds.), **The institutional construction of organizations**. Thousand Oaks, CA: Sage.

Baum, J. A. & Korn, H. 1999. Dynamics of dyadic competitive interaction. **Strategic Management Journal**, 20(3): 251-278.

Baumol, W. J. 1982. Contestable markets: An uprising in the theory of industry structure. **American Economic Review**, 72(1): 1-15.

Baumol, W. J., Panzar, J. C., & Wilig, R. P. 1982. **Contestable markets and the theory of industry structure**. New York: Harcourt, Brace and Jovanovich.

Bendor, J., Kramer, R. M., & Stout, S. 1991. When in doubt... **Journal of Conflict Resolution**, 35: 691-719.

Berger, A. N., Cummins, J. D., & Weiss, M. A. 2000. Conglomeration versus strategic focus: Evidence from the insurance industry. **Journal of Financial Intermediation**, 9: 323-362.

Berger, P. G. & Ofek, E. 1999. Causes and effects of corporate refocusing programs. **The Review of Financial Studies**, 12: 311-345.

Bergh, D. & Lawless, M. 1998. Portfolio restructuring and limits to hierarchical governance: the effects of environmental uncertainty and diversification strategy. **Organization Science**, 9(1): 87-102.

Bergh, D. D. 1997. Predicting divestiture of unrelated acquisitions: An integrative model of ex ante conditions. **Strategic Management Journal**, 18(9): 715-731.

Bergh, D. D. & Lim, E. N.-K. 2008. Learning how to restructure: Absorptive capacity and improvisational views of restructuring actions and performance. **Strategic Management Journal**, 29: 593-616.

Bertrand, J. 1883. Revue de la theorie mathematique de la riches et des recherches sur les principles mathematique de al theorie des richesses. **Journal des Savant**: 499-508.

Bettis, R. A. & Weeks, D. 1987. Financial returns and strategic interaction: The case of instant photography. **Strategic Management Journal**, 8: 549-563.

Bhabra, G. S., Bhabra, H. S., & Boyle, G. W. 1999. **Investment opportunities, leverage, and the wealth gains from acquisition program announcements.** Dunedin: University of Otago.

Bikhchandani, S. D., Hirschleifer, D., & Welch, I. 1992. A theory of fads, fashion, custom, and cultural change as informational cascades. **Journal of Political Economy**, 100(5): 992-1026.

Blaug, M. 2001. Is competition such a good thing? Static efficiency versus dynamic efficiency. **Review of Industrial Organization**, 19(1): 37-48.

Bogner, W. 1991. **Patterns of intra-industry competition: A dynamic analysis of theoretical foundations of strategic groups**. University of Illinois, Urbana Champaign.

Bogner, W., Thomas, H., & McGee, J. 1996. A longitudinal study of the competitive positions and entry paths of European firms in the US pharmaceutical market. **Strategic Management Journal**, 17(2): 85-107.

Bogner, W., Mahoney, J. T., & Thomas, H. 1998. Paradigm shift: The parallel origin, evolution and function of strategic group analysis with the resource-based theory of the firm. **Advances in Strategic Management**, 15: 63-102.

Born, P. & Viscusi, W. K. 2006. The catastrophic effects of natural disasters on insurance markets. **Journal of Risk and Uncertainty**, 33: 55-72.

Bourgeois, L. J. 1981. On the measurement of organizational slack. **Academy of Management Review**, 6(1): 29-39.

Box-Steffensmeier, J. M. & Zorn, C. 2002. Duration models for repeated events. **Journal of Politics**, 64(4): 1069–1094.

Box-Steffensmeier, J. M. & Jones, A. 2004. **Event history analysis: A guide for social scientists**. Cambridge: Cambridge University Press.

Brandenburger, A. M. & Nalebuff, B. J. 1996. **Co-opetition: A revolution mindset that combines competition and cooperation**. New York: Doubleday.

Brauer, M. 2006. What have we acquired and what should we acquire in divestiture research? A review and research agenda. **Journal of Management**, 32: 751-785.

Brauer, M. 2009. Corporate and divisional manager involvement in divestitures - A contingent analysis. **British Journal of Management**, 20(3): 341-362.

Bresser, R., Dunbar, R. L., & Jithendranathan, T. 1994. Competitive and collective strategies: An empirical examination of strategic groups. In P. Shrivastava & A. S. Huff & J. Dutton (Eds.), **Advances in Strategic Management**, Vol. 10B: 187-211. Greenwich, CT: JAI Press.

Bresser, R. 2008. Performance implications of delayed competitive responses: Evidence from the US retail industry. **Strategic Management Journal**, 29: 1077-1096.

Bromiley, P., Govekar, M., & Marcus, A. 1988. On using event-study methodology in strategic management research. **Technovation**, 8: 25-42.

Bromiley, P. 1991. Testing a causal model of corporate risk taking and performance. **Academy of Management Journal**, 34(1): 37-59.

Bromiley, P. 2004. **The behavioral foundation of strategic management**. Hoboken, NJ: John Wiley & Sons.

Brown, S. & Warner, J. B. 1980. Measuring security price performance. **Journal of Financial Economics**, 8: 205-258.

Bruton, G. D., Oviatt, B. M., & White, M. A. 1994. Performance of acquisitions of distressed firms. **Academy of Management Journal**, 37: 972-989.

Budzinski, O. 2008. Monoculture versus diversity in competition economics. **Cambridge Journal of Economics**, 32(2): 295-324.

Burgelman, R. A. 1996. A process model of strategic business exit in dynamic environments. **Strategic Management Journal**, 17: 193-214.

Cabantous, L. & Gond, J.-P. 2009. Turning terrorism into market: How calculability and power frame the genesis of markets, **Academy of Management Annual Meeting**. Chicago, Ill.: Academy of Management.

Calinski, R. B. & Harabasz, J. 1974. A dendrite method for cluster analysis. **Communications in Statistics**, 3(1): 1-27.

Calvo, G. A., Izquierdo, A., & Talvi, E. 2006. Sudden stops and phoenix miracles in emerging markets. **American Economic Review**, 96(2): 405-410.

Carroll, C., Pandian, M., & Thomas, H. 1994. Assessing the height of mobility barriers: A methodology and an empirical test in the UK retail grocery industry. **British Journal of Management**, 5(1): 1-18.

Caves, R. & Porter, M. 1977. From entry barriers to mobility barriers. **Quarterly Journal of Economics**, 91: 421-434.

Chang, S. J. 1996. An evolutionary perspective on diversification and corporate restructuring: Entry, exit, and economic performance during 1981-1989. **Strategic Management Journal**, 17(8): 587-611.

Chang, W. C. 1983. On using principal components before separating a mixture of two multivariate normal distributions. **Applied Statistics**, 32(3): 267-275.

Chatterjee, A. & Hambrick, D. C. 2007. It's all about me: Narcissistic Chief Executive Officers and their effects on company strategy and performance. **Administrative Science Quarterly**, 52: 351-386.

Chatterjee, K. & Samuelson, W. F. 2001. **Game theory and business applications**.

Chatterjee, S. & Wernerfelt, B. 1991. The link between resources and type of diversification: Theory and evidence. **Strategic Management Journal**, 12: 33-48.

Chatterjee, S. 2009. The key to successful acquisition programmes. **Long Range Planning**, 42(2): 137-163.

Chattopadhyay, P., Glick, W. H., & Huber, G. P. 2001. Organizational actions in response to threats and opportunities. **Academy of Management Journal**, 44: 937-955.

Chen, M. J. 1988. **Competitive strategic interaction: A study of competitive actions and responses**. Unpublished doctoral dissertation, University of Maryland.

Chen, M. J. & MacMillan, I. 1992. Nonresponse and delayed response to competitive moves: The roles of competitor dependence and action irreversibility. **Academy of Management Journal**, 35: 539-570.

Chen, M. J., Smith, K. D., & Grimm, C. M. 1992. Action characteristics as predictors of competitive responses. **Management Science**, 38: 439-455.

Chen, M. J. & Miller, D. 1994. Competitive attack, retaliation and performance: An expectancy-valence framework. **Strategic Management Journal**, 15: 85-102.

Chen, M. J. & Hambrick, D. C. 1995. Speed, stealth, and selective attack: How small firms differ from large firms in competitive behavior. **Academy of Management Journal**, 38: 453-482.

Chen, M. J. 1996. Competitor analysis and interfirm rivalry: Toward a theoretical integration. **Academy of Management Review**, 21: 100-134.

Chen, M. J., Su, K. H., & Tsai, W. 2007. Competitive tension: The awareness-motivation-capability perspective. **Academy of Management Journal**, 50: 101-118.

Chen, M. J. 2009a. **Competitive dynamics research program: An introduction.** Atlanta, Georgia: University of Virginia.

Chen, M. J. 2009b. Competitive dynamics research: An insider's odyssey. **Asia Pacific Journal of Management**, 26(1): 5-25.

Chen, M. J., Lin, H. C., & Michel, J. G. 2009. **Prospering in a hypercompetitive environment: The roles of TMT dynamics and competitive behavior**. Paper presented at the Academy of Management Annual Meeting, Washington, D.C.

Chen, X., Doerpinghaus, H., Lin, B.-X., & Yu, T. 2008. Catastrophic losses and insurer profitability: Evidence from 9/11. **The Journal of Risk and Insurance**, 75(1): 39-62.

Child, J. 1997. Strategic choice in the analysis of action, structure, organizations and environment: Retrospect and prospect. **Organization Studies**, 18(1): 43-76.

Clapham, S. E. & Schwenk, C. R. 1991. Self-serving attributions, managerial cognition, and company performance. **Strategic Management Journal**, 12(3): 219-229.

Clark, E. & Montgomery, C. 1998. Deterrence, reputations, and competitive cognition. **Management Science**, 44(1): 62-82.

Clark, J. M. 1940. Toward a concept of workable competition. **American Economic Review**, 30: 241-256.

Cleves, M. 1999. **Analysis of multiple failure-time survival data.** http://www.stata.com/support/faqs/stat/stmfail.html

Cohen, J. 1960. A coefficient of agreement for nominal scales. **Educational and Psychological Measurement**, 20: 37-46.

Cohen, W. M. & Levinthal, D. A. 1990. Absorptive capacity: A new perspective on learning and innovation. **Administrative Science Quarterly**, 35: 128-152.

Coleman, J. 1981. **Longitudinal data analysis**. New York: Basic Books.

Comment, R. & Jarrell, G. 1995. Corporate focus and stock returns. **Journal of Financial Economics**, 37(1): 67-87.

Conn, R. L., Cosh, A., Guest, P. M., & Hughes, A. 2004. **Why must all good things come to an end? The performance of multiple acquirers**. Paper presented at the Academy of Management 2004 Annual Meeting, New Orleans, LA.

Cool, K. & Schendel, D. 1987. Strategic group formation and performance: The case of the US pharmaceutical industry, 1963-1982. **Management Science**, 33: 1102-1124.

Cool, K. & Schendel, D. 1988. Performance differences among strategic group members. **Strategic Management Journal**, 9(3): 207-223.

Cool, K. & Dierickx, I. 1993. Rivalry, strategic groups and firm profitability. **Strategic Management Journal**, 14(1): 47-59.

Cournot, A. 1938. **Research into the mathematical principles of the theory of wealth. English edition of Cournot**. New York: Kelly.

Cox, D. R. 1972. Regression models and life tables. **Journal of the Royal Statistical Society**, 34(2): 187-220.

Cummings, J. D., Harrington, S. E., & Klein, R. W. 1991. Cycles and crises in property-casualty insurance: Causes and implications for public policy. **Journal of Insurance Regulation**, 11: 50-93.

Cyert, R. M. & March, J. G. 1963. **A behavioral theory of the firm**. Malden, MA: Blackwell Publishers.

D'Aveni, R. 1994. **Hypercompetition: Managing the dynamics of strategic maneuvering**. New York: Free Press.

Daems, H. & Thomas, H. 1994. **Strategic groups, strategic moves and performance**. Oxford: Pergamon.

Daley, L., Mehrota, V., & Sivakumar, R. 1997. Corporate focus and value creation: Evidence from spin-offs. **Journal of Financial Economics**, 45(1): 257-281.

De Soete, G. 1986. Optimal variable weighting for ultrametric and additive tree clustering. **Quality & Quantity**, 20: 169-180.

Denning, K. C. 1988. Spin-offs and sales of assets: An examination of security returns and divestment motivations. **Accounting and Business Research**, 19(73): 32-42.

Desai, H. & Jain, P. 1999. Firm performance and focus: Long-run stock market performance spinoffs. **Journal of Financial Economics**, 54(1): 75-101.

DeSarbo, W. S., Carroll, J. D., Clark, L. A., & Green, P. E. 1984. Synthesized clustering: A method for amalgamating alternative clustering bases with different weighting of variables. **Psychometrika**, 49(1): 57-78.

DeSarbo, W. S. & Grewal, R. 2008. Hybrid strategic groups. **Strategic Management Journal**, 29(3): 293-317.

DeSarbo, W. S., Grewal, R., & Wang, R. 2009. Dynamic strategic groups: Deriving spatial evolutionary paths. **Strategic Management Journal**, 30(forthcoming).

Dess, G. G. & Beard, D. W. 1984. Dimensions of organizational task environment. **Administrative Science Quarterly**, 29(1): 52-73.

Dess, G. G., Gupta, A., Hennart, J., & Hill, C. W. L. 1995. Conducting and integrating strategy research at the international, corporate and business levels: Issues and directions. **Journal of Management**, 21: 357-393.

Dierickx, L. & Cool, K. 1989. Asset stock accumulation and sustainability of competitive advantage. **Management Science**, 35: 1504-1511.

Diesing, P. 1971. **Patterns of discovery in the social sciences**. Chicago, IL: Aldine-Atherton.

DiMaggio, P. J. & Powell, W. W. 1983. The iron cage revisited: Institutional isomorphism and collective rationality in organizational fields. **American Sociological Review**, 48: 147-160.

Dittmar, A. & Shivdasani, A. 2003. Divestitures and divisional investment policies. **The Journal of Finance**, 58(6): 2711-2743.

Doherty, N. 1980. A portfolio theory of insurance capacity. **The Journal of Risk and Insurance**, 47(3): 405-420.

Donaldson, L. 1985. **In defense of organization theory**. Cambridge: Cambridge University Press.

DowJones; **Dow Jones Stoxx Global 1800 Insurance**; http://www.stoxx.com/indices/components.html?symbol=DJW0INS; 24 November 2008, 2008.

Downling, M. J. & Ruefli, T. W. 1992. Technological innovation as a gateway to entry: The case of the telecommunications equipment industry. **Research Policy**, 21(1): 63-77.

Dranikoff, L., Koller, T., & Schneider, A. 2002. Divestiture: Strategy's missing link. **Harvard Business Review**, 80(5): 74-83.

Duda, R. O. & Hart, P. E. 1973. **Pattern classification and scene analysis**. New York: Wiley.

Duhaime, I. M. & Grant, J. H. 1984. Factors influencing divestment decision-making: Evidence from a field study. **Strategic Management Journal**, 5: 301-318.

Duncan, R. B. 1972. Characteristics of organizational environments and perceived environmental uncertainty. **Administrative Science Quarterly**, 17: 313-327.

Durand, R. 2006. **Organizational evolution and strategic management**. Thousand Oaks, CA: SAGE.

Duriau, V. J., Reger, R. K., & Ndofor, H. 2000. Content analysis of firms' web sites: Methodological foundations, software solutions, and implementation issues, **Academy of Management Conference**. Toronto, Canada.

Eisenhardt, K. M. & Bourgeois, L. 1988. Politics of strategic decision making in high-velocity environments: Towards a midrange theory. **Academy of Management Journal**, 31(4): 737-770.

Elango, B. 2009. Impact of insurers' product variety on performance across underwriting cycles. **Management Decision**, 47(2): 359-374.

Eling, M. & Marek, S. 2011a. Corporate governance and risk taking: Evidence from European insurance markets (under review), **Working Paper Series University of Ulm.** Ulm: University of Ulm.

Eling, M. & Marek, S. 2011b. Internal and external drivers for risk taking in U.K. and German insurance markets (under review), **Working Paper Series University of Ulm.** Ulm: University of Ulm.

Ellis, H. C. 1965. **The transfer of learning**. New York: MacMillan.

Emerald. 2011. **Outstanding paper awards**; http://www.emeraldinsight.com/authors/literati/awards.htm?year=2011&journal=jsma&PHPSESSID=k6l89s96kodus87hqqogmkfjf0; June 20, 2011.

Ensley, M. D., Pearce, C. L., & Hmieleski, K. M. 2006. The moderating effect of environmental dynamism on the relationship between entrepreneur leadership behavior and new venture performance. **Journal of Business Venturing**, 21: 243-263.

Everitt, B. 1980. **Cluster analysis** (2 ed.). London: Heinemann Educational Books.

Fama, E. F., Fisher, L., Jensen, M. C., & Roll, R. 1969. The adjustment of stock prices to new information. **International Economic Review**, 10: 1-21.

Ferguson, T. D., Deephouse, D. L., & Ferguson, W. L. 2000. Do strategic groups differ in reputation? **Strategic Management Journal**, 21(12): 1195-1214.

Ferrier, W. J., Smith, K. G., & Grimm, C. M. 1999. The role of competitive action in market share erosion and industry dethronement: A study of industry leaders and challengers. **Academy of Management Journal**, 42: 372-388.

Ferrier, W. J. 2001. Navigating the competitive landscape: The drivers and consequences of competitive aggressiveness. **Academy of Management Journal**, 44: 858-877.

Ferrier, W. J. & Lee, H. 2002. Strategic aggressiveness, variation, and surprise: How the sequential pattern of competitive rivalry influences stock market returns. **Journal of Managerial Issues**, 14: 162-180.

Festinger, L. 1950. Informal social communication. **Psychological Review**, 57: 271-282.

Fetch Technologies; **How it works**; http://www.fetch.com/why/how-it-works; Feb 25, 2011.

Fiegenbaum, A. & Thomas, H. 1986. Dynamic and risk measurement perspectives on Bowman's risk-return paradox for strategic management: An empirical study. **Strategic Management Journal**, 7: 395-407.

Fiegenbaum, A. & Thomas, H. 1988. Attitudes toward risk and the risk-return paradox: Prospect theory explanations. **Academy of Management Journal**, 31(1): 85-105.

Fiegenbaum, A. 1990. Prospect theory and the risk-return association: An empirical examination in 85 industries. **Journal of Economic Behavior & Organization**, 14(2): 187-203.

Fiegenbaum, A., Sudharshan, D., & Thomas, H. 1990. Strategic time periods and strategic groups research: Concepts and an empirical example. **Journal of Management Studies**, 27: 133-148.

Fiegenbaum, A. & Thomas, H. 1990. Strategic groups and performance: The US insurance industry 1970-1984. **Strategic Management Journal**, 11(3): 197-215.

Fiegenbaum, A. & Thomas, H. 1993. Industry and strategic group dynamics: Competitive strategy in the insurance industry, 1970-1984. **Journal of Management Studies**, 30(1): 69-105.

Fiegenbaum, A. & Thomas, H. 1995. Strategic groups as reference groups: Theory, modeling and empirical examination of industry and competitive strategy. **Strategic Management Journal**, 16(6): 461-476.

Fiegenbaum, A., Hart, S., & Schendel, D. 1996. Strategic reference point theory. **Strategic Management Journal**, 17(3): 219-235.

Fiegenbaum, A., Thomas, H., & Tang, M.-J. 2001. Linking hypercompetition and strategic group theories: Strategic maneuvering in the US insurance industry. **Managerial and Decision Economics**, 22(4-5): 265-279.

Fields, T. D., Lys, T. Z., & Vincent, L. 2001. Empirical research on accounting choice. **Journal of Accounting and Economics**, 31(1-3): 255-307.

Finkelstein, S. & Hambrick, D. 1990. Top management team tenure and organizational outcomes: The moderating role of managerial discretion. **Administrative Science Quarterly**, 35(3): 484-503.

Fowler, K. L. & Schmidt, D. R. 1989. Determinants of tender offer post-acquisition financial performance. **Strategic Management Journal**, 10: 339-350.

Fowlkes, E. B. & Mallows, C. L. 1983. A method for comparing two hierarchical clusterings. **Journal of the American Statistical Association**, 78: 113-136.

Fransella, F. & Bannister, D. 1977. **A manual for repertory grid technique**. New York: Academic Press.

Friedl, J. 2006. **Mastering regular expressions**. Cambridge, MA: O'Reilly.

Friedman, M. 1962. **Capitalism and freedom**. Chicago: Chicago University Press.

Fuente-Sabaté, J. M. d. l., Rodríguez-Puerta, J., Vicente-Lorente, J. D., & Zúñiga-Vicente, J. A. 2007. Do stable strategic time periods exist? Towards new methodological and theoretical insights. **Managerial and Decision Economics**, 28(3): 171-180.

Gary, M. S. 2005. Implementation strategy and performance outcomes in related diversification. **Strategic Management Journal**, 26: 643-664.

Geletkanycz, M. & Hambrick, D. 1997. The external ties of top executives: Implications for strategic choice and performance. **Administrative Science Quarterly**, 42(654-681).

Ghemawat, P. & Cassiman, B. 2007. Introduction to the special issue on strategic dynamics. **Management Science**, 53(4): 529-536.

Gimeno, J. & Woo, C. Y. 1996. Hypercompetition in a multimarket environment: The role of strategic similarity and multimarket contact in competitive de-escalation, **Organization Science**, Vol. 7: 322-341.

Gimeno, J. 1999. Reciprocal threats in multimarket rivalry: Staking out "spheres of influence" in the US airline industry. **Strategic Management Journal**, 20(2): 101-128.

Gnyawali, D. R. & Madhavan, R. 2001. Cooperative networks and competitive dynamics: A structural embeddedness perspective. **Academy of Management Review**, 26(3): 431-445.

Goll, I. & Rasheed, A. A. 1997. Rational decision-making and firm performance: The moderating role of environment. **Strategic Management Journal**, 18(7): 583-591.

Goll, I. & Rasheed, A. A. 2004. The moderating effect of environmental munificence and dynamism on the relationship between discretionary social responsibility and firm performance. **Journal of Business Ethics**, 49: 51-54.

Goll, I. & Rasheed, A. A. 2009. Environmental jolts and strategic change in the US airline industry: Deregulation and 9/11, **Annual Meeting of the Academy of Management**. Chicago.

Gort, M. 1969. An economic disturbance theory of mergers. **Quarterly Journal of Economics**, 83(4): 624-642.

Grace, M. F. & Barth, M. M. 1993. **The regulation and structure of nonlife insurance in the United States**, Vol. 1155. Washington: World Bank.

Greve, H. R. 1998a. Performance, aspirations and risky organizational change. **Administrative Science Quarterly**, 43(1): 58-86.

Greve, H. R. 1998b. Managerial cognition and the mimetic adoption of market positions: What you see is what you do. **Strategic Management Journal** 19(10): 967-988.

Greve, H. R. 2003. **Organizational learning from performance feedback: A behavioral perspective on innovation and change**. Cambridge, UK: Cambridge University Press.

Greve, H. R. 2008a. Organizational routines and performance feedback. In M. Becker (Ed.), **Handbook of organizational routines**: 187-204. Cheltenham: Edward Elgar.

Greve, H. R. 2008b. Multimarket contact and sales growth: Evidence from insurance. **Strategic Management Journal**, 29(3): 229-249.

Group of Thirty. 2006. **Reinsurance and international financial markets**. Washington, DC: Group of Thirty.

Gulati, R. 1995. Social structure and alliance formation patterns: A longitudinal analysis. **Administrative Science Quarterly**, 40(4): 619-652.

Hair, J. F., Black, W. C., Babin, B. J., & Anderson, R. E. 2009. **Multivariate Data Analysis** (7 ed.). Upper Saddle River: Pearson.

Hakansson, N. H. 1982. Changes in the financial market: Welfare and price effects and the basic theorems of value conservation. **The Journal of Finance**, 37: 977-1004.

Haleblian, J. & Finkelstein, S. 1999. The influence of organizational acquisition experience on acquisition performance: A behavioral learning perspective. **Administrative Science Quarterly**, 44: 29-56.

Haleblian, J., Devers, C. E., McNamara, G., Carpenter, M., & Davison, R. B. 2009. Taking stock of what we know about mergers and acquisitions: A review and research agenda. **Journal of Management**, 35(3): 469-502.

Hambrick, D. 2004. The disintegration of strategic management: it's time to consolidate the gains. **Strategic Organization**, 2(1): 91-98.

Hambrick, D. C. & Finkelstein, S. 1987. Managerial discretion: A bridge between polar views of organizational outcomes. **Research in Organizational Behavior**, 9: 369-406.

Hambrick, D. C., Cho, T., & Chen, M. 1996. The influence of top management team heterogeneity on firms' competitive moves. **Administrative Science Quarterly**, 41: 659-684.

Hand, J. & Skantz, T. 1997. The bad news in equity carveouts, **Working Paper. University of North Carolina**.

Hannan, M. T. & Freeman, J. 1984. Structural inertia and organizational change. **American Sociological Review**, 49(2): 149-164.

Hannan, M. T. & Freeman, J. 1989. **Organizational ecology**. Cambridge, MA: Harvard University Press.

Hansen, G. S. & Hill, C. W. L. 1991. Are institutional investors myopic? A time-series study of four technology-driven industries. **Strategic Management Journal**, 14(8): 607-618.

Harrington, S. E. & Niehaus, G. 1999. Volatility and underwriting cycles. In G. Dionne (Ed.), **Handbook of insurance**. Boston: Kluwer Academic Publishers.

Hatten, H. J. & Hatten, M. L. 1987. Strategic groups, asymmetrical mobility barriers and contestability. **Strategic Management Journal**, 8(4): 329-342.

Haugen, R. A. 1971. Insurance risk under alternative investment and financing strategies. **Journal of Risk and Insurance**, 38(1): 71-80.

Haunschild, P. R., Davis-Blake, A., & Fichman, M. 1994. Managerial overcommitment in corporate acquisition process. **Organization Science**, 5: 528-540.

Haunschild, P. R. & Miner, A. S. 1997. Modes of interorganizational imitation: The effects of outcome salience and uncertainty. **Administrative Science Quarterly**, 42(3): 472-500.

Hausman, J. 1978. Specification tests in econometrics. **Econometrica**, 46: 1251-1272.

Haveman, H. A. 1993. Follow the leader: Mimetic isomorphism and entry into new markets. **Administrative Science Quarterly**, 38: 593.

Hawley, A. H. 1950. **Human Ecology: A theory of community structure**. New York: Ronald.

Hayek, F. A. 1968. Competition as a discovery procedure. **The Quarterly Journal of Austrian Economics**, 5(3): 9-23.

Haynes, M., Thompson, S., & Wright, M. 2002. The impact of divestment on firm performance: Empirical evidence from a panel of UK companies. **The Journal of Industrial Economics**, 50(2): 173-196.

Haynes, M., Thompson, S., & Wright, M. 2003. The determinants of divestment: Evidence from a panel of UK firms. **Journal of Economic Behavior & Organization**, 52(1): 147-166.

Haynes, M., Thompson, S., & Wright, M. 2007. Executive remuneration and corporate divestment: Motivating managers to make unpalatable decisions. **Journal of Business Finance and Accounting**, 34(5-6): 792-818.

Hayward, M. L. 2002. When do firms learn from their acquisition experience? Evidence from 1990-1995. **Strategic Management Journal**, 23(1): 21-39.

Hayward, M. L. A. & Hambrick, D. C. 1997. Explaining the premiums paid for large acquisitions: Evidence of CEO hubris. **Administrative Science Quarterly**, 42(1): 103-127.

Hearth, D. & Zaima, J. K. 1984. Voluntary corporate divestitures and value. **Financial Management**, 13(1): 10-16.

Hedberg, B., Nystrom, P., & Starbuck, W. 1976. Camping on seesaw: Prescriptions for a self-designing organization. **Administrative Science Quarterly**, 21: 41-65.

Hergert, M. 1988. Causes and consequences of strategic grouping in US manufacturing industries. **International Studies of Management and Organization**, 18(1): 26-49.

Herriot, S. R., Levinthal, D., & March, J. G. 1985. Learning from experience in organizations. **American Economic Review**, 75: 298-302.

Hill, C. W. L. & Hoskisson, R. 1987. Strategy and structure in the multiproduct firm. **Academy of Management Journal**, 12: 331-341.

Hilliard, D., Purpura, S. J., & Wilkerson, S. 2006. Computer assisted topic classification for mixed methods social science research. **Journal of Information Technology and Politics**, 4(4).

Hite, G., Owers, J., & Rogers, R. C. 1987. The market for interfirm asset sales, partial sell-offs and total liquidations. **Journal of Financial Economics**, 12: 229-252.

Hitt, M. A. & Tyler, B. B. 1991. Strategic decision models: Integrating different perspectives. **Strategic Management Journal**, 12(5): 327-351.

Hitt, M. A., Ireland, R. D., & Hoskisson, R. E. 1995. **Strategic management: Competitiveness and globalization**. St. Paul: West Publishing.

Hodgkinson, G. P. 1997. The cognitive analysis of competitive structures: A review and critique. **Human Relations**, 50(6): 625-654.

Hoskisson, R. E., Hitt, M., Wan, W. P., & Yiu, D. 1999. Theory and research in strategic management: Swings of a pendulum. **Journal of Management**, 25(3): 417-456.

Houthoofd, N. & Heene, A. 1997. Strategic groups as subsets of strategic scope groups in the Belgian brewing industry. **Strategic Management Journal**, 18(8): 653-666.

Hrebiniak, L. & Joyce, W. 1985. Organizational adaptation: Strategic choice and environmental determinism. **Administrative Science Quarterly**, 30(3): 336-350.

Hsieh, K.-Y. & Chen, M.-J. 2010. Responding to rivals' actions: Beyond dyadic conceptualization of interfirm rivalry, **2010 Academy of Management Annual Meeting**. Montreal, Canada.

Huff, A. S. 1982. Industry influences on strategy reformulation. **Strategic Management Journal**, 3(2): 119-131.

Huff, A. S., Huff, J. O., & Thomas, H. 1994. The dynamics of strategic change. In H. Daems & H. Thomas (Eds.), **Strategic groups, strategic moves and performance**. Oxford: Pergamon.

Huh, M.-H. & Lim, Y. B. 2009. Weighting variables in K-means clustering. **Journal of Applied Statistics**, 36(1): 67-78.

Hunt, M. 1972. **Competition in the major home appliance industry, 1960-1970**. Harvard University, Boston, MA.

Ingram, P. & Baum, J. A. C. 1997. Opportunity and constraint: Organization's learning from the operating and competitive experience of industries. **Strategic Management Journal**, 18(1): 75-98.

Iyer, D. & Miller, K. 2008. Performance feedback, slack, and the timing of acquisitions. **Academy of Management Journal**, 51(4): 808-822.

Jacobson, R. 1992. The "Austrian" school of strategy. **Academy of Management Review**, 17(4): 782-807.

Jain, P. C. 1985. The effect of voluntary sell-off announcements on shareholder wealth. **The Journal of Finance**, 40: 209-224.

Jauch, L. R., Osborn, R. N., & Martin, T. N. 1980. Structured content analysis of cases: A complementary method for organizational research. **Academy of Management Review**, 5: 517-526.

Jensen, M. C. & Ruback, R. S. 1983. The market for corporate control: The scientific evidence. **Journal of Financial Economics**, 11: 5-50.

Jensen, M. C. 1986. Agency costs of free cash flow, corporate finance and takeovers. **American Economic Review**, 76: 323-329.

Jensen, M. C. 1989. The eclipse of the public corporation. **Harvard Business Review**, 67(5): 61-74.

Jick, T. 1979. Mixing qualitative and quantitative methods. Triangulation in action. **Administrative Science Quarterly**, 24: 602-661.

John, K., Lang, L., & Netter, J. 1992. The voluntary restructuring of large firms in response to performance decline. **The Journal of Finance**, 47: 891-918.

John, K. & Ofek, E. 1995. Asset sale and increase in focus. **Journal of Financial Economics**, 37: 105-126.

Johnson, G., Scholes, K., & Whittington, R. 2005. **Exploring corporate strategy. Text and cases** (7 ed.). New York: Prentice-Hall.

Johnson, R. A. 1996. Antecedents and outcomes of corporate refocusing. **Journal of Management**, 22: 439-483.

Kahneman, D. & Tversky, A. 1979. Prospect theory: An analysis of decision under risk. **Econometrica**, 47(2): 263-291.

Kahneman, D. & Tversky, A. 2000. **Choices, values, and frames**. New York, NY: Cambridge University Press.

Kaiser, K. & Stouratis, A. 2001. Agency costs and strategic considerations behind sell-offs: The UK evidence. **European Financial Management**, 7: 319-349.

Katrishen, F. A. & Scordis, N. A. 1998. Economies of scale in services: A study of multinational insurers. **Journal of International Business Studies**, 29(2): 305-323.

Kelley, H. H. & Michela, J. L. 1980. Attribution theory and research. **Annual Review of Psychology**, 31: 457-501.

Kelly, G. A. 1955. **The psychology of personal constructs**. New York: Norton.

Ketchen, D. J., Thomas, J. B., & Snow, C. C. 1993. Organizational configurations and performance: A comparison of theoretical approaches. **Academy of Management Journal**, 36(6): 1278-1313.

Ketchen, D. J. & Shook, C. L. 1996. The application of cluster analysis in strategic management research. **Strategic Management Journal**, 17(6): 441-458.

Ketchen, D. J., Snow, C. C., & Hoover, V. L. 2004. Research on competitive dynamics: Recent accomplishments and future challenges. **Journal of Management**, 30(6): 779-804.

Kiefer, N. M. 1988. Economic duration data and hazard functions. **Journal of Economic Literature**, 26(2): 646-679.

Killström, P. 2005. **Strategic groups and performance of the firm - Towards a competitive environment in the Finnish telecommunications industry**. University of Helsinki, Helsinki.

Kim, Y. & Lee, B. 2002. Patterns of technological learning among the strategic groups in the Korean electronic part industry. **Research Policy**, 31(4): 543-567.

King, G. & Lowe, A. 2003. An automated information extraction tool for international conflict data with performance as good as human coders: A rare events evaluation design. **International Organization**, 57(3): 617-642.

Kirzner, I. 1973. **Competition and Entrepreneurship**. Chicago: University of Chicago Press.

Kirzner, I. M. 1997. Entrepreneurial discovery and the competitive market process: An Austrian approach. **Journal of Economic Literature**, 35(1): 60-85.

Klein, A. 1986. The timing and substance of divestiture announcements: Individual, simultaneous and cumulative effects. **The Journal of Finance**, 41: 685-696.

Koka, B. R., Madhavan, R., & Prescott, J. E. 2006. The evolution of interfirm networks: Environmental effects on patterns of network change. **Academy of Management Review**, 31(3): 721-737.

Kreps, D., Milgrom, P., Roberts, J., & Wilson, R. 1982. Rational cooperation in the finitely repeated prisoners' dilemma. **Journal of Economic Theory**, 27: 245-252.

Kreps, D. M. 1990. **Game theory and economic modeling**. Oxford, England: Oxford University Press.

Krishnaswami, S. & Subramaniam, V. 1999. Information asymmetry, valuation, and the corporate spin-off decision. **Journal of Financial Economics**, 53: 73-112.

Kusewitt, J. B. 1985. An exploratory study of strategic acquisition factors relating to performance. **Strategic Management Journal**, 6: 151-169.

Laamanen, T. 2007. On the role of acquisition premium in acquisition research. **Strategic Management Journal**, 28(13): 1359-1369.

Laamanen, T. & Keil, T. 2008. Performance of serial acquirers: Toward an acquisition program perspective. **Strategic Management Journal**, 29(6): 663-672.

Lang, L. & Schulz, R. M. 1994. Tobin's q, corporate diversification, and firm performance. **Journal of Political Economy**, 102(6): 1248-1280.

Lang, L., Poulsen, A., & Stulz, R. 1995. Asset sales, firm performance, and the agency costs of managerial discretion. **Journal of Financial Economics**, 37: 3-37.

Lant, T. K., Milliken, F. J., & Batra, B. 1992. The role of managerial learning and interpretation in strategic persistence and reorientation: An empirical exploration. **Strategic Management Journal**, 13(8): 585-608.

Larraza-Kintana, M., Wiseman, R., Gomez-Mejia, L., & Welbourne, T. M. 2000. **Framing compensation, and employment risk influence on CEO risk taking behavior.** Tempe, AZ: Arizona State University.

Lasfer, M., Sudarsanam, P. S., & Taffler, R. J. 1996. Financial distress, asset sales and lender monitoring. **Financial Management**, 25(3): 57-66.

Lawless, M. W., Bergh, D. D., & Wilsted, W. D. 1989. Performance variations among strategic group members: An examination of individual firm capability. **Journal of Management**, 15(4): 649-661.

Lawrence, P. R. & Lorsch, J. W. 1967. Differentiation and Integration in complex organizations. **Administrative Science Quarterly**, 12(1): 1-47.

Lee, H., Smith, K. G., Grimm, C. M., & Schomburg, A. 2000. Timing, order and durability of new product advantages with imitation. **Strategic Management Journal**, 21: 23-30.

Lee, J., Lee, K., & Rho, S. 2002. An evolutionary perspective on strategic group emergence: A genetic algorithm-based model. **Strategic Management Journal**, 23(8): 727-746.

Lehner, J. M. 2000. Shifts of reference points for framing of strategic decisions and changing risk-return association. **Management Science**, 46(1): 63-76.

Levinthal, D. A. & March, J. G. 1993. The myopia of learning. **Strategic Management Journal**, 14(Winter special issue): 95-112.

Levitt, B. & March, J. G. 1988. Organizational learning. **Annual Review of Sociology**, 14: 319-340.

Li, M. & Simerly, R. L. 1998. The moderating effect of environmental dynamism on the ownership and performance relationship. **Strategic Management Journal**, 19(2): 169-179.

Li, W. & Lu, Y. 2011. CEO dismissal, institutional development, and environmental dynamism. **Asia Pacific Journal of Management**, 28(forthcoming).

Lieberman, M. B. & Montgomery, C. 1998. First -mover (dis)advantages: Retrospective and link with the resource-based view. **Strategic Management Journal**, 19.

Lieberman, M. B. & Asaba, S. 2006. Why do firms imitate each other? **Academy of Management Review**, 31(2): 366-385.

Lincoln, J. R. 1984. Analyzing relations in dyads: Problems, models, and an application to interorganizational research. **Sociological Research Methods**, 13(1): 45-76.

Long, J. S. 2009. **The workflow of data analysis using Stata**. College Station, TX: Stata Press.

Lopes, L. L. 1987. Between hope and fear: The psychology of risk. **Advances in Experimental Social Psychology**, 20: 255-295.

Lowe, W. 2003. The statistics of text: New methods for content analysis. **http://citeseerx.ist.psu.edu/viewdoc/summary?doi=10.1.1.129.5225**.

MacKinley, A. C. 1997. Event studies in economics and finance. **Journal of Economic Literature**, 35: 13-39.

MacMillan, I., McCaffrey, M., & Van Wijk, G. 1985. Competitor's responses to easily imitated new products: Exploring commercial banking product introductions. **Strategic Management Journal**, 6: 75-86.

Mahalanobis, P. C. 1936. On the generalized distance in statistics. **Proceedings of the National Institute of Sciences of India**, 1(2): 49-55.

Maier, N., Parodi, F., & Verna, S. 2008. dTa, 1.1.2 ed. Rome: Open Source.

Makarenkov, V. & Legendre, P. 2001a. Optimal variable weighting for ultrametric and additive trees and k-means partitioning: Methods and software. **Journal of Classification**, 18(2): 1432-1342.

Makarenkov, V. & Legendre, P. 2001b. **OVW: Optimal variable weighting for ultrametric and additive tree clustering, and k-means partitioning**: 6. Département de sciences biologiques: Université de Montréal.

Mandelbrot, B. 1968. Information theory and psycholinguistics. In R. C. Oldfield & J. C. Marchall (Eds.), **Language**. London: Penguin Books.

Mankins, M. C., Harding, D., & Weddigen, R.-M. 2008. How the best divest. **Harvard Business Review**, 86(10): 92-99.

Mansfield, E. 1961. Technical change and the rate of imitation. **Econometrica**, 29: 741-766.

March, J. G. & Simon, H. A. 1958. **Organizations**. New York: John Wiley & Sons.

March, J. G. & Shapira, Z. 1987. Managerial perspectives on risk and risk taking. **Management Science**, 33(11): 1404-1418.

March, J. G. & Shapira, Z. 1992. Variable risk preferences and the focus of attention. **Psychological Review**, 99(1): 172-183.

Markides, C. C. 1992. Consequences of corporate restructuring: Ex ante evidence. **Academy of Management Journal**, 35: 398-412.

Más Ruíz, F. J. 1999. Dynamic analysis of competition in marketing: Strategic groups in Spanish banking. **International Journal of Bank Marketing**, 17(5): 233-250.

Mascarenhas, B. 1989. Strategic group dynamics. **Academy of Management Journal**, 32(2): 333-352.

Mascarenhas, B. & Aaker, D. A. 1989. Mobility barriers and strategic groups. **Strategic Management Journal**, 10(5): 475-485.

Mason, E. S. 1949. The current state of the monopoly problem in the US. **Harvard Law Review**, 62: 1265-1285.

McGee, J. & Thomas, H. 1986. Strategic groups: Theory, research and taxonomy. **Strategic Management Journal**, 7(2): 141-160.

McGee, V. & Carleton, W. 1970. Piecewise regression. **Journal of the American Statistical Association**, 65(331): 1109-1124.

McGrath, R. G., Chen, M.-J., & MacMillan, I. C. 1998. Multimarket maneuvering in uncertain spheres of influence: Resource diversion strategies. **Academy of Management Review**, 23(4): 724-740.

McNamara, G., Deephouse, D. L., & Luce, R. A. 2003. Competitive positioning within and across a strategic group structure: The performance of core, secondary and solitary firms. **Strategic Management Journal**, 24(2): 161-181.

McNamara, G. M., Luce, R. A., & Thompson, G. H. 2002. Examining the effect of complexity in strategic group knowledge structures on firm performance. **Strategic Management Journal**, 23(2): 153-170.

McNulty, P. 1968. Economic theory and the meaning of competition. **Quarterly Journal of Economics**, 82(4): 639-656.

McWilliams, A. & Siegel, D. 1997. Event studies in management research: theoretical and empirical issues. **Academy of Management Journal**, 40(3): 626-657.

Mehra, A. & Floyd, S. W. 1998. Product market heterogeneity, resource imitability and strategic group formation. **Journal of Management**, 24(4): 511-531.

Meindl, J. R., Ehrlich, S. R., & Dukerich, J. M. 1985. The romance of leadership. **Administrative Science Quarterly**, 30: 78-102.

Meyer, A. D. 1982. Adopting to environmental jolts. **Administrative Science Quarterly**, 27: 515-537.

Meyer, A. D., Brooks, G. R., & Goes, J. B. 1990. Environmental jolts and industry revolutions: Organizational responses to discontinuous change. **Strategic Management Journal**, 11(Summer special issue): 93-110.

Miles, G., Snow, C. C., & Sharfman, M. P. 1993. Industry variety and performance. **Strategic Management Journal**, 14(3): 163-177.

Miles, J. A. & Rosenfeld, J. D. 1983. The effect of voluntary spin-off announcement on shareholder wealth. **The Journal of Finance**, 38: 1597-1606.

Miller, D. & Friesen, P. 1980. Momentum and revolution in organizational adaptation. **Academy of Management Journal**, 23(4): 591-614.

Miller, D. 1994. What happens after success: The perils of excellence. **Journal of Management Studies**, 31(3): 325-358.

Miller, D. & Chen, M. J. 1994. Sources and consequences of competitive inertia: A study of the US airline industry. **Administrative Science Quarterly**, 39(1): 1-23.

Miller, D. & Chen, M. J. 1996a. The simplicity of competitive repertoires: An empirical analysis. **Strategic Management Journal**, 17(6): 419-439.

Miller, D. & Chen, M. J. 1996b. Nonconformity in competitive repertoires: A sociological view of markets. **Social Forces**, 74: 1209-1234.

Miller, K. D. & Chen, W.-R. 2004. Variable organizational risk preferences: Tests of the March-Shapira model. **Academy of Management Journal**, 47(1): 105-115.

Miller, K. D. & Tsang, E. W. 2011. Testing management theories: Critical realist philosophy and research methods. **Strategic Management Journal**, 32(2): 139-158.

Milligan, G. W. & Cooper, M. C. 1985. An examination of procedures for determining the number of clusters in a dataset. **Psychometrika**, 50: 159-179.

Milligan, G. W. 1996. Clustering validation: Results and implications for applied analysis. In P. Arabie & L. J. Hubert & G. De Soete (Eds.), **Clustering and classification**. River Edge, NJ: World Scientific.

Milliken, F. J. & Lant, T. K. 1991. The effect of an organization's recent performance history on strategic persistence and change. In P. Shrivastava & A. S. Huff & J. Dutton (Eds.), **Advances in Strategic Management**, Vol. 7: 129-156. Greenwich, CT: JAI Press.

Mises, L. 1949. **Human action: A treatise on economics**. New Haven: Yale University Press.

Montgomery, C. A., Thomas, A. R., & Kamath, R. 1984. Divestiture, market valuation, and strategy. **Academy of Management Journal**, 27: 830-840.

Myers, S. C. & Majluf, N. 1984. Corporate financing and investment decisions when firms have information that investors do not have. **Journal of Financial Economics**, 13: 187-221.

Nair, A. & Kotha, S. 2001. Does group membership matter? Evidence from the Japanese steel industry. **Strategic Management Journal**, 22(3): 221-235.

Nair, A. & Filer, L. 2003. Cointegration of firm strategies within groups: A long-run analysis of firm behavior in the Japanese steel industry. **Strategic Management Journal**, 24(2): 145-159.

Nanda, V. 1991. On the good news in equity carve-outs. **The Journal of Finance**, 46: 1717-1737.

Nanda, V. & Narayanan, M. 1999. Disentangling value: financing needs, firm scope, and divestitures. **Journal of Financial Intermediation**, 8: 174-204.

Nees, D. B. 1978. The divestment decision process in large and medium-sized diversified companies: A descriptive model based on clinical research. **International Studies of Management & Organization**, 8(4): 67-93.

Nees, D. B. 1981. Increase your divestment effectiveness. **Strategic Management Journal**, 2: 119-130.

Nelson, R. R. & Winter, S. G. 1982. **An evolutionary theory of economic change**. Cambridge, MA: Harvard University Press.

Neter, J., Wasserman, W., & Kutner, M. H. 1985. **Applied linear statistical models**. Homewood, IL: Irwin.

OECD. 2003. **Science, technology and industry scoreboard 2003** - Towards a knowledge-based economy. Paris: OECD.

Oetzel, J. & Bannerjee, S. 2008. A case of the tortoise versus the hare? Deregulation process, timing, and firm performance in emerging markets. **International Business Review**, 17(1): 54-77.

Oler, D., Harrison, J., & Allen, M. 2008. The danger of misinterpreting short-window event study findings in strategic management research: An empirical illustration using horizontal acquisitions. **Strategic Organization**, 6(2): 151-184.

Ordover, J. A., Sykes, A. O., & Willig, R. D. 1982. Herfindahl concentration, rivalry and mergers. **Harvard Law Review**, 95(8): 1857-1874.

Osborne, J. D., Stubbart, C. I., & Ramaprasad, A. 2001. Strategic groups and competitive enactment: A study of dynamic relationships between mental models and performance. **Strategic Management Journal**, 22(5): 435-454.

Oster, S. M. 1982. Intra-industry structure and the ease of strategic change. **Review of Economics and Statistics**, 64: 376-383.

Palmer, T. B. & Wiseman, R. B. 1999. Decoupling risk taking from income stream uncertainty: A holistic model of risk. **Strategic Management Journal**, 20: 1037-1062.

Park, K. M. 2007. Antecedents of convergence and divergence in strategic positioning: The effects of performance and aspiration on the direction of strategic change. **Organization Science**, 18(3): 386-402.

Park, N. 2004. A guide to using event study methods in multi-country settings. **Strategic Management Journal**, 25: 655-668.

Pennings, J. M. 1987. Structural contingency theory: A multivariate test. **Organization Studies**, 8: 223-240.

Pennings, J. M., Barkema, H., & Douma, S. 1994. Organizational learning and diversification. **Academy of Management Journal**, 37: 608-640.

Penrose, E. 1959. **The theory of the growth of the firm**. New York: Wiley.

Peteraf, M. & Shanley, M. 1997. Getting to know you: A theory of strategic group identity. **Strategic Management Journal**, 18(S1): 165-186.

Peterson, P. P. 1989. Event studies: A review of issues and methodology. **Quarterly Journal of Business and Economics**, 28(3): 36-66.

Pettigrew, A. 1990. Longitudinal field research on change: Theory and practice. **Organization Science**, 1(3): 267-292.

Pettigrew, A. & Whipp, R. 1991. **Managing change for competitive success**. Oxford: Blackwell.

Pfeffer, J. & Salancik, G. R. 1978. **The external control of organizations: A resource dependence perspective**: Harper & Row.

Porac, J. F., Thomas, H., & Baden-Fuller, C. 1989. Competitive groups as cognitive communities: The case of Scottish knitwear manufacturers. **Journal of Management Studies**, 26(4): 397-416.

Porac, J. F. & Thomas, H. 1990. Taxonomic mental models in competitor definition. **The Academy of Management Review**, 15(2): 224-240.

Porac, J. F. & Thomas, H. 1994. Cognitive categorization and subjective rivalry among retailers in a small city. **Journal of Applied Psychology**, 79(1): 54-66.

Porter, M. 1979. The structure within industries and companies' performance. **Review of Economics and Statistics**, 61: 214-227.

Porter, M. E. 1980. **Competitive strategy: Techniques for analyzing industries and competitors**. New York, NY: Free Press.

Porter, M. E. 1981. The contributions of industrial organization to strategic management. **Academy of Management Journal**, 6(4): 609-620.

Porter, M. E. 1985. **Competitive advantage**. New York: Free Press.

Powell, M. & DiMaggio, P. J. 1991. **The new institutionalism in organizational analysis**. Chicago: University Press of Chicago.

Pruett, M. & Thomas, H. 1994. Introduction. In H. Daems & H. Thomas (Eds.), **Strategic groups, strategic moves and performance**: vii-xii. Oxford: Pergamon.

Quinn, J. B. 1980. **Strategies for change: Logical incrementalism**. Homewood: Richard D. Irwin.

Ravenscraft, D. J. & Scherer, F. M. 1991. Divisional sell-off: A hazard function analysis. **Managerial and Decision Economics**, 12: 429-438.

Reger, R. K. & Huff, A. S. 1993. Strategic groups: A cognitive perspective. **Strategic Management Journal**, 14(2): 103-123.

Rhoades, S. A. 1983. **Power, empire building, and mergers**. Lanham, MD: Lexington Books.

Rindova, V., Ferrier, W. J., & Wiltbank, R. 2010. Value from gestalt: How sequences of competitive actions create advantage for firms in nascent markets. **Strategic Management Journal**, 31(13): 1474-1497.

Rosenfeld, J. D. 1984. Additional evidence on the relationship between divestiture announcements and shareholder wealth. **The Journal of Finance**, 39: 1437-1448.

Rumelt, R. 1984. Toward a strategic theory of the firm. In R. Lamb (Ed.), **Competitive Strategic Management**: 556–570. Englewood Cliffs, NJ: Prentice-Hall.

Sanders, W. G. 2001. Behavioral responses of CEOs to stock ownership and stock option pay. **Academy of Management Journal**, 44: 477-492.

Schendel, D. & Hofer, C. W. 1979. **Strategic management: A new view of business policy and planning**. Boston, MA: Little Brown.

Scherer, F. M. & Ross, S. 1990. **Industrial market structure and economic performance** (3 ed.). Boston: Houghton Mifflin.

Schill, M. J. & Zhou, C. 2001. Pricing an emerging industry: Evidence from Internet subsidiary carve-outs. **Financial Management**, 30(3): 5-33.

Schimmer, M. 2010. Strategic group dynamics: A behavioral perspective. **Annual Meeting of the Academy of Management**. Montreal, QC.

Schipper, K. & Smith, K. G. 1983. Effects of recontracting on shareholder wealth: The case of voluntary spin-offs. **Journal of Financial Economics**, 12: 437-467.

Schipper, K. & Thompson, R. 1983. Evidence on the capitalized value of merger activity for acquiring firms. **Journal of Financial Economics**, 11: 85-119.

Schipper, K. & Smith, A. 1986. A comparison of equity carve-outs and seasoned equity offerings. **Journal of Financial Economics**, 15(1-2): 153-186.

Schomburg, A., Grimm, C., & Smith, K. 1994. Avoiding new product warfare: The role of industry structure. In P. Shrivastava & A. S. Huff & J. Dutton (Eds.), **Advances in Strategic Management**, Vol. 10. Greenwich: JAI Press.

Schumpeter, J. 1934. **The Theory of Economic Development**. Boston, MA: Harvard University Press.

Schumpeter, J. 1943. **Capitalism, socialism, and democracy**. New York: Harper.

Sen, A. 1993. Internal consistency of choice. **Econometrica**, 61(3): 495-521.

Shapiro, G. & Markoff, J. 1997. **Text analysis for the social sciences: Methods for drawing statistical inferences from text and transcripts**. Mahwah, NJ: Lawrence Erlbaum Associates.

Short, J. C., Ketchen, D. J., Palmer, T. B., & Hult, G. T. M. 2007. Firm, strategic group, and industry influences on performance. **Strategic Management Journal**, 28(2): 147-167.

Sicherman, N. W. & Pettway, R. H. 1987. Acquisition of divested assets and shareholder wealth. **The Journal of Finance**, 42: 1261-1273.

Siggelkow, N. 2001. Change in the presence of fit: The rise, the fall, and the renaissance of Liz Claiborne. **Academy of Management Journal**, 4: 838-857.

Simon, H. A. 1959. Theories of decision-making in economics and behavioral science. **American Economic Review**, 49: 253-283.

Simon, H. A. 1972. Complexity and the representation of patterned sequences of symbols. **Psychological Review**, 79(5): 369-382.

Singh, H. & Zollo, M. 1998. The impact of knowledge codification, experience trajectories and integration strategies on the performance of corporate acquisitions, **Working paper series**: 42: The Wharton Financial Institutions Center.

Slovin, M. B., Sushka, M. E., & Ferraro, S. 1991. A comparison of information conveyed by equity carve-outs, spin-offs, and asset sell-offs. **Journal of Financial Economics**, 37(1): 89-104.

Smith, A. 1776. **The wealth of nations**. Glasgow.

Smith, K., Grimm, C., Chen, M., & Gannon, M. 1989. Predictors of response time to competitive strategic actions: Preliminary theory and evidence. **Journal of Business Research**, 18(3): 245-259.

Smith, K. G., Grimm, C., Gannon, M., & Chen, M. 1991. Organizational information processing, competitive responses, and performance in the domestic airline industry. **Academy of Management Journal**, 34: 60-85.

Smith, K. G., Grimm, C. M., & Gannon, M. J. 1992. **Dynamics of competitive strategy**. Newbury Park, CA: Sage Publications.

Smith, K. G., Young, G., Becerra, M., & Grimm, C. 1996. **An assessment of the validity of competitive dynamics research**. Paper presented at the Academy of Management (Best Paper Proceedings), Cincinnati, OH.

Smith, K. G., Ferrier, W. J., & Grimm, C. M. 2001a. King of the hill: Dethroning the industry leader, **Academy of Management Executive**, Vol. 15: 59-70: Academy of Management.

Smith, K. G., Ferrier, W. J., & Ndofor, H. 2001b. Competitive dynamics research: Critique and future directions. In M. A. Hitt (Ed.), **The Blackwell handbook of strategic management**: 315-361. Oxford: Blackwell Business.

Sneath, P. H. & Sokal, R. R. 1973. **Numerical taxonomy**. San Francisco, CA: Freeman.

Sneath, P. H. 1980. The risk of not recognizing from ordinations that clusters are distinct. **Classification Society Bulletin**, 4: 22-43.

Spencer, J. C. 1989. **Industry recipes**: Blackwell Publishers.

Starbuck, W. 1976. Organizations and their environments. In M. Dunnette (Ed.), **Handbook of industrial and organizational psychology**. Chicago: Rand McNally & Co.

Staw, B. M. & Szwajkowski, E. 1975. The scarcity-munificence component of organizational environments and the commission of illegal acts. **Administrative Science Quarterly**, 20: 345-354.

Staw, B. M., Sandelands, L. E., & Dutton, J. E. 1981. Threat rigidity effects in organizational behavior: A multilevel analysis. **Administrative Science Quarterly**, 26(4): 501-524.

Staw, B. M., McKechnie, P. I., & Puffer, S. M. 1983. The justification of organizational performance. **Administrative Science Quarterly**, 28(4): 582-600.

Stigler, G. J. 1964. A theory of oligopoly. **Journal of Political Economy**: 44-61.

Stigler, G. J. 1968. Competition. In D. L. Sills (Ed.), **International encyclopedia of the social sciences**: 181-186. London: Macmillan.

Swiss Re. 2008. **Sigma Research**; http://www.swissre.com/pws/research%20publications/sigma%20ins.%20research/sigma%20insurance%20research.html; 21.07.2008.

Tabachnick, B. G. & Fidell, L. S. 2006. **Using multivariate statistics**. Boston: Allyn & Bacon.

Tan, F. B. & Hunter, M. G. 2002. The repertory grid technique: A method for the study of cognition in information systems. **MIS Quarterly**, 26(1): 39-57.

Tetlock, P. C. 2007. Giving content to investor sentiment: The role of media in the stock market. **The Journal of Finance**, 62: 1139-1168.

Tetlock, P. C., Saar-Tsechansky, M., & Macskassy, S. 2008. More than words: Quantifying language to measure firms' fundamentals. **The Journal of Finance**, 63: 1437-1467.

Thomas, H. & Venkatraman, N. 1988. Research on strategic groups: Progress and prognosis. **Journal of Management Studies**, 25: 537-555.

Thomas, H. & Carroll, C. 1994. Theoretical and empirical links between strategic groups, cognitive communities, and networks of interacting firms. In H. Daems & H. Thomas (Eds.), **Strategic groups, strategic moves and performance**: 7-30. Oxford: Pergamon.

Thomas, H. & Pollock, T. 1999. From IO economics SCP paradigm through strategic groups to competence-based competition: Reflections on the puzzle of competitive strategy. **British Journal of Management**, 10(2): 127-140.

Thomson Media. 2001. Divestiture activity in 2000. **Mergers & Acquisitions: The Dealmaker's Journal**, 36(2): 47-50.

Tosi, H. & Slocum, J. W. 1984. Contingency theory: Some suggested directions. **Journal of Management**, 10: 9-26.

Tushman, M. 1979. Work characteristics and sub-unit communication structure: A contingency analysis. **Administrative Science Quarterly**, 24: 82-97.

Tyco; **7,200 laid off as Tyco divests**; http://secure.theengineer.co.uk/Articles/268722/7,200+laid+off+as+Tyco+divests.htm; 20 November 2008, 2008.

Uotila, J., Maula, M., Keil, T., & Zahra, S. 2009. Exploration, exploitation, and financial performance: Analysis of S&P500 corporations. **Strategic Management Journal**, 30(2): 221-231.

Vassolo, R., Sanchez, J. G., & Mesquita, L. F. 2010. Industry evolution and the sustainability of advantage in conditions of macroeconomic turbulence, **2010 Academy of Management Annual Meeting**. Montreal.

Vermeulen, F. & Barkema, H. G. 2001. Learning through acquisitions. **Academy of Management Journal**, 44(3): 457-476.

Vermeulen, F. & Barkema, H. 2002. Pace, rhythm, and scope: Process dependence in building a profitable multinational corporation. **Strategic Management Journal**, 23: 637-653.

Vichi, M. & Kiers, H. A. L. 2001. Factorial k-means analysis for two-way data. **Computational Statistics and Data Analysis**, 37(1): 49-64.

Vijh, A. M. 1999. Long term returns from equity carveouts. **Journal of Financial Economics**, 51: 273-308.

Vijh, A. M. 2002. The positive announcement period returns on equity carveouts: Asymmetric information or divestiture gains? **Journal of Business**, 75(1): 153-190.

von Neumann, J. & Morgenstern, O. 1944. **Theory of games and economic behavior**. Princeton, NJ: Princeton University Press.

von Neumann, J. & Morgenstern, O. 1953. **Theory of games and economic behavior** (3 ed.). London: John Wiley & Sons.

Voss, I. & Müller-Stewens, G. 2006. Strategische M&A-Kompetenz im Rahmen von Akquisitionsstrategien - Komponenten, Erfolgsfaktoren und Aufbau. In F. Keuper & M. Häfner & C. Glahn (Eds.), **Der M&A-Prozess. Konzepte, Ansätze und Strategien für die Pre- und Post-Phase**: 3-32. Wiesbaden: Gabler.

Waldman, D. A., Ramirez, G. G., House, R. J., & Puranam, P. 2001. Does leadership matter? CEO leadership attributes and profitability under conditions of perceived environmental uncertainty. **Academy of Management Journal**, 44(1): 134-143.

Walsh, J. P. 1995. Managerial and organizational cognition. **Organization Science**, 6: 280-324.

Wan, W. P. & Yiu, D. W. 2009. From crisis to opportunity: Environmental jolt, corporate acquisitions, and firm performance. **Strategic Management Journal**, 30(7): 791-801.

Wang, L. & Zajac, E. J. 2007. Alliance or acquisition? A dyadic perspective on interfirm resource combinations. **Strategic Management Journal**, 28: 1291-1317.

Ward, J. H. 1963. Hierarchical grouping to optimize an objective function. **Journal of the American Statistical Association**, 58(301): 236-244.

Watzlawick, P., Weakland, J. H., & Fisch, R. 1974. **Change: Principles of problem formation and problem resolution**. New York: Norton.

Welch, I. 1989. Seasoned offerings, imitation costs, and the underpricing of initial public offerings. **Journal of Finance**, 44: 421-449.

Wernerfelt, B. 1984. A resource-based view of the firm. **Strategic Management Journal**, 5(2): 171-180.

Weston, J. F. & Chung, K. S. 1990. Takeovers and corporate restructuring: An overview. **Business Economics**, 25(2): 6-11.

White, L. H. 2008. **The research program of Austrian economic**: Emerald Group.

Wiggins, R. & Ruefli, T. 1995. Necessary conditions for the predictive validity of strategic groups: Analysis without reliance on clustering techniques. **Academy of Management Journal**, 38(6): 1635-1656.

Williams, R.; **Nonlinear relationships**; http://nd.edu/~rwilliam/stats2/l61.pdf; 08.08.2010, 2010.

Wiseman, R. M. & Bromiley, P. 1996. Toward a model of risk in declining organizations: An empirical examination of risk, performance and decline. **Organization Science**, 7(5): 524-543.

Wright, P. & Ferris, S. P. 1997. Agency conflict and corporate strategy: The effect of divestment on corporate value. **Strategic Management Journal**, 18: 77-83.

Yasai-Ardekani, M. 1989. Effects of environmental scarcity and munificence on the relationship of context to organizational structure. **Academy of Management Journal**, 32: 131-156.

Yeung, K. Y. & Ruzzo, W. L. 2001. Principal component analysis for clustering gene expression data. **Bioinformatics**, 17(9): 763-774.

Young, G., Smith, K. G., & Grimm, C. M. 1996. "Austrian" and industrial organization perspectives on firm-level competitive activity and performance. **Organization Science**, 7: 243-254.

Young, G., Smith, K. G., Grimm, C. M., & Simon, D. 2000. Multimarket Contact and Resource Dissimilarity: A Competitive Dynamics Perspective. **Journal of Management**, 26(6): 1217-1236.

Yu, T. 2003. **Dynamics of multinational rivalry**. Texas A&M University, College Station, TX.

Yu, T. & Cannella, A. A. 2007. Rivalry between multinational enterprises: An event history approach. **Academy of Management Journal**, 50: 665-686.

Zajac, E. J. & Kraatz, M. S. 1993. A diametric forces model of strategic change: Assessing the antecedents and consequences of restructuring in the higher education industry. **Strategic Management Journal**, 14(Special Issue): 83-102.

Zipf, G. K. 1932. **Selected studies of the principle of relative frequency in language**. Cambridge, MA: Harvard University Press.

Zollo, M. & Winter, S. 2002. Deliberate learning and the evolution of dynamic capabilities. **Organization Science**, 13: 339-351.

Zollo, M. & Singh, H. 2004. Deliberate learning in corporate acquisitions: Post-acquisition strategies and integration capability in U.S. bank mergers. **Strategic Management Journal**, 25(13): 1233-1256.

Zuchhini, L. & Kretschmer, T. 2011. Competitive pressure: Competitive dynamics as reactions to multiple rivals, **Annual Meeting of the Academy of Management**. St. Antonio, TX.

Zuckerman, E. 2000. Focusing the corporate product: securities analysts and de-diversification. **Administrative Science Quarterly**, 45(3): 591-619.

Zuckermann, E. 2000. Focusing the corporate product: Securities analysts and de-diversification. **Administrative Science Quarterly**, 45(3): 591-619.

Zuniga-Vicente, J. A., Fuente-Sabaté, J. M. d. l., & Rodríguez-Puerta, J. 2004a. A study of industry evolution in the face of major environmental disturbances: Group and firm strategic behavior of Spanish banks. **British Journal of Management**, 15(3): 219-245.

Zuniga-Vicente, J. A., Fuente-Sabaté, J. M. d. l., & Suarez-Gonzalez, I. 2004b. Dynamics of the strategic group membership-performance linkage in rapidly changing environments. **Journal of Business Research**, 57(12): 1378-1390.

Appendices

Appendix 1: Empirical Foundation of the Dissertation

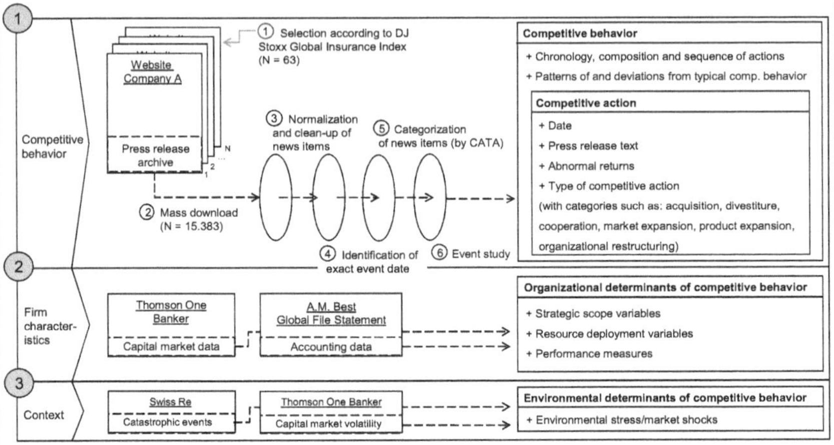

(1) Competitive behavior:

- We collected the competitive actions of the firms listed in Table A1 for the time period ranging from 1998 to 2007
- We positioned all competitive actions in time by a self-developed date identifier (see Appendix 4), which works with a negligible failure rate of approx. 1%.
- The press releases of all competitive actions can be analyzed by means of a filter-and-printout mechanism that eases manual coding or by two automatized keyword-based mechanisms (see Appendix 2):
  1. Event categorization: Based on a set of categories, each linked to a list of keywords, we identify for each press release which category of competitive action it describes. We let the different event category "compete" for each press release in a two step process. First, we assess how much more often each category's keywords occur in the press release than in the average press release in which at least one of the keywords occurs once. We then compare these normalized indicators across the different categories, and decide upon the action category which the distinct press release most probably describes (see Uotila, Maula, Keil, & Zahra, 2009 for a similar approach).
  2. Event scaling: Besides of assigning a press release to an event category, we can also measure the portion of specific words within each press release. This feature is particularly useful when studying bipolar scales (such as exploration vs. exploitation).
- Cumulative Abnormal Returns (CARs) were calculated for all events (beta factors were calculated individually for each event with reference to the correct home market index over an observation window of 250 days preceding the respective event) with flexible event window lengths of up to 21 days.

Table A1: Firms in the Database on Strategic Moves

Company	Company (cont.)	Company (cont.)
ACE Ltd[1]	Genworth Financial[2]	Safeco[1,2]
Aegon[1,2]	Great-West Lifeco[2]	Sampo[1,2]
Aflac	Groupama	Scor[1]
Allianz[1,2]	Hannover Re[1,2]	Sompo Japan Insurance[1]
Allstate[1]	Hartford Financial Services[1]	Storebrand[2]
AIG[1]	ING[1,2]	Sun Life Financial[2]
Amlin[1]	Insurance Australia[1]	Swiss Life[2]
Assicurazioni Generali[1,2]	Irish Life & Permanent[2]	Swiss Re[2]
Assurant	Legal & General[2]	T&D Holdings
Aviva[1,2]	Manulife Financial	Topdanmark[1]
AXA[1,2]	Mapfre[1]	Torchmark
Axis Capital Holdings	MetLife[2]	Travelers[1,2]
Baloise[1,2]	Mitsui	Unipol[1]
Brit Insurance[1,2]	Munich Re[1,2]	Unum Group[2]
Chubb[1,2]	Nipponkoa Insurance[1]	Vienna Insurance[1]
Cincinnati Financial[1]	Old Mutual[1,2]	WR Berkley
CNP Assurances	Power Financial	White Mountains Insurance[1,2]
Everest Re Group	Principal Financial Group	XL Capital[1]
Fairfax Financial	Progressive[1]	Zurich Financial Services[1,2]
Fondaria[1,2]	Prudential[2]	
Fortis[1,2]	Prudential Financial	
Friends Provident	RSA Insurance[1,2]	

Notes: [1] firms included in the sample of the study "From Crisis to Opportunity: How Market Shocks Impact Interfirm Rivalry" (constituting 9,613 press releases); [2] firms included in the sample of the study "Performance Effects of Corporate Divestiture Programs" (constituting 7,445 press releases); total sample includes 15,383 press releases.

(2) Firm characteristics:

- Range of years included in the database: 1999-2008
- Detailed consolidated and unconsolidated balance sheet and profit & loss account data (divided in technical and non-technical accounts) for more than 12,000 insurers worldwide (with 5,000 from the U.S.).
- Detailed data on the different lines of business for all U.S. firms allows for in-depths analyses of the firms' diversification levels.
- A.M. Best firm ratings.
- Organizational relationships can be tracked (i.e., parent/affiliate relationships).
- All data can be efficiently accessed via an Excel-Plugin, or by means of proprietary software.
- The database was previously used in various management, finance and insurance research.

(3) Context:

- Operational risks factors: We collected data on the total insured catastrophe losses in USD as well as the numbers of various types of catastrophes.
- Investment risk factors: As for the investment risks of insurance firms, we retrieved the price volatilities of the two major asset classes into which insurers invest. For stocks we refer to the S&P 500 Index, for bonds to the Lehman Brothers U.S. Aggregate Index. Both indices are the standard references for their respective U.S. asset markets.

Appendix 2: Event Categorization, Scaling and Coding

Event categorization and scaling:

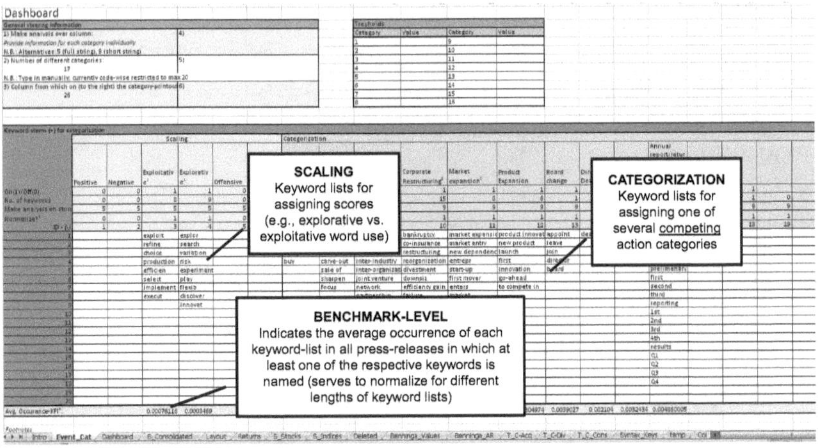

Export and manual coding form:

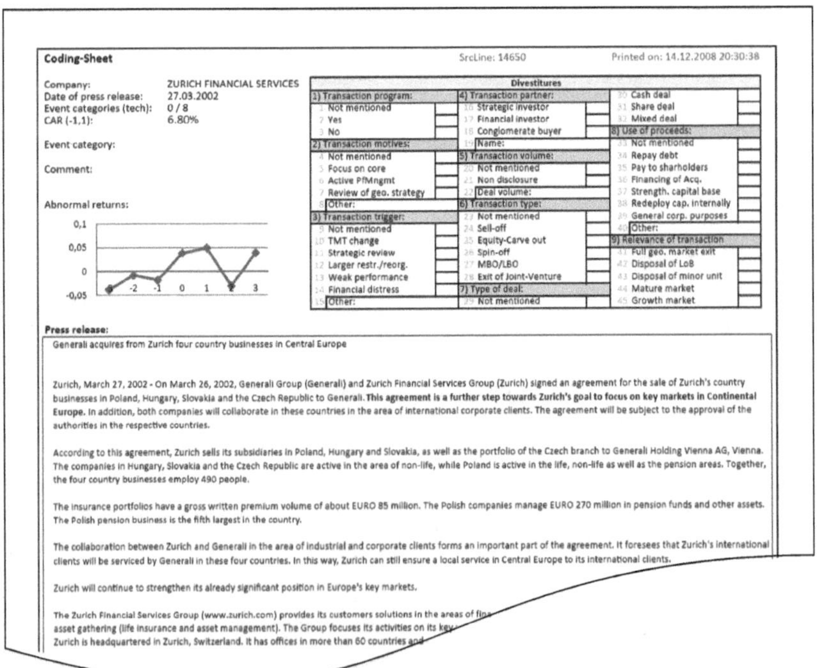

Appendix 3: Chart of Strategic Group Analyses

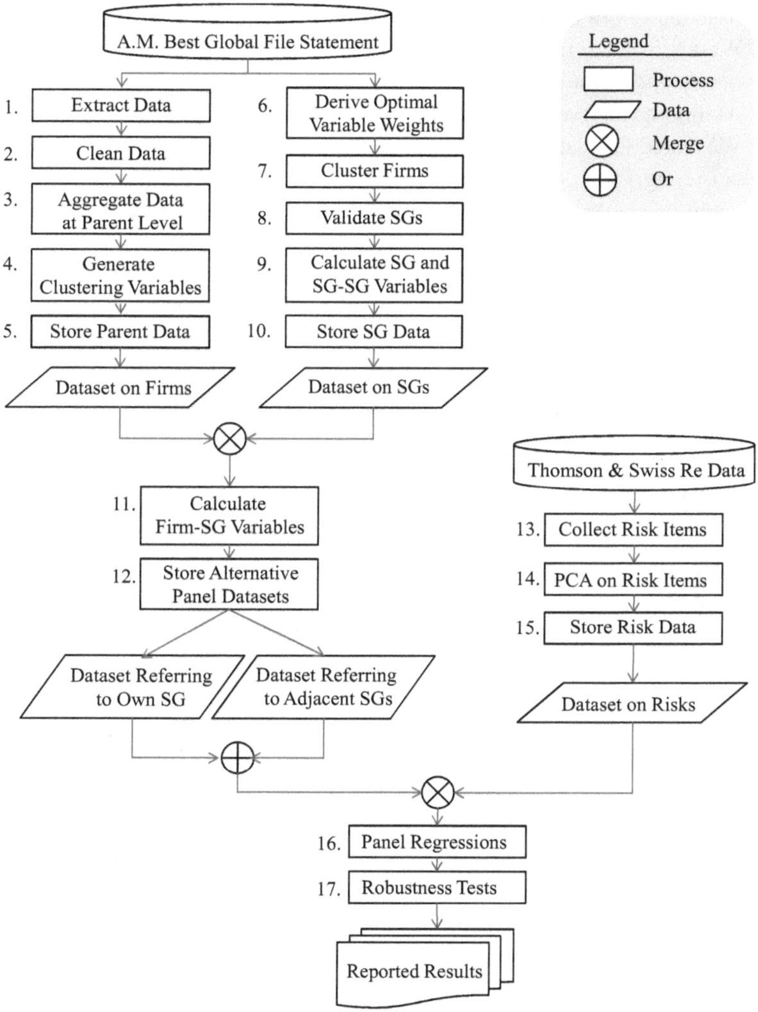

1. In an initial step, we retrieved various data items from the A.M. Best Global File Statement 2009.3. This included information on all 4.879 legal insurance entities operating in the U.S. market between 1999 and 2008, and information on which entity is affiliated with which parent organization.

2. We then set a flag to all entities that showed missing data in more than one year. If data was missing for one year only, we filled this gap by extrapolating from the values of the enclosing year(s).
3. We aggregated, resp. recalculated all items at the level of the U.S. holding-/parent-organization.
4. At this parent-level, we calculated the clustering variables shown in Table 3-1.
5. We stored this dataset as a separate file, titled "Dataset on Firms". It holds all clustering variables, performance KPIs, and further descriptive variables that could be created independent of information on the industry's strategic group structure.
6. To reduce the "masking effect" of unvalidated clustering variables, we assigned variable weights to the clustering variables (Makarenkov & Legendre, 2001a) by using the algorithm provided by Makarenkov and Legendre (2001b). The algorithm required a set of presumably correct strategic group clusters, which we received from four industry experts.
7. Based on the variable weights provided by the algorithm, we then clustered the full sample of firms in a two-staged process. In a first step, we applied Ward's (1963) method of hierarchical clustering to explore the ideal number of clusters in our data. Following the stopping rules pseudo-F test (Calinski & Harabasz, 1974) and Je(2)/Je(1) index (Duda & Hart, 1973), which both suggested five clusters of firms in our sample, we applied the k-means clustering algorithm in a second step and set k to 5. This step then yielded the clusters of firms that we then considered as the strategic group structure of the U.S. insurance industry.
8. We validated this strategic group structure by several means. First, we screened the clustering solutions of all years by examining the clusters on scatterplots of all clustering variable-combinations. Second, we generated a printout that lists all firms and their assigned clusters. With the help of the industry experts involved in step six, we verified that all well-known (i.e., "ideal type") firms were assigned to the correct clusters (Milligan, 1996).
9. Based on the cluster solutions for the ten year study period, we calculated for all years the cluster centroids (i.e., the location of each cluster in the multi-dimensional strategic space) and the performance differentials between the different clusters.
10. We stored this dataset as a separate file labeled as "Dataset on SGs".
11. After merging the "Dataset on Firms" with the "Dataset on SGs", we could calculate variables that required information on both firms and strategic groups. These variables include the dependent variables, as well as the PRA-variables.

12. In the next step, we derived two different panel-datasets, the "Dataset Referring to Own SG" and the "Dataset Referring to Adjacent SGs". The first dataset includes data necessary to test our hypotheses that relate to the own strategic group, whereas the second dataset includes data that can be used to test theory on the repositionings of firms vis-à-vis adjacent strategic groups.[4]
13. We received contextual data from two sources, the Thomson One Banker module that covers various databases such as Worldscope and Compustat, and from the research portal of Swiss Re Sigma Research, which was available to the public when the data was collected in July 2008 (Swiss Re, 2007). Swiss Re has abandoned this service in the course of the year 2010.
14. We explored several risk items by means of a principal component analysis: (1) Yearly costs of insured catastrophic losses stemming from weather-related natural catastrophes, earthquakes and tsunamis as well as man-made disasters; (2) numbers of distinct catastrophic events per year and category; (3) annual volatility of the Lehman Aggregate Bond Index; (4) annual volatility of the S&P 500 index. Following the Kaiser criterion for determining the number of factors, items (1) and (2) load on one factor, while the items (3) and (4) load on a second factor. The Eigenvalue of the potential third factor is only 0.65. For the sake of parsimoniousness, we used only item (1) to refer to environmental dynamism and GWP growth to refer to environmental munificence.
15. We stored these risk items in a dataset labeled "Dataset on Risks".
16. After merging the "Dataset Referring to Own SG" with the "Dataset on Risks", we ran panel regressions to test our hypotheses. Given clear indication of the Hausman-Test, we specified all regressions as fixed effects models with robust clustered standard errors.
17. To validate the regression results, we applied robustness test. Specifically, we reran our analyses with various sub-samples of the full dataset, incorporating portions of the full sample between 40% and 90%. Our results remained stable across all samples.

[4] While an earlier version of this study also analyzed the movement vectors to adjacent strategic groups (Schimmer, 2010), we narrowed the study's scope and focused on the movement vectors referring to the own strategic group. The "Dataset Referring to Adjacent SGs" has eventually not been used for the purpose of this dissertation.

Appendix 4: Exemplary VBA Macro

Macro identifying the press release date

For the role of this macro within the analysis process, see Appendix 1, step 4.

```
Option Explicit
Option Compare Text
Public Line As Integer
Dim basebook As Workbook, casebook As Workbook
Dim ConsString As String
Dim DatumFormat As Integer, DatumFormat2 As Integer, DatumA As Integer
Dim ItemDate As Date
Dim checkyear As Integer
Dim ApplCase As String

Sub Identify_AnnouncementDate()
Dim x As Integer
Dim timestamp As String
Set basebook = ThisWorkbook
Application.ScreenUpdating = False

   For Line = 2 To Cells(Rows.Count, 2).End(xlUp).Row
     ConsString     = basebook.Sheets("Consolidated").Cells(Line, 5).Value
     checkyear      = basebook.Sheets("Consolidated").Cells(Line, 20).Value
     DatumFormat    = basebook.Sheets("Consolidated").Cells(Line, 21).Value
     DatumFormat2   = basebook.Sheets("Consolidated").Cells(Line, 22).Value
     DatumA         = basebook.Sheets("Consolidated").Cells(Line, 23).Value


        'Call for Date-Identification
        ItemDate = DatumFinder(ConsString, DatumFormat, DatumA)
        basebook.Sheets("Consolidated").Cells(Line, 24).Value = ApplCase
        'Testing of Sequence required!!
            If ItemDate = 0 Then
                If DatumFormat2 <> 0 Then
                ItemDate = DatumFinder(ConsString, DatumFormat2, DatumA)
                End If
                If ItemDate = 0 Then
                For x = 0 To 7
                    ItemDate = DatumFinder(ConsString, x, DatumA)
                    If ItemDate <> 0 Then
              basebook.Sheets("Consolidated").Cells(Line, 24).Value = ApplCase
                    Exit For
                    End If
                        If x = 7 And ItemDate = 0 Then
                      basebook.Sheets("Consolidated").Cells(Line, 4).Value = " "
                      basebook.Sheets("Consolidated").Cells(Line, 7).Value = "No
                      date in NewsItem-String"
                        Exit For
                        End If
                Next x
                End If
            End If

            basebook.Sheets("Consolidated").Cells(Line, 4).Value = ItemDate

            'Create UniqueID
```

```
            timestamp = Format(ItemDate, "yyyymmdd")
            basebook.Sheets("Consolidated").Cells(Line, 1).Value =
basebook.Sheets("Consolidated").Cells(Line, 2).Value & "_" & timestamp
    Next Line
End Sub


Public Function DatumFinder(txt As String, DatumFormat As Integer, DatumArt As
Integer) As Date

'DatumFormat:
'                   0 - DD.MM.YYYY       --> TK = "."
'                   1 - MM/DD/YYYY       --> TK = "/"
'                   2 - DD/MM/YYYY       --> TK = "/"
'                   3 - MM DD, YYYY      --> TK = ", "
'                   4 - MMMM DD, YYYY    --> TK = ", "
'                   5 - DD MM, YYYY and DD MMMM, YYYY             --> TK = ", "
'                   6 - DD MMMM YYYY    --> TK1 = "199"; TK2 = "200"
'                   7 - DD MM or MM DD or DDDD MMMM or MMMM DDDD  --> TK = " "
'
'                   0-2 --> bytesimple = 0 --> same routine
'                   3-7 --> bytesimple = 1 --> individual routines

'DatumArt:          0 - oldest date
'                   1 - youngest date
'                   2 - first date
'                   3 - last date


Dim TK As String, TK1 As String, TK2 As String
Dim p1 As Long
Dim Erg As Date
Dim zwErg As Date
Dim Tag As Integer, Monat As Integer, Jahr As Integer
Dim T1 As String, T2() As String
Dim Flag As String, byteSimple As Byte
Dim strDay As String, strMonth As String, strYear As String, see As String,
PstrMonth As String
Dim intDay As Integer, intMonth As Integer, intYear As Integer
Dim x As Integer, lv21 As Integer, lv22 As Integer, p2 As Integer, p3 As Integer,
p0 As Integer, counter As Integer, lv221 As Integer, lv222 As Integer
Dim vartype
byteSimple = 0
Flag = "o.k."

Select Case DatumFormat
    Case 0
        TK = "."
        Tag = 0
        Monat = 1
        Jahr = 2
        byteSimple = 0
    Case 1
        TK = "/"
        Tag = 1
        Monat = 0
        Jahr = 2
        byteSimple = 0
    Case 2
```

```
        TK = "/"
        Tag = 0
        Monat = 1
        Jahr = 2
        byteSimple = 0
    Case 3
        byteSimple = 1
        TK = ", "
    Case 4
        byteSimple = 1
        TK = ", "
    Case 5
        byteSimple = 1
        TK = ", "
    Case 6
        byteSimple = 1
        TK1 = "199"
        TK2 = "200"
    Case 7
        byteSimple = 1
        TK = " "
End Select

If byteSimple = 0 Then 'Add checkyear for byteSimple = 0 case
    Dim check1 As Boolean, check2 As Boolean

    Do
        p1 = InStr(p1 + 1, txt, TK)
        If p1 = 0 Then Exit Do
        'see = Mid$(txt, p1 + 4, 1)                          'debugging
        'see2 = Mid$(txt, p1 + 2, 1) 'Mid$(txt, p1 - 1, 1) 'debugging
        'see3 = Mid$(txt, p1 - 3, 10)                         'debugging
    check1 = (Mid$(txt, p1 + 3, 1) = TK) Or (Mid$(txt, p1 + 2, 1) = TK)
    check2 = IsNumeric(Mid$(txt, p1 + 4, 1)) And IsNumeric(Mid$(txt, p1 + 1, 1))
        If check1 = True And check2 = True Then
            If p1 = 2 Then
            T1 = Mid$(txt, 1, 9)
            Else
            T1 = Mid$(txt, p1 - 2, 10)
            End If
            T2 = Split(T1, TK)
If Not IsNumeric(T2(2)) Then T2(2) = Left(T2(2), 2)  'check number of year digits
            If T2(Jahr) = checkyear And T2(Monat) > 0 And T2(Tag) > 0 Then
            zwErg = DateSerial(T2(Jahr), T2(Monat), T2(Tag))
                If IsNumeric(T2(0)) Then
                    If IsNumeric(T2(1)) Then
                        If IsNumeric(T2(2)) Then
                            Select Case DatumArt
                                Case 0
                                    If Erg = 0 Then
                                        Erg = zwErg
                                    Else
                                        If zwErg < Erg Then Erg = zwErg
                                        Flag = "Check Date"
                                    End If
                                Case 1
                                    If Erg = 0 Then
                                        Erg = zwErg
                                    Else
```

```
                                        If zwErg > Erg Then Erg = zwErg
                                        Flag = "Check Date"
                                    End If
                                Case 2
                                    If Erg = 0 And counter = 0 Then
                                    Erg = zwErg
                                    counter = 1
                                    Else
                                    If zwErg <> Erg Then Flag = "Check Date"
                                    End If
                            End Select
                        End If
                    End If
                End If
            End If
            p1 = p1 + 3
        End If

    If p1 > Len(txt) - 30 Then Exit Do
    Loop
    basebook.Sheets("Consolidated").Cells(Line, 7).Value = Flag
    ApplCase = "0-2"
    DatumFinder = Erg
    counter = 0
End If

Select Case DatumFormat
    Case 3
    Do
            p1 = InStr(p1 + 1, txt, TK)
            If p1 = 0 Then Exit Do
                    strYear = Mid(txt, p1 + 2, 5)
                    If IsNumeric(Mid(txt, p1 + 2, 5)) Then
                    strDay = Mid(txt, p1 - 2, 2)
                    strMonth = Mid(txt, p1 - 6, 3)
                    intDay = Val(strDay)
                        If intDay = 0 Then
                        intDay = Val(Mid(strDay, 2, 1))
                        strMonth = Mid(txt, p1 - 5, 3)
                        End If
                    intMonth = translatestrMonth(strMonth)
                    strYear = Mid(txt, p1 + 2, 5)
                    intYear = Val(strYear)
                    End If
                    If intMonth > 0 And intYear = checkyear And intDay > 0 Then
                    zwErg = DateSerial(intYear, intMonth, intDay)
                    Select Case DatumArt
                            Case 0
                                If Erg = 0 Then
                                    Erg = zwErg
                                Else
                                    If zwErg < Erg Then Erg = zwErg
                                    Flag = "Check Date"
                                End If
                            Case 1
                                If Erg = 0 Then
                                    Erg = zwErg
                                Else
                                    If zwErg > Erg Then Erg = zwErg
```

```
                                  Flag = "Check Date"
                              End If
                          Case 2
                              Erg = zwErg
                              Exit Do
                      End Select
                      intMonth = 0
                  End If
        If p1 > Len(txt) - 30 Then Exit Do
        Loop
        basebook.Sheets("Consolidated").Cells(Line, 7).Value = Flag
        ApplCase = 3
        DatumFinder = Erg

    Case 4
    Dim x2 As Integer
         Do
            p1 = InStr(p1 + 1, txt, TK)
            If p1 = 0 Then Exit Do
                    strYear = Mid(txt, p1 + 2, 4)

                    If Right(strYear, 1) = "%" Then GoTo shortend4:
                    If IsInteger(Val(strYear)) = False Then GoTo shortend4:

                    If Val(strYear) = checkyear Then
                    strDay = Mid(txt, p1 - 2, 2)
                    intDay = Val(strDay)
                        If intDay = 0 Then
                            intDay = Val(Mid(strDay, 2, 1))
                                If intDay = 0 Then
                                x2 = 0
                                    While x2 < 6
                                    strDay = Mid(txt, p1 - x2, 2)
                                    intDay = Val(strDay)    'debugging
                                    x2 = x2 + 1
                                    see = Mid(txt, p1 - x2, 2)    'debugging
                                   If Val(Mid(txt, p1 - x2 - 1, 2)) < intDay Then
                                        intDay = Val(Mid(txt, p1 - x2, 2))
                                        GoTo shortcut4:
                                        End If
                                    Wend
                                GoTo shortend4:
                                End If
                            'strMonth = Mid(txt, p1 - 5, 3)
                        End If
          '-------- Positioning, and measurement of length of month string ----
shortcut4:
                        x = 0
                            Do
                            x = x + 1
                            lv21 = InStr(p1 - 3 - x - x2, txt, " ")
                            If lv21 < p1 Then Exit Do
                            Loop
                        p2 = lv21
                        see = Mid(txt, p2 + 1, 10)   'debugging
                        '---------
                        x = 0

                        Do
```

```
                    x = x + 1
                    PstrMonth = Mid(txt, p2 - x, x)
                        If x > 10 Then
                        intMonth = 0
                        Exit Do
                        End If
                            If translatestrMonth(PstrMonth) > 0 Then
                                intMonth = translatestrMonth(PstrMonth)
                                x = 0
                                Exit Do
                            End If
                    Loop

                'intMonth = translatestrMonth(strMonth)
                strYear = Mid(txt, p1 + 2, 5)
                intYear = Val(strYear)
                End If

                If intMonth > 0 And intYear = checkyear Then
                zwErg = DateSerial(intYear, intMonth, intDay)
                Select Case DatumArt
                        Case 0
                            If Erg = 0 Then
                                Erg = zwErg
                            Else
                                If zwErg < Erg Then Erg = zwErg
                                Flag = "Check Date"
                            End If
                        Case 1
                            If Erg = 0 Then
                                Erg = zwErg
                            Else
                                If zwErg > Erg Then Erg = zwErg
                                Flag = "Check Date"
                            End If
                        Case 2
                            If Erg = 0 Then
                            Erg = zwErg
                            Else
                                If zwErg < Erg Then
        Flag = "There is an earlier date in the text than the first one mentioned"
                                End If
                            End If
                            'Exit Do
                    End Select
                    intMonth = 0
                End If
shortend4:
        If p1 > Len(txt) - 30 Then Exit Do
        Loop
        basebook.Sheets("Consolidated").Cells(Line, 7).Value = Flag
        ApplCase = 4
        DatumFinder = Erg

    Case 5
         Do
            p1 = InStr(p1 + 1, txt, TK)
            If p1 = 0 Then Exit Do
                    strYear = Mid(txt, p1 + 2, 5)
```

```
                If IsNumeric(strYear) Then
                'MsgBox txt  'debugging
        '--- Positioning, and measurement of length of month string ---
                    x = 0
                    Do
                    x = x + 1

                    lv21 = InStr(p1 - x, txt, " ")
                    If lv21 < p1 Then Exit Do
                    Loop
                    p2 = lv21
                    see = Mid(txt, p2, 10)
                    '---------
                    x = 0
                        Do
                        x = x + 1
                        If x = p2 Then
                        lv22 = 0
                        Exit Do
                        End If
                        lv22 = InStr(p2 - x, txt, " ")
                        If lv22 < p2 Then Exit Do
                        Loop
                    p3 = lv22
                    If (p2 - p3 - 1) > 2 Then p3 = p2 - 3
              '---------------------------------------------------------
                see = Mid(txt, p3 + 1, p2 - p3 - 1)
                strDay = Mid(txt, p3 + 1, p2 - p3 - 1)
                strMonth = Mid(txt, p2 + 1, p1 - p2 - 1)
                intDay = Val(strDay)
                    If intDay = 0 Then
                    intDay = Val(Mid(strDay, 2, 1))
                    strMonth = Mid(txt, p1 - 5, 3)
                    If intDay = 0 Then
                    x2 = 0
                    While x2 < 6
                    strDay = Mid(txt, p3 + 1 - x2, 2)
                    intDay = Val(strDay)                'debugging
                    x2 = x2 + 1
                    see = Mid(txt, p3 + 1 - x2, 2)      'debugging
                   If Val(Mid(txt, p3 + 1 - x2 - 1, 2)) < intDay Then
                        intDay = Val(Mid(txt, p3 + 1 - x2, 2))
                        GoTo shortcut5:
                        End If
                    Wend
                    End If
                    End If
shortcut5:
                intMonth = translatestrMonth(strMonth)
                strYear = Mid(txt, p1 + 2, 5)
                intYear = Val(strYear)
                End If

                If intMonth > 0 And intYear = checkyear Then
                zwErg = DateSerial(intYear, intMonth, intDay)
                Select Case DatumArt
                        Case 0
                            If Erg = 0 Then
```

```
                                Erg = zwErg
                            Else
                                If zwErg < Erg Then Erg = zwErg
                                Flag = "Check Date"
                            End If
                        Case 1
                            If Erg = 0 Then
                                Erg = zwErg
                            Else
                                If zwErg > Erg Then Erg = zwErg
                                Flag = "Check Date"
                            End If
                        Case 2
                            Erg = zwErg
                            Exit Do
                    End Select
                    intMonth = 0
                End If

        If p1 > Len(txt) - 30 Then Exit Do
        Loop
        basebook.Sheets("Consolidated").Cells(Line, 7).Value = Flag
        ApplCase = 5
        DatumFinder = Erg

    Case 6
         Dim pre1 As Integer, pre2 As Integer
         Do
            pre1 = InStr(pre1 + 1, txt, TK1)
            pre2 = InStr(pre2 + 1, txt, TK2)
                If pre1 < pre2 Then
                    If pre1 = 0 Then
                    p1 = pre2
                    Else
                    p1 = pre1
                    End If
                Else
                    If pre2 = 0 Then
                    p1 = pre1
                    Else
                    p1 = pre2
                    End If
                    If pre1 = 0 And pre2 = 0 Then
                    p1 = 0
                    End If
                End If

            If p1 < 2 Then Exit Do
            see = Mid(txt, p1, 4)              'debugging
            If IsNumeric(Mid(txt, p1, 4)) Then
                x = 0
                Do
                x = x + 1
                lv21 = InStr(p1 - x, txt, " ")
                If lv21 < p1 - 1 Then Exit Do
                'If x = p1 - 1 Then Exit Do
                If x > p1 - 2 Then
                lv21 = p1 - 2
                Exit Do
```

```
                End If

                Loop
                p2 = lv21
                '----------------------------
                x = 0
                Do
                x = x + 1
                If x > p1 - 3 Then
                lv22 = p1 - 3
                Exit Do
                End If
                If lv22 <= p2 Then Exit Do
                lv22 = InStr(p2 - x, txt, " ")
                Loop
                p3 = lv22

                'see = Mid(txt, p2 + 1, p1 - p2 - 2)        'debugging
                strMonth = Mid(txt, p2 + 1, p1 - p2 - 2)
                intMonth = translatestrMonth(strMonth)
                If intMonth <> 0 Then
                strYear = Mid(txt, p1, 4)
                intYear = Val(strYear)
                'see = Mid(txt, p3 + 1, p2 - p3 - 1)        'debugging
                strDay = Mid(txt, p3 + 1, p2 - p3 - 1)
                intDay = Val(strDay)
                        If intDay = 0 Then
                            For x = 2 To 1 Step -1
                            see = Mid(txt, p2 - x, x)
                            intDay = Val(Mid(txt, p2 - x, x))
                            If intDay <> 0 Then GoTo shortend6:
                            Next x
                                If intDay = 0 Then
                                    For x = 4 To 3 Step -1
                                    see = Mid(txt, p2 - x, 2 - (4 - x))
                            intDay = Val(Mid(txt, p2 - x, 2 - (4 - x)))
                                    If intDay <> 0 Then GoTo shortend6:
                                    Next x
                                End If
shortend6:
                        End If
                End If
            End If

If intMonth > 0 And intMonth < 13 And intDay > 0 And intYear = checkyear Then
                    zwErg = DateSerial(intYear, intMonth, intDay)
                    Select Case DatumArt
                            Case 0
                                If Erg = 0 Then
                                    Erg = zwErg
                                Else
                                    If zwErg < Erg Then Erg = zwErg
                                    Flag = "Check Date"
                                End If
                            Case 1
                                If Erg = 0 Then
                                    Erg = zwErg
                                Else
                                    If zwErg > Erg Then Erg = zwErg
```

```
                                        Flag = "Check Date"
                                    End If
                                Case 2
                                    Erg = zwErg
                                    Exit Do
                            End Select
                            intMonth = 0
                        End If

        If p1 > Len(txt) - 30 Then
        'Flag = "No date in NewsItem"
        Exit Do
        End If

        If p1 > Len(txt) - 30 Then Exit Do
        Loop
        basebook.Sheets("Consolidated").Cells(Line, 7).Value = Flag
        ApplCase = 6
        DatumFinder = Erg

    Case 7
        Do
            p1 = InStr(p1 + 1, txt, TK)
            If p1 = 0 Then Exit Do
            'see = Mid(txt, p1, 4)              'debugging
                x = 0
                Do
                x = x + 1
                    If p1 - x <= 1 Then
                    lv21 = 0
                    Exit Do
                    End If
                lv21 = InStr(p1 - x, txt, " ")
                If lv21 < p1 Then Exit Do
                Loop
                p0 = lv21
                '----------------------------
                x = 0
                Do
                lv22 = InStr(p1 + 1, txt, " ")
                If lv22 > p1 Or lv22 = 0 Then
                    If lv22 > p1 Then
                    Exit Do
                    End If
                        If lv22 = 0 Then
                        lv22 = p2 + 1
                        Exit Do
                        End If
                End If
                Loop
                p2 = lv22

                'debugging:
                'see1 = Mid(txt, p1 + 1, 2)
                'see2 = Mid(txt, p0 + 1, p1 - p0 - 1)
                If p1 > p2 Then GoTo shortend:
                If IsNumeric(Mid(txt, p1 + 1, p2 - p1 - 1)) And
IsNumeric(translatestrMonth(Mid(txt, p0 + 1, p1 - p0 - 1))) Then
```

```
                   If Val(translatestrMonth(Mid(txt, p0 + 1, p1 - p0 - 1))) > 0
And Val(translatestrMonth(Mid(txt, p0 + 1, p1 - p0 - 1))) < 13 Then
                    strMonth = Mid(txt, p0 + 1, p1 - p0 - 1)
                    intMonth = translatestrMonth(strMonth)
                    intYear = checkyear
                    strDay = Mid(txt, p1 + 1, p2 - p1 - 1)
                    intDay = Val(strDay)
                   End If
                End If
                If IsNumeric(translatestrMonth(Mid(txt, p0 + 1, p1 - p0 - 1)))
And IsNumeric(Mid(txt, p0 + 1, p1 - p0 - 1)) = True And IsNumeric(Mid(txt, p1 +
1, p2 - p1 - 1)) Then
                    strMonth = Mid(txt, p1 + 1, p2 - p1 - 1)
                    intMonth = translatestrMonth(strMonth)
                    intYear = checkyear
                    strDay = Mid(txt, p0 + 1, p1 - p0 - 1)
                    intDay = Val(strDay)
                End If

             If intMonth > 0 And intDay > 0 And intYear = checkyear Then
                    zwErg = DateSerial(intYear, intMonth, intDay)
                    Select Case DatumArt
                            Case 0
                                If Erg = 0 Then
                                    Erg = zwErg
                                Else
                                    If zwErg < Erg Then Erg = zwErg
                                    Flag = "Check Date"
                                End If
                            Case 1
                                If Erg = 0 Then
                                    Erg = zwErg
                                Else
                                    If zwErg > Erg Then Erg = zwErg
                                    Flag = "Check Date"
                                End If
                            Case 2
                                Erg = zwErg
                                Exit Do
                        End Select
                        intMonth = 0
                    End If

        If p1 > Len(txt) - 30 Then Exit Do
        Loop
shortend:
        basebook.Sheets("Consolidated").Cells(Line, 7).Value = Flag
        ApplCase = 7
        DatumFinder = Erg
End Select
End Function


Public Function translatestrMonth(txt As String) As Integer

'see = txt          'debugging
'see = Len(txt)     'debugging

Dim intMonth As Integer
```

```
If txt = "Jan" Or txt = "Jan." Or txt = "January" Or txt = "Januar" Then
intMonth = 1
End If
If txt = "Feb" Or txt = "Feb." Or txt = "February" Or txt = "Februar" Then
intMonth = 2
End If
If txt = "Mar" Or txt = "Mar." Or txt = "March" Or txt = "März" Then
intMonth = 3
End If
If txt = "Apr" Or txt = "Apr." Or txt = "April" Then
intMonth = 4
End If
If txt = "May" Or txt = "Mai" Then
intMonth = 5
End If
If txt = "Jun" Or txt = "Jun." Or txt = "June" Or txt = "Juni" Then
intMonth = 6
End If
If txt = "Jul" Or txt = "Jul." Or txt = "July" Or txt = "Juli" Then
intMonth = 7
End If
If txt = "Aug" Or txt = "Aug." Or txt = "August" Then
intMonth = 8
End If
If txt = "Sep" Or txt = "Sep." Or txt = "September" Or txt = "Sept" Or txt =
"Sept." Then
intMonth = 9
End If
If txt = "Oct" Or txt = "Oct." Or txt = "October" Or txt = "Oktober" Then
intMonth = 10
End If
If txt = "Nov" Or txt = "Nov." Or txt = "November" Then
intMonth = 11
End If
If txt = "Dec" Or txt = "Dec." Or txt = "December" Or txt = "Dezember" Then
intMonth = 12
End If
translatestrMonth = intMonth
End Function

Public Function IsInteger(vValue) As Boolean
 If vartype(vValue) = 2 Or vartype(vValue) = 5 Then
 IsInteger = True
 Else
 IsInteger = False
 End If
  '    IsInteger = (vartype(vValue) = vbInteger)
End Function
```

Kolibri 360 GmbH
Ferdinand-Jühlke-Straße 7
99095 Erfurt, Deutschland
produktsicherheit@kolibri360.de